"Even as more of Abraham Kuyper's voluminous writings become available to Anglophone audiences, revisiting his seminal English-language source, the Stone Lectures of 1898, is a worthwhile and important endeavor. In the intervening century, Kuyper's addresses at Princeton Seminary have been the main touchstone for worldwide familiarity with Kuyper and neo-Calvinism more broadly. This edited volume provides a valuable point of entry to that reception as well as to the significance of the legacy for both today and tomorrow. We should be grateful to the editors and contributors for providing an accessible as well as substantive guide to some of the most salient features of Kuyper's fertile thought."

Jordan J. Ballor, general editor, Abraham Kuyper Collected Works in Public Theology, and director of research at the Center for Religion, Culture, and Democracy

"What does Abraham Kuyper have to offer to our fractured, twenty-first-century world? With one eye on Kuyper's own context and another on the challenges facing Christians attempting to bring their faith to bear on public life today, this volume of essays offers an essential guide to the relevance—and limitations—of Kuyperian thought in our contemporary moment."

Kristin Kobes Du Mez, author of *Jesus and John Wayne: How White Evangelicals Corrupted a Faith and Fractured a Nation*

"I have felt ambivalent about Kuyper's Stone Lectures since I first encountered them. The world and life vision set forth in the lectures are vital to my theological outlook. But Kuyper's racist asides trouble me deeply, especially when set against tragic appropriations by later interpreters. *Calvinism for a Secular Age* thus offers a welcome tonic, amplifying my gratitude and acknowledging my grief, making it an essential companion to Kuyper's lectures. It clarifies his aims, complicates his legacy, and challenges his flaws. When necessary, it moves forward by reading Kuyper against himself. Most importantly, it continues Kuyper's project, offering a generative and generous vision for all of life, one sorely needed in our secular age."

Justin Ariel Bailey, associate professor of theology at Dordt University and author of *Reimagining Apologetics: The Beauty of Faith in a Secular World*

"In recent months, Kuyper has been misquoted and co-opted by some to justify nefarious political agendas and misinterpreted by others who have argued he should be 'canceled.' The Joustras provide a timely resource for those seeking to be honest heirs of Kuyperian thought while being committed to refining, at times renouncing, and finally innovating out of this tradition. It is a creative engagement with the complex man whose blatant sins stand alongside the many gifts he offers to those who seek to live all of their lives in light of the gospel of Christ."

Cory Willson, Jake and Betsy Tuls Associate Professor of Missiology and Missional Ministry, director of the Institute for Global Church Planting and Renewal, Calvin Theological Seminary

"How might an ancient faith connect with modern questions of science, politics, the arts, race, religion, and more? This outstanding collection of essays explores the intersection between faith and public life with a rich and profound theological imagination. This book represents a long-awaited gift for readers of Reformed theology and Abraham Kuyper. Some of the best Kuyper scholars in the world are gathered herein to bring new life and new perspective to Kuyper's groundbreaking Lectures on Calvinism."

Matthew Kaemingk, chair and director of the Richard John Mouw Institute of Faith and Public Life at Fuller Theological Seminary

"Looking to Abraham Kuyper as a guide who can help us navigate the complexities of this cultural and political moment, this timely volume provides an accessible introduction to Kuyper's thought as it probes ways that we can continue to learn from Kuyper's contributions. Each essay, from one among an exceptional lineup of contributors, invites us to consider what faithful Christian engagement looks like in such important areas as politics, science, and the arts. These essays not only mine the wisdom of Kuyper's thought from the past, but they urge us to imagine what it means that God is renewing and redeeming all things today. This volume will be of interest to all who believe that the gospel involves both personal devotion and public engagement."

Kristen Deede Johnson, dean and vice president for academic affairs, professor of theology and Christian formation, Western Theological Seminary

JESSICA R. JOUSTRA AND
ROBERT J. JOUSTRA, EDS.

CALVINISM
FOR A
SECULAR
AGE

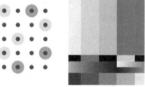

A TWENTY-FIRST-
CENTURY READING OF
ABRAHAM KUYPER'S
STONE LECTURES

ivp
Academic
An imprint of InterVarsity Press
Downers Grove, Illinois

InterVarsity Press
P.O. Box 1400, Downers Grove, IL 60515-1426
ivpress.com
email@ivpress.com

InterVarsity Press® is the book-publishing division of InterVarsity Christian Fellowship/USA®, a movement of
students and faculty active on campus at hundreds of universities, colleges, and schools of nursing in the United
States of America, and a member movement of the International Fellowship of Evangelical Students. For
information about local and regional activities, visit intervarsity.org.

All Scripture quotations, unless otherwise indicated, are taken from The Holy Bible, New International Version®,
NIV®. Copyright © 1973, 1978, 1984, 2011 by Biblica, Inc.™ Used by permission of Zondervan. All rights reserved
worldwide. www.zondervan.com. The "NIV" and "New International Version" are trademarks registered in the
United States Patent and Trademark Office by Biblica, Inc.™

Cover design and image composite: David Fassett
Interior design: Jeanna Wiggins
Images: dried gold leaf © Anne Antonini / EyeEm / Getty Images
        city illustration © Ben Grib Design / Moment / Getty Images
        globe illustration © CSA Images / Getty Images
        microscope © Noun Project Website
        data science icons © pressureUA / iStock / Getty Images Plus
        science icons © pressureUA / iStock / Getty Images Plus
        gold picture frame © seraficus / E+ / Getty Images
        tv test pattern © Serhii Brovoko / iStock / Getty Images Plus
        Abraham Kuyper VU: https://commons.wikimedia.org/wiki/File:Abraham_Kuyper_VU.jpg

ISBN 978-1-5140-0146-2 (print)
ISBN 978-1-5140-0147-9 (digital)

Printed in the United States of America ∞

InterVarsity Press is committed to ecological stewardship and to the conservation of natural resources in all our
operations. This book was printed using sustainably sourced paper.

Library of Congress Cataloging-in-Publication Data
Names: Joustra, Jessica Renee, 1987- editor. | Joustra, Robert, editor.
Title: Calvinism for a secular age : a twenty-first-century reading of
    Abraham Kuyper's Stone lectures / edited by Jessica R. Joustra, Robert
    J. Joustra.
Description: Downers Grove, IL : IVP Academic, [2021] | Includes
    bibliographical references and index.
Identifiers: LCCN 2021047362 (print) | LCCN 2021047363 (ebook) | ISBN
    9781514001462 (print) | ISBN 9781514001479 (digital)
Subjects: LCSH: Kuyper, Abraham, 1837-1920. Lectures on Calvinism. |
    Calvinism.
Classification: LCC BX9422.5.K883 C35 2021 (print) | LCC BX9422.5.K883
    (ebook) | DDC 284/.2—dc23
LC record available at https://lccn.loc.gov/2021047362
LC ebook record available at https://lccn.loc.gov/2021047363

| P | 25 | 24 | 23 | 22 | 21 | 20 | 19 | 18 | 17 | 16 | 15 | 14 | 13 | 12 | 11 | 10 | 9 | 8 | 7 | 6 | 5 | 4 | 3 | 2 |
| Y | 37 | 36 | 35 | 34 | 33 | 32 | 31 | 30 | 29 | 28 | 27 | 26 | 25 | 24 | 23 | 22 |

To Jacob

One generation commends your works to another

CONTENTS

PREFACE

JAMES D. BRATT

ON AUGUST 21, 1898, Abraham Kuyper boarded the Cunard liner *Lucania* for a six-day voyage to the United States. He had read a lot about America and thought about it even more, so he was eager for some firsthand experience of its people and places. His trip would last for nearly four months and take him around the whole northeastern quadrant of the country—from New York to Iowa, Connecticut to Maryland. His first objective, however, was to travel to Princeton, New Jersey, where he would receive an honorary doctorate from the university there and deliver the Stone Lectures at Princeton Theological Seminary.[1]

Kuyper was not shy about receiving the honorary degree. In his acceptance speech he recalled how he had been nominated for one such twenty years before back home in the Netherlands, only to see his political opponents block the measure. "The degree you now bestow upon me," he told the assembly, thus provided "a little revenge upon my antagonists, and revenge with honor—why not admit it?—always offers something sweet to the human heart."[2] This little vignette offers our first glimpse into Kuyper as a person—a combatant yearning for respect, yet a sincere Christian remembering the virtue of humility. The ceremony also called on his sense of drama, for it took place in Princeton's august Nassau Hall, named after the Netherlands' royal House of Orange, with ex–United States president Grover Cleveland present in the audience.

---

[1] For detail and analysis of Kuyper's American trip, see James D. Bratt, *Abraham Kuyper: Modern Calvinist, Christian Democrat* (Grand Rapids, MI: Eerdmans, 2013), 261-79.
[2] Bratt, *Modern Calvinist*, 264.

Kuyper's lectures at Princeton Seminary involved a quieter sort of drama. On the one hand, he was sure of a friendly audience since the seminary was the bastion of orthodoxy in the Presbyterian Church in the USA;[3] his unabashed devotion to Calvinism would go down well there. On the other hand, he meant more by "Calvinism" than people at Princeton were used to. Yes, he assured them, the tradition did involve the uncompromising doctrine and system of church governance by which Princeton Seminary had long defined itself. But there was more to it than that, he continued. Calvinist history displayed a record of wide-ranging political and cultural activism, and Reformed theology mandated taking part in the affairs of the world in that believers were to act not just as citizens and neighbors but also as self-consciously Christian citizens and neighbors. Such holistic engagement, the dream of creating not just a pure church but a "holy commonwealth," was associated in Princeton's mind with the "New School" Presbyterianism that had drafted heavily on New England Puritanism, and against those two "News" Princeton Seminary had been keeping vigilant guard for nearly its entire history.[4]

If it was not enough to idealize the Puritans, as Kuyper did—he called them, in fact, the "core" of the American nation—he sounded two more themes troubling to the Princeton heart.[5] First, his epistemology (his theory of knowledge) drew deeply on German Idealist models that Princeton always rejected. Such were the stakes innocently hiding in Kuyper's notion of "world-and-life-view." Kuyper's approach opposed Princeton's commitment to the philosophy of Common Sense Realism, derived from the Scottish Enlightenment, which held that reality comes to us objectively through our five senses, to be processed as "facts" by a

---

[3]This was known colloquially at the time as the "Northern" Presbyterian Church in contradistinction from the "Southern" Presbyterian Church in the United States, which was more uniformly conservative in its theology.

[4]E. Brooks Holifield, *Theology in America: From the Age of the Puritans to the Civil War* (New Haven, CT: Yale University Press, 2003), 341-96.

[5]Quotation from Abraham Kuyper, "Calvinism: Source and Stronghold of Our Constitutional Liberties," in James D. Bratt, ed., *Abraham Kuyper: A Centennial Reader* (Grand Rapids, MI: Eerdmans, 1998), 286.

neutral and dispassionate reason. On this understanding, Christianity is a rational system of convictions based on factual evidence and to be defended by logic and reason; in fact, it was ultimately the most (maybe the only) fully rational system. Kuyper insisted to the contrary that we all inevitably perceive and process our impressions of the world within a pre-rational interpretive grid—that the Christian intellectual enterprise is therefore to make sure that this grid is as faithful as possible to the testimony of Scripture and then to build within it by a consistent logic, defending the results against all comers. Similarly, Christians must pursue their work in culture and politics according to a consistent, self-critical program grounded in careful study of the Bible, theology, and history.[6]

To these twin challenges—his picture of a comprehensive and dynamic Christianity, and his concept of knowledge as a struggle among perspectives—Kuyper added one more. Charles Hodge, long Princeton's foremost theologian, had once asserted that no fundamentally new idea had ever been broached at the seminary. Kuyper issued quite a different mandate. As he stated at the beginning of his final lecture, "Calvinism and the Future," the need of the day was "not to copy the past, as if Calvinism were a petrifaction, but to go back to the living root of the Calvinist plant, to clean and to water it, and so to cause it to bud and to blossom once more, now fully in accordance with our actual life in these modern times, and with the demands of the times to come."[7] Moreover, this reflected no faddish desire for relevance but simply fleshed out Calvinism's core commitment to the sovereignty of God:

> The world after the fall is no lost planet, only destined now to afford the Church a place in which to continue her combats; and humanity is no aimless mass of people which only serves the purpose of giving birth to the elect. On the contrary, the world now, as well as in the beginning, is the theater for the mighty works of God, and humanity remains a

---

[6]On Common Sense Realism, see Mark Noll, *America's God: From Jonathan Edwards to Abraham Lincoln* (New York: Oxford University Press, 2002), 93-113, 253-68.

[7]Abraham Kuyper, *Lectures on Calvinism* (1931; repr., Grand Rapids, MI: Eerdmans, 1999), 171.

creation of His hand, which, apart from salvation, completes under this present dispensation, here on earth, a mighty process, and in its historical development is to glorify the name of Almighty God.[8]

Kuyper was aiming these challenges well beyond Princeton Seminary; he was speaking to American Protestantism as a whole. We will review his relative success on this score later when considering where his lectures were received and how. First we need to fathom the program behind them. Kuyper saw great stakes at hand in the issues of his day, which helps explain the audacious language and grand historical sweep we encounter in the Stone Lectures. To our postmodern ears, so tuned to irony and suspicion, "audacious" can quickly become "outrageous," and the grand, grandiose. For the times, however, neither the language nor the sense of historical sweep was that unusual. Just two years before, Americans had heard William Jennings Bryan accept the Democratic presidential nomination by warning the monied interests of the land, "You shall not press down upon the brow of labor this crown of thorns, you shall not crucify mankind upon a cross of gold!"[9] Likewise, Theodore Roosevelt said to his nominating convention in 1912: "We stand at Armageddon, and we battle for the Lord!"[10] Such rhetoric could be heard Left, Right, and Center; it was the convention of the day.

To this mix Kuyper added his own steeping in German Idealist notions of history, most memorably carved out by Georg W. F. Hegel.[11] True, Kuyper decried Hegel's translation of God into the World Spirit, but he shared completely the concept that world history proceeded by the dialectical play of leading "principles" as these were incarnated in various nations, systems, civilizations, and religions. Already as a

---

[8]Kuyper, *Lectures on Calvinism*, 162.

[9]"Bryan's 'Cross of Gold' Speech: Mesmerizing the Masses," History Matters, accessed May 1, 2020, http://historymatters.gmu.edu/d/5354/.

[10]Lewis L. Gould, "1912 Republican Convention: Return of the Rough Rider," *Smithsonian Magazine*, August 2008, www.smithsonianmag.com/history/1912-republican-convention-855607/.

[11]Bratt, *Modern Calvinist*, 31-32, 58-59.

young pastor in a quiet Dutch village in 1865 Kuyper saw this drama playing out in contemporary Europe; history had come down, he said, to a confrontation between the traditional theistic view of the world represented in Christianity and a stark, remorseless naturalism that was utterly materialistic in its philosophical grounding and in its pre-scriptions for human life.[12] By the 1890s the foe had become pan-theism, with traditional Christianity's resources divided between Roman Catholic and Protestant. ("Calvinism" in Kuyper's mind always represented the purest distillation of the spirit or "principle" animating Protestantism.[13])

To this struggle Kuyper had devoted his life both as a thinker and a doer. Since the forces controlling history were ultimately spiritual, he saw culture (rather than politics or economics) as the front line of en-gagement and so focused his energies on the church and school. But as educational policy came to the fore in national politics in the Nether-lands (as in many other countries) in the 1870s, he took a seat in the Dutch Parliament to advocate for a religiously pluralistic public school system. He took advantage of new provisions in Dutch law to publish a newspaper that knit together a nationwide community of committed, and now better informed, Calvinist citizens. To coordinate their action he founded a new political party; to provide leadership for what by now was emerging as a whole movement he founded a university.

All these were in place by 1880. He next undertook what he hoped would be a thorough reformation of the national Reformed church, but that plan fell short of his goal. So he turned his focus back to politics, and in the ten years leading up to his Princeton lectures his movement went from strength to strength. Two dramatic expansions of the franchise—in 1887 and 1897—benefited Kuyper's party more than any other. The harsh depression of the late 1880s finally prompted his movement to start paying attention to economics, and in the great reform measures

---

[12]Bratt, *Modern Calvinist*, 46-47.
[13]Bratt, *Modern Calvinist*, 212-14.

instituted in the 1890s the Netherlands laid the foundations for much better prospects in public health and prosperity. The same years saw Kuyper's greatest successes as a scholar. He finished his three-volume *Encyclopedia of Sacred Theology* in 1894 and began the long series of magazine articles on his distinctive doctrine of common grace that would be published in three volumes in 1902.[14]

In short, for all the tones of foreboding and declension that run through the *Lectures on Calvinism*, Kuyper came to Princeton on a rising tide. He had declared the same to his followers in a scintillating speech in 1896: "Brothers, *I believe in the future,* I believe in it with all my heart!"[15] God was still sovereign over history and creation, and God had mighty works in mind for the faithful in the years ahead. One of those, perhaps, was Kuyper's elevation to prime minister in 1901. With that a remarkable movement that he had birthed and led over a thirty-year course of innovation and development came of age. Kuyper arrived in Princeton to get American Calvinists to start thinking about something similar.

But the times proved not to be ripe on this side of the Atlantic. Kuyper's *Lectures* would be remembered and honored but in places he largely overlooked rather than where he had hoped, and a fuller reach for his influence would only come much later. This outcome was forecast in two other lecture tours Kuyper took upon leaving Princeton. The first followed the chain of Dutch American immigrant communities across the Midwest, from western Michigan to Chicagoland and northwest Iowa. The other retraced the trail of the New England diaspora, from Chicago back to Cleveland, Rochester, and Hartford, then down to Dutch Reformed and Presbyterian citadels in New Jersey and Philadelphia.

---

[14]On Kuyper's church reform, see Bratt, *Modern Calvinist*, 149-71; on politics and economics in these years, 215-32, 298-301; on his scholarship, 183-87, 197-204, 206-7.

[15]Quoted in Bratt, *Modern Calvinist*, 239 (emphasis original).

To take the second trip first: these stops bore Kuyper along the axes of the northeastern Protestant establishment that still ruled America's economy and culture at the end of the nineteenth century. Here lay the seed of the Puritan dream of a righteous society, mixed with Scots and Dutch Calvinist commitments to education and con-stitutional order.[16] Kuyper affirmed all of it, but he worried that the churches of these tribes were too involved with their ethical fruits to pay attention to the disease of modernist theology threatening their religious roots. His message along this route consequently echoed the *Lectures'* call for a critical scrutiny of the mixed spirits in the age and to separate the wheat from the chaff accordingly. But his audience either misunderstood or ignored his challenge. The powers in American Protestantism were poised on the verge of the great Pro-gressive campaign to reform, revitalize, and reorder the country on a more stable basis. The division of the spirits would come only in the 1920s, after World War I had burned up crusading zeal, and neither the modernist nor the fundamentalist side in that clash had room for Kuyper's initiatives.

The trip through Dutch America proved more propitious, with a twist. That community was divided between two denominations: the Reformed Church in America (RCA), which descended from colonial New Netherland and so bore some establishment airs itself; and the Christian Reformed Church (CRC), which prized the community's roots in various secession movements from the national Reformed church back in the Netherlands. Kuyper had long corresponded with key Midwestern leaders in the RCA—in fact, he used them to gain an audience with President William McKinley during his visit to Wash-ington, DC. McKinley proved a huge disappointment, and Kuyper's anticipation of influence through the strategically situated RCA went

---

[16]For comparative profiles of these two lineages, see James D. Bratt, "Calvinism in North Amer-ica," in *John Calvin's Impact on Church and Society, 1509–2009,* ed. Martin Ernst Hirzel and Martin Sallmann (Grand Rapids, MI: Eerdmans, 2009), 49-66. On Kuyper's message to them, see Bratt, *Modern Calvinist,* 272-73, 277-78.

a-glimmering as well. The few who followed his flame in these circles had a small audience and little legacy.[17]

That flame would burn longer and stronger in the more separatist CRC instead. Here a self-segmentation within American society against the common shibboleths of American culture gave greater room for Kuyper's critical spirit. At the same time, here his call for positive Christian engagement with the world proved to be the very word of life for bright, ambitious youth who were reared under, and chafed against, the denomination's sectarian spirit. Up through World War II the CRC centered its agenda on a zealous fight against doctrinal deviation and any form of "worldliness." Kuyper gave orthodox reasons and a well-grounded method for getting beyond those strictures. One of the clearest results has been the string of national-class philosophers produced by the denomination's Calvin University.[18] More broadly symbolic, William B. Eerdmans Publishing Company, situated in the heart of this community, has kept the *Lectures* in print since acquiring its rights in 1931.

Kuyper's influence broadened later in the century along two lines. First, post–World War II emigration from the Netherlands to Canada brought to North America thousands of people who had been reared under the full panoply of Kuyper's institutions in their homeland and sought, with some success, to build likewise in their new land. Through their home in the bi-national CRC their influence spread in the United States as well.[19] Second, a half-century after their traumatic shaming in the 1920s, many Protestant fundamentalists emerged to reengage the American scene as evangelicals. The anti-scientific and world-flight

---

[17]Bratt, *Modern Calvinist*, 264-68, 276-79.

[18]The presiding spirit in this enterprise was William Harry Jellema; among his students were Cornelius Van Til, William Frankena, O. K. Bouwsma, Nicholas Wolterstorff, and Alvin Plantinga. More broadly, see James D. Bratt, "De Erfenis van Kuyper in Noord Amerika" [Kuyper's Legacy in North America], in *Abraham Kuyper: zijn volksdeel, zijn invloed*, ed. C. Augustijn, J. H. Prins, and H. E. S. Woldring (Delft: Meinema, 1987), 203-28; and James D. Bratt, "The Reformed Churches and Acculturation," in *The Dutch in America: Immigration, Settlement, and Cultural Change*, ed. Robert P. Swierenga (New Brunswick, NJ: Rutgers University Press, 1984), 191-208.

[19]Bratt, "Kuyper's Legacy," 203-28.

impulses of their heritage left them looking for resources fit for this enterprise, and Kuyper's program offered a robust option. First, its perspectival epistemology made more sense than the outmoded rationalism of Common Sense Realism that fundamentalism had inherited from Princeton. Second, its mandate for world engagement under the promises of God for the future offered a positive alternative to the violent fantasies of dispensationalism, the other pole of the fundamentalist mind. This is the audience for Lexham Press's new publication of a broad span of Kuyper's volumes in public theology.[20]

So how should Kuyper's *Lectures* be used going forward? His core insight will always remain valuable: that our faith involves not just Sunday but weekday; not just the spiritual but the material; not just theology and piety and personal behavior but science and politics, art and leisure, labor and business. This is not just a gospel mandate but simple reality: even apathy amounts to a commitment of sorts, and to flee the world is in its own way to affirm it as the best one possible, however far it might fall from the divine righteousness to which we are called to bear witness.

Another valuable legacy lies in how Kuyper pays attention to the interconnectedness of things. Our prime convictions *do* shape our knowledge and actions, just as social institutions and political policies and artistic productions bear out control axioms and desires. It is not hard to see power blocs embodying different ideals and value systems moving like tectonic plates beneath the landscape of our own times, and it is essential that we search these out and assess them by both the standards of Scripture and the wisdom of history. That is, we need Kuyper's call for Christians to develop a deep and not superficial or merely

---

[20]Mark Noll, *The Scandal of the Evangelical Mind* (Grand Rapids, MI: Eerdmans, 1994), 215-17, 224-25, 237. On the Lexham Press series, see "Abraham Kuyper Collected Works in Public Theology," Lexham Press, accessed April 20, 2020, https://lexhampress.com/product/55067 /abraham-kuyper-collected-works-in-public-theology.

emotional or simply reactive understanding of the world. That is a vital prelude for truly loving our neighbor.

Of course, we don't have to see connections in the grand Hegelian way, which, as the *Lectures* demonstrate often enough, is prone to exaggeration and overgeneralization. We are rightly more aware of nuance and the ironic inconsistencies—even contradictions—in things. For instance, Kuyper brought to America the Continental European perception that supporters of the (French) "Revolution" will line up consistently against those of traditional Christianity. But in the United States that dial had to be twisted ninety degrees: *both* sides in the American Revolution numbered Christians and devotees of Enlightenment Reason. The opposition between good and evil, we have come to learn along with Alexander Solzhenitsyn, does not run between groups of people but right down the middle of every human heart.[21] Thus, we first need to apply Kuyper's critical mandate to ourselves before lowering on our opponents.

It is also important to consider our metaphors and tone. Kuyper favored political terms: authority, law, obedience, the lordship of Christ. We should attend to, and benefit from, other terms from the treasury of Scripture as well. How might politics, art, science, and economy appear under the image of Christ as a shepherd walking before us, a friend by our side, or a radiant Spirit within? What if we bore down into the peace that Christ promises us rather than, with Kuyper, just the war that the gospel will provoke? We should not think here in exclusive terms of either-or, but at least be mindful of the whole menu of terms and tones at our disposal.

All that said, however, Kuyper's *Lectures* still serve as a model for how a Christian can—and how Christians together must—take on the whole world. If we differ from him in some points of method and language, if other incidents and examples and developments than his necessarily loom larger in our field of observation, we can nonetheless be summoned to engage our life and times with some of the energy, conviction, and brilliance that Kuyper shows in the Stone Lectures.

---

[21]Alexander Solzhenitsyn, *The Gulag Archipelago* (New York: Harper & Row, 1974), 168.

ACKNOWLEDGMENTS

THE GREAT CHURCH HISTORIAN Jaroslav Pelikan calls tradition the "living faith of the dead."[1] Too much important theology, philosophy and doctrine has become what he calls a kind of *traditionalism*, the dead faith of the living. A tradition alive, as Alasdair MacIntyre would have it, must be in dialogue; debated, renewed, refined, and updated. Kuyper—and Calvin—would have preferred perhaps *semper reformanda*, always reforming.

The book is dedicated to our son, Jacob Scott Joustra, but it is the fruit of our parents—Ray and Mary Joustra, and Scott and Renee Driesenga— and of our intellectual and spiritual parents, our "doctor fathers," and our beloved friends and colleagues, many of whom joined us in this project. They, and others, such as Matthew Kaemingk, Justin Bailey, Stephanie Summers, Harry Van Dyke, and more, witness beautifully to the *life* of this tradition.

This book is also the fruit of institutions, of people organized together for common purpose, across generations. Redeemer University, our academic home, funded and supported this work through internal research grants and our very capable research office, administered by the indispensable Nicole Benbow. Johanna Lewis, our research assistant at Redeemer, did extraordinary work checking and correcting bibliographies and footnotes. The Reid Trust Foundation also financially supported the book and its authors, without which much of this would simply not have been possible. Cardus NextGen, Redeemer University's Faculty Development Week, and Redeemer Presbyterian's Center for Faith and Work all served as generous forums and

---

[1]Jaroslav Pelikan, *The Vindication of Tradition* (New Haven, CT: Yale University Press), 65.

inspiration for some of the book's content. The Theological University of Kampen, which hosted Jess first as a postdoctoral researcher and then later as a research fellow, remains a home and harbor for so much excellence in research on neo-Calvinism and Abraham Kuyper. Its summer fellowship for doctoral students—the Advanced Theological Studies Fellowship—is one we highly commend to aspiring doctoral students reading this book.

We also think of other institutions, the consortium of organizations that host the European neo-Calvinist Symposium—Fuller Theological Seminary, the Free University of Amsterdam, the University of Edinburgh—at which we met, as so many Calvinists do, at a conference in Rome on the papal encyclical *Rerum Novarum* and the Kuyper Conference hosted now at Calvin University, by Jordan Ballor and others, who have done so much to bring the archive of Kuyper (and others) into the English language.

Here, in short, is our note of thanks to this extraordinary cloud of witnesses, who are not deaf to the sins of our fathers and mothers, but who press on despite and in the midst of it, to find the good news, the good work, that the Lord has done. A tradition's life is measured best not, probably, in its institutions or journals or ideas, but in its *persons*, and if that is so, the neo-Calvinist tradition is blossoming beautifully all around the world.

This book, like all Calvinistic projects, is fundamentally, therefore, a work of gratitude, first to the Lord our God, but then also to all of you above, and those unnamed, who pattern themselves—also—on this living faith of the dead.

INTRODUCTION

ROBERT J. JOUSTRA

ABRAHAM KUYPER (1837–1920), newspaper and university founder, pastor, church maker and breaker, and Dutch prime minister, was, truth be told, a troublemaker. Don't get us wrong: he was a true Renaissance man as at least one slightly overly rosy biography has put it,[1] a man of deep piety and a passionate follower of Jesus Christ, but he also had that quality of driven, singularly gifted men, of alienating those closest to him.[2] His theology provoked spirited backlash in people like Klaas Schilder, who did not suffer from an inability to express his own feelings.[3] In politics, Kuyper alienated rivals, allies, and even the Queen herself, especially after one incident in which Kuyper published Her Majesty's private remarks in his newspaper. The consequences of Kuyper's views on *pillarization*, the idea that modern society should not erase difference but create distinct, meaningful space for difference, created a Dutch education system still much in debate today and, of course, also became a rallying call for racial segregation in former Dutch colonies like South Africa. Its specter is very bleak and has led some to conclude that Kuyper's ideas are irredeemably colonial and racist.

Why look at such a person, then? He was sensational, to be sure, but sensational in a kind of small historical way, in his own little context of

---

[1] James Edward McGoldrick, *God's Renaissance Man: Abraham Kuyper* (Darlington, UK: Evangelical Press, 2000).

[2] James Bratt, the author of the definitive English biography of Abraham Kuyper, writes that Kuyper was "a great man, but not a nice one." James Bratt, *Abraham Kuyper: Modern Calvinist, Christian Democrat* (Grand Rapids, MI: Eerdmans, 2013), xxii.

[3] A fine example of that response now exists in a new translation in English, with a foreword by Richard Mouw. Klaas Schilder, *Christ and Culture*, trans. William Helder and Albert H. Oosterhoff (Hamilton, ON: Lucerna CRTS Publications, 2016).

the Netherlands, itself a sleepy little low country in the north of Europe and a one-time global power, long past its zenith. Maybe we could justify this tiny exploration if we lived in Holland, if we were all Dutch boys and girls learning our parochial history. But it might seem like an odd choice for an English-language introduction intended for Christians of faith in North America, a hundred years later, wrestling with questions that seem far removed from Kuyper's world.

We want to make at least four arguments for why Abraham Kuyper is for "such a time as this" in our initial orientation: one biographical and three more conceptual (that is, about the content of what Kuyper thought and taught). Kuyper is hardly the panacea for faithful Christian cultural and political engagement today in North America, but he is a very solid signpost, a guide, to help us in the increasingly turbulent and treacherous waters of polarized politics and tribal religion.

A CASE FOR GETTING
TO KNOW ABRAHAM KUYPER

Kuyper's Holland was a Christian nation, or at least that's how they saw themselves. Europe was Christian too; they certainly saw *themselves* that way, as a center of civilization, education, and morality. And at the end of the nineteenth century there seemed to be an overwhelming amount of evidence to prove it: a mass industrialization driven by scientific innovation that quickly overwhelmed and dominated the ancient empires of China, India, and Mesopotamia. European technical and scientific knowledge vastly outstripped their contemporaries, until they were without rival and until, in fact, they dominated the entire world in an age of empire, of which the Dutch were early and successful enthusiasts. This was the world Kuyper was born into.

Yet something was clearly wrong.

These Christian empires were invested less in the fraternity of humankind under the gospel than in scrambling for territory, resources, even slaves. The rise of so-called Christian Europe was marked by an uneven piety, to put it kindly, and the results of these Christian nations and their rivalry would be a global cataclysm from which the world would not soon recover. Its story and its collateral carnage would, in fact, dominate the entire century.

There was, in other words, a simultaneous and breathtaking expansion of technology, political power, and economic growth and a kind of moral and spiritual hollowing out of the family and the nation, a growing disconnect between what people said they believed and what they did, between what people knew they *ought* to be and how they really *lived*.

The (European) Christian church served as poor respite. Wrote Kuyper in his early years, "Church life was cold and formal. Religion was almost dead. There was no Bible in the schools. There was no life in the nation."[4] Or again, "People had been satisfied with [Christian] appearances alone and failed to bring the gospel to the heart," and connecting this directly to the catastrophe of the Great War (1914–1918), he concludes that "the sad outcome was that in Europe the torch of division and discord was set alight."[5] But were Europeans not blessed nations under God? Was not Christian Europe, at the turn of the twentieth century, a chosen people to bring light to the nations? Hardly, wrote Kuyper in disgust on the eve of that war: "The genuinely devout in every one of them [Christian nations] had not lagged a bit in baptizing their country's cause as the Lord's,"[6] the result of which, in Kuyper's mind, was a moral and material collapse that would consume the world.

Sound familiar? If you're American, it should. The globe is getting awfully crowded for America's superpower ambitions, which have run unchecked since the end of the Cold War and the "rise of the rest," as Fareed Zakaria puts it.[7] America has stumbled economically,

---

[4] Abraham Kuyper, *Lectures on Calvinism* (1931; repr., Grand Rapids, MI: Eerdmans, 1999), iii.

[5] Abraham Kuyper, *Pro Rege: Living Under Christ's Kingship: Volume 3*, ed. John Kok with Nelson D. Kloosterman, trans. Albert Gootjes (Bellingham, WA: Lexham Press, 2019), 256.

[6] Bratt, *Modern Calvinist*, 370.

[7] Fareed Zakaria, *The Post-American World: Release 2.0* (New York: W. W. Norton, 2012).

geopolitically, and politically, and all the while massive new powers are pulling huge populations of people into the global economy. Even (especially?) if you are an evangelical Christian in the United States today, the fissure running down the center of what was once American evangelicalism is now a chasm so wide it is doubtful it can be crossed even by its own people. To say that traditional religion in America is in crisis borders on cliché.

Yet you could go read your European history at the turn of the twentieth century and find in it the same ideas and language as you would about America at the turn of the twenty-first: a chosen people, blessed by God, bringing light to the nations. All the while, the evidence of its decline mounts. All the while the world holds its breath as new, bellicose powers arise and we hope to avoid the worst of our history and inclinations.

"You cannot step in the same river twice," the ancient Greeks knew. This historical analogy is far from perfect, but the point is simply that Abraham Kuyper matters for such a time as this because the crises of our times are, in a perennial way, reminiscent of the crises of Kuyper's. He, too, lived through the turn of a very violent century marked by extremely radical change. Our attitudes of history can run so narcissistic sometimes that we forget that as significant as the digital revolution, space flight, and iPhones may be, the telegram, the internal combustion engine, the electric light, and fixed nitrogen transformed a world at a speed and in a fashion that would take the breath away of even the most ambitious Silicon Valley entrepreneur.

Abraham Kuyper, in other words, was not just a man of uncommon insight, piety, and ambition; he was also a product of his time, maybe in the most crucial sense a time of massive upheaval and global change. And in that time, he founded newspapers, churches, schools, and served as prime minister of a minor European state, all the while clinging to his passion for his Christian religion. We would expect such a wide-ranging man to have made mistakes, maybe bad ones, but we might also want to sit at his feet to see how he held Scripture in one hand and his times in the other, how he read them together in pursuit of this same Jesus we call Lord today.

WORLD- AND LIFE-VIEWS:
"EVERY SQUARE INCH"

Abraham Kuyper loved Calvinism. We might even characterize his passion for Calvinism as unusual; most Calvinists today try to appear as nonthreatening, beer drinking, bearded hipsters. Kuyper was none of those things. His passion for Calvinism as "a true world and life system" is the first of his Stone Lectures that Richard Mouw discusses in this book, lectures that would eventually become *Lectures on Calvinism*.

Kuyper loved Calvinism not for some special genius of John Calvin but because he thought that in Calvinism the truest teaching of the Christian gospel came through. For Kuyper, Calvinism represented the fullest meaning of a catholic gospel—universal good news. The "promiscuity" of this gospel, as one of Kuyper's favorite confessions, the Canons of Dort put it, is universal because it calls us to obedience in *every* area of life, and the good news itself is not just for humankind but for *all* of creation. His lectures on Calvinism are basically just working this out: What does the good news of Jesus Christ mean for art? Or science? Or politics? And what would a consistent Christian foundation for these areas look like? Might we call such consistent Christian foundations something like a "worldview"?

With this concept of worldview, Kuyper captured that people really do *believe* things and that, while we may not even be aware of what those beliefs are, these function in a real way to control our behavior, attitudes, and ultimately the whole of our lives. Kuyper is sometimes criticized here for being too intellectual, as though beliefs are just ideas, concepts, things educated people read about and debate. But this reads Kuyper and his blue-collar theology wrong: beliefs are about what's in our hearts, about what we *love*, not just what we think. A belief is really only proper and basic if it gets to the heart of how we think things really are, if it shapes and is shaped by the things we would give our lives for.

That is what Kuyper meant by worldview, and it is not something only religious people have.

Conforming such a worldview to the Christian gospel was one of his lifelong tasks. The task for Kuyper was not creating a worldview *ex nihilo* but rather discipling our already existing worldviews to the gospel of Jesus Christ. We all have such basic beliefs and desires long before we get into the business of theorizing or praying about them. Christian worldview, for Kuyper, was an extension of the psalmist's prayer—to test our hearts and see if there is any offensive way in us. In this respect, Kuyper anticipated nearly half a century early the postmodernist impulse that there is *always* some belief system or desire underneath knowledge, that there can be no neutral way of knowing.

But he also went beyond the clever deconstructions of the postmodernists. Kuyper not only argued such belief systems and desires persisted but also that love, trust, and obedience to some principle or power was fundamental to the human condition. We trust and love either God or some created thing, ourselves included. For Kuyper this was no mere intellectual project; it was a matter of faith. Calvinism, he thought, was the most consistent and faithful Christian world- and life-view, concerned with all of life and all of what God is owed. H. Evan Runner, a later twentieth-century disciple of Kuyper, would simply say in his favorite phrase, "life is religion."

CONFIDENT PLURALISM:
LOVING FAITHFUL INSTITUTIONS

A radical kind of social project emerges from the logical conclusions of Kuyper's worldview argument. If knowledge and desire are never neutral, and if all of life is claimed by Jesus Christ—intellectual, emotional, blue collar, white collar, and so on—then how can the church go about discipling people under this radical kingdom vision?

Here is the worldview that has launched a thousand Christian institutions, of which Kuyper and his heirs built many. By far, the most
enduring and all-encompassing Protestant Christian social, educational, and political organizations have been built with this worldview,
working to integrate the kingdom of God with the work of their hands.
Other Christian social visions exist, to be sure, but they usually either
elevate some form of work and ministry (pastoral ministry, for example) or subsume the Christian work of business, art, or politics as a
means to the conversion of hearts and minds. The cosmic scope of
Kuyper's theology meant Christian farmers praying about how to sow
and reap under the call of Christ (as in the Christian Farmers Federation) or Christian laborers praying and practicing steel-form construction as obedience to Christ and his kingdom (as in the Christian
Labour Association of Canada).

It was a key argument of Kuyper that all vocations, trades, and practices have buried within them habits and beliefs that either conform
to or react against the kingship of Jesus Christ (thesis or anti-thesis).
The usual complaint is the so-called neutral work of science or math,
where to the modern mind it is unclear how a faithful Christian's work
on linear algebra differs meaningfully from the hedonist atheist. The
math, as they say, is the math. Bringing worldview into it doesn't
change it one bit, or if it does, not for the better. What is missed in
these complaints is the already persisting worldviews behind modern
mathematics and science: presumptions about the knowability of the
universe, the logical, repetitious, and discoverable nature of reality,
none of which are the natural or necessary conclusions of a randomly
generated universe. Laws like "do not steal" seem religious in a way
that laws like those of thermodynamics are not. But that is only because we are busy trading off the religious past of the great scientific
minds of history, who bequeathed to us a scientific method charged
with trust in a kind of universe suspiciously laden with wonder,
goodness, and discoverability.

So if, as Kuyper said, "not one square inch" (not even math!) is unclaimed by Christ, then we must get busy building the kind of institutions and intergenerational conversations that will foster the discipleship Christ demands. We must have a public faith, as some have said[8]—one that is not simply about the piety of prayer closets and Sunday mornings but a faith as cosmic as the redemption of Jesus Christ.

And so we must also practice what legal theorist John Inazu might call confident pluralism,[9] a public practice of faith that deliberately and unapologetically advances our understanding of Christ's kingdom: a faith lived out loud, in public, and with others who may not necessarily share it.

Inazu does not come to his term accidentally, and it elicits the third and final area we think makes the study of Kuyper necessary for our day: the problem of living together amid deep difference. If Christians are living their convictions out loud, what happens when Christians disagree, or (more to the point) what happens when Christians, atheists, Buddhists, Hindus, Muslims, and so on, of all tribes and persuasions, live *their* faith out loud? Pluralism in Kuyper's day looked like Protestants and Catholics having separate school systems. Pluralism in our day looks like Muslims and Jews having family courts, libertarian capitalism and radical ecology, and the now ever-present Muslim headscarf.

Are we still so sure about all this pluralism?

CAN WE LIVE TOGETHER?
THE POINT OF KUYPER'S PLURALISM

Kuyperian philosopher Nicholas Wolterstorff writes that it is "often said, for instance, that everyone has a 'set of presuppositions' or a 'perspective on reality' to bring to a theoretical inquiry. That may be true.

---

[8]Miroslav Volf, *A Public Faith: How Followers of Christ Should Serve the Common Good* (Grand Rapids, MI: Brazos Press, 2011).

[9]John Inazu, *Confident Pluralism: Surviving and Thriving Through Deep Difference* (Chicago: University of Chicago Press, 2016).

But saying such things cannot be the end of the matter. It must at best be the beginning."[10]

Like Wolterstorff, we in the twenty-first century are probably more aware than most in human history of the huge array of rival presuppositions, or perspectives on reality, that people and cultures bring. But also, like Wolterstorff, we know that such diversity is at best a beginning, a context, within which we live, not an end in itself. How to evaluate this potpourri of pluralism, some of which seems dangerous and unsettling? How, to put it to the point, can a Christian live amid the kind of wide diversity it would simply call sin in its own home? Can such a peaceful settlement really exist between religious rivals that, especially under a Kuyperian system, we know are not simply at odds about a *piece* of life but, in a sense, *all* of life?

Here Kuyper advanced what his students have come to call *principled pluralism*, a kind of constitutional arrangement for politics that places principled and procedural limits on pluralism but does not demand we all agree "on why" (as Jacques Maritain famously put it). This is also the cornerstone of what has been called Christian social democracy, or what Kuyperian political philosopher Jonathan Chaplin calls the Christian diversity state.[11] It is probably ironic that this has ended up being one of Kuyper's more enduring legacies, a way to imagine peaceful politics amid radically diverse world- and life-views, when he was himself such a passionate champion of Calvinistic politics and religion as the only sure path of obedience and prosperity. But it is not accidental, because while Kuyper, like others after him, would not give "one inch" on what they owed to Christ, they also recovered and rearticulated a Christian vision for political life beyond tribal polarization

---

[10]Nicholas Wolterstorff, *Reason Within the Bounds of Religion*, 2nd ed. (1984; repr., Grand Rapids, MI: Eerdmans, 1999), 22.

[11]Jonathan Chaplin, "Rejecting Neutrality, Respecting Diversity: From 'Liberal Pluralism' to 'Christian Pluralism,'" *Christian Scholar's Review* 35, no. 2 (Winter 2006): 143-75. Chaplin's magisterial work on a Kuyperian, Dooyeweerdian political theory cannot pass us by without a recommendation: Jonathan Chaplin, *Herman Dooyeweerd: Christian Philosopher of State and Civil Society* (Notre Dame, IN: University of Notre Dame Press, 2016).

and toward an overlapping set of principles and procedures for the common good. And Kuyper did so for specifically Calvinist reasons—a pattern of theology and philosophy that we could do much worse than study to understand and apply in our own day. Ultimately, Kuyper believed that the vitality of a nation and its common life was very much a reflection of its inner spiritual life—a two-way street out of which either renewal or decline would surely come.

FOR SUCH A TIME AS THIS

Abraham Kuyper can seem very contemporary when we read him, and it is our argument that he is a wonderful model for us partly for that reason. There is a great deal we could cover in talking through the work and life of the man Kuyper, not least because of the many new English-language translations of his primary works like *Common Grace, Pro Rege, On the Church, On Islam,* and so on.[12] He was an uncommonly productive man in writing, speaking, and movement and institution building.

But perhaps his most famous work, certainly in America, is his slender *Lectures on Calvinism,* which shows so much of the energy and vision of his theology and politics. We confine ourselves to these lectures in this introductory guide, not because we do not endorse the rest of his work (we do!) but because we think this is the right way to understand his intent and influence in truly interdisciplinary areas (you could say *all*) of human life. These were lectures intended for a North American audience, delivered at Princeton for non-initiates, like us, to help introduce them to the breadth and depth of Kuyper's Calvinistic program. Each of our experts therefore begins with explaining Kuyper's context and argument with each lecture ("What Did Kuyper Say?") but then also gives us a "biography" of each lecture: What kind of influence in North America has it had ("What Did They Do?")? What did the people who heard it think of it, and what sorts of ripples do we see, even

---

[12]See www.abrahamkuyper.com.

now, more than a hundred years later, in North America? Finally, they will also name some blind spots, weaknesses, and areas where later students of Kuyper either found mistakes or brought improvement ("What Should We Do?"). At least one key area is an additional chapter in this guide, which at Princeton in 1898 Kuyper did not address but which today we must: race. No small amount of work has been done on this topic by Kuyper's students, and it is undoubtedly a set of areas in which Kuyper's Christian worldview was dangerously incomplete or in some cases simply wrong.[13]

As we read Kuyper's best intentions out of his *Lectures on Calvinism* in the pages ahead, we must therefore also remember that as contemporary as he may sound, he is also—for us—a man out of time. And he was also a Calvinist, and so all too aware that his best efforts were often marked with the depredations of sin. We will see those echoes too.

The point, at the end, is to paint a portrait not of a saint but of a man, a sometimes crank, who nonetheless worked with "fear and trembling" to bring the whole of life, including his own, under the lordship of Jesus Christ. In that effort, he was far from perfect, but then, so are we. And so, in that project, and in that work, we are all colaborers in "the fields of the Lord,"[14] and it is in that spirit that we invite you to explore the life and legacy of Abraham Kuyper.

---

[13]In this volume, we focus on Kuyper's comments on race within the Stone Lectures, though Kuyper's troubling discussion of race can be found in many other places as well.

[14]As one favorite phrase of Kuyperian Calvin Seerveld put it, which also became the title of an edited anthology of his work. Craig Bartholomew, ed., *In the Fields of the Lord: A Calvin Seerveld Reader* (Carlisle, UK: Piquant, 2000).

KUYPER AND LIFE-SYSTEMS

RICHARD J. MOUW

WHAT DID KUYPER SAY?

One of my students once thanked me for assigning Abraham Kuyper's *Lectures on Calvinism* in the course he had taken from me. Reading these lectures, he said, was a great experience for him. But then he added a mild complaint about the first of Kuyper's lectures. "I think there should be a 'warning label' right there at the beginning. There is a bit of an arrogant spirit in the way he makes Calvinism look good and the other perspectives—including the Christian ones—look bad. And then he makes you wade through a lot of technical stuff as he is making his points. I was glad to get on to the next chapters, which I really liked!"

I was not surprised by his complaint about getting started in reading the Stone Lectures. I have gone through them many times over the years, and even though I understand the points that Kuyper is making, I don't find it easy reading. And like the student, I find some of Kuyper's references to other Christian traditions to be a bit too polemical in tone. Kuyper gets more interesting for me when he turns to specific areas of cultural engagement in the subsequent chapters, showing how Calvinism can help us understand why God cares about religious beliefs and practices, politics, science, and the arts.

Still, important topics are covered in these early pages, and it is good to get a sense of why Kuyper finds it necessary to contrast Calvinism with these other perspectives before he moves on to more specific areas. And it also helps to know why his tone is a bit strident as he sets up his overall framework.

Kuyper was well aware that the Presbyterian folks who attended these lectures at Princeton—mainly pastors and professors—were feeling beleaguered by attacks on the traditional Calvinism that had long characterized the theology at Princeton Seminary. And Kuyper himself had recently gone through some theological struggles back home in the Netherlands, resulting in a serious division in the ranks of the Dutch Reformed there. So, he wanted to offer words of encouragement to his hearers. He wanted to assure them that the defense of Calvinism is no lost cause—indeed, Calvinism provides a very exciting overall perspective on how we are to live our lives as people who want to serve the Lord in all things.

To make his case, Kuyper explained to his audience that he was going to explore some new dimensions in Calvinism, ones that often were not given adequate attention by those who, over the past centuries, professed loyalty to the theology of John Calvin. Kuyper made it clear that his intention in discussing Calvinism in these lectures was "not to restore its worn-out form"; rather, he was going to show how Calvinism, as a system of thought that flows from a deep "life principle," fulfills in an exciting way "the requirements of our own century."[1]

It may not have been the wisest thing for Kuyper to talk about not wanting to rehabilitate Calvinism in "its worn-out form." He certainly wasn't meaning to reject the Calvinism of the past, and it probably would have been better to assure his audience about that. Kuyper clearly endorsed the basics of the Calvinist portrayal of how an individual can get right with God. We were created to live in an obedient fellowship with God, but in rebelling against our Creator we have become deeply

---

[1] Abraham Kuyper, *Lectures on Calvinism* (1931; repr., Grand Rapids, MI: Eerdmans, 1999), 41.

stuck in our own sinfulness. If we are to be rescued from our depravity, it has to happen from God's direction. And God did move toward us by sending Jesus into the world to take our sin on himself. So we are saved by grace alone.

Kuyper firmly believed in all of that, including all of the traditional Calvinist formulations about election and predestination and the "eternal security" of the believer. His intention in these lectures was to show how Calvinism offers us all of that—but also a lot more. Yes, God saves us from our helpless sinful condition. But what does he save us *for*? And here is where the bigger Calvinist picture begins to unfold. We are saved—as members of a community of believers—to show forth the lordship of Christ over all things.

To put it in simple terms, in these lectures Kuyper wants to portray Calvinism as a big-picture perspective on the Christian life. This is why he gives so much attention in this first lecture to the importance of seeing Calvinism as a "life-system."[2] If all we have is a theology about individual salvation, we can easily be taken in by the answers to the broader questions about human well-being generated by what he sees as the four other life-systems providing influential guidance for human living at that time: paganism, Islamism, Roman Catholicism, and modernism. To resist these competing influences, he argues, we must be clear about what Calvinism has to teach us about what he identifies as the "three fundamental relations of all human life": how we human creatures relate to God, how we relate to our fellow humans, and how we relate to the larger world in which we find ourselves.[3]

Foundational to all of this for Kuyper is our understanding of who God is. The supreme authority of the God of the Bible is basic to Kuyper's understanding of reality. As the Creator of all things, God is distinct from all he has called into being. God did not have to create a world in order to be fully God. That view stands in stark contrast to the

---

[2]Kuyper, *Lectures on Calvinism*, 9-40.
[3]Kuyper, *Lectures on Calvinism*, 19.

pantheistic understanding, which equates the divine with the "all" of the universe. Kuyper was passionate about that classical conception of the Wholly Other-ness of God.

The denial of this vast "being" gap between the Creator and his creation is at the heart of human sinfulness. God alone is worthy of our ultimate trust, and when we put that trust in something less than God— something creaturely—we are engaged in idolatry, and this is the root of all sin. By turning our ultimate allegiance toward something within the creation, we mess up those "three fundamental relations of all human life."[4] By refusing to honor God's authority, we cut ourselves off from the blessings of living in fellowship with our Creator, and this in turn disrupts our relations with our fellow humans as well as with our ways of relating to the nonhuman world.

What's at stake in all of this for Kuyper is the insistence that Christian faith is more than a purely "personal" matter. It is not less than that, of course. We human beings got into the mess that we are in because our first parents made the very personal decision to trust the serpent's promise that if they would disobey God and eat the forbidden fruit, they themselves would "be like God" (Gen 3:5). But that personal act of rebellion has wide-reaching consequences for human life—which is why Kuyper goes on in these lectures to explain how restoring our personal relationship with God through Christ's atoning work has profound implications for how we view church, politics, science, and artistic endeavors.

Before getting into the details of those specific areas of Christian service, though, Kuyper wants us to see how the life-system he sets forth differs from other major life-systems that are at work in the world. He is especially concerned about one of these in particular. In present life, he says, it is modernism and Christianity that "are wrestling with one another, in mortal combat."[5] He sees a close connection in this regard

---

[4]Kuyper, *Lectures on Calvinism*, 19.
[5]Kuyper, *Lectures on Calvinism*, 11.

between the modernist life-system and the French Revolution of the late eighteenth century.

Two decades earlier Kuyper had founded the Anti-Revolutionary Party, of which he had served as the party's leader in the Dutch Parliament. In choosing "Anti-Revolutionary" for the name of his political party, he signaled his conviction that the ideology of the French Revolution was diametrically opposed to Christian life and thought. The revolutionaries in France were committed to abolishing everything associated with belief in God. Central to their thinking was the insistence on the radical supremacy of the independent human self. In that sense, the ideology of the French Revolution was the philosophical expression of the serpent's promise that human beings can be their own gods, with human reason functioning as the ultimate source of meaning and value.

As Kuyper explains the modernist perspective in more detail in this first lecture, he introduces some complications. In addition to the French atheistic themes, he sees some "pantheist" German philosophical ideas at work in modernism, particularly the ways that the traditional Christian belief in divine providence had been incorporated into evolutionistic thought, with the conviction regarding the inevitably of human progress. For our purposes here, though, we do not need to follow the philosophical details of Kuyper's exposition as long as we grasp his basic point, which is that modernism is a life-system that seeks to eliminate all the influences of Christian faith from human life and thought.

While that modernist project clearly remains a major challenge to the Christian faith in the twenty-first century, Kuyper's other two non-Christian life-systems are still very much in the picture for our Western culture—more so than they were in Kuyper's time. He was thinking globally, and for him, paganism and Islam were a major presence primarily in other parts of the world. As he put it, the pagan understanding of spiritual things could be seen in both "the lowest Animism" and "the highest Buddhism." What every form of paganism has in common, he observes, is an understanding of the divine that "does not rise to the conception of the independent existence of a God beyond and above the creature."[6] In that sense, paganism is a presence in our current surroundings, not only in popular "New Age" thinking but also in the outlook expressed in the popular motto, "I'm not religious at all, but I do consider myself to be quite spiritual!"

And, of course, Islam has become a highly visible presence in Western cultures. When I was growing up, what we knew about Muslims was mainly from what returning missionaries told us when they visited our congregations to report about their ministries in Arab countries. Now I see Muslims daily, in supermarkets and schoolyards.

Islam presents a unique religious phenomenon for Kuyper. Muslims certainly do not confuse the Creator with some aspect of his creation. The God to whom they pray is very much above and beyond the created order. Indeed, in Kuyper's telling, the problem with Islam is that it creates *too great* a spiritual distance between Allah and the world. It makes God's being *so* distinct from created reality, he says, that it "*isolates God from the creature*, in order to avoid all commingling with the creature."[7] The result, as one Calvinist expert on Islam has put it more recently, is that

> in Islam there is little room for a life of personal fellowship with God. Allah is so great and so exalted, and his will is so completely dominating, that very little is left on the human side. . . . Even the sense of personal responsibility toward him and the need for forgiveness and reconciliation, find no possibility of development.[8]

As opposed to these other life-systems, for Kuyper, Christianity gets it right in spelling out the big picture. The Bible tells us of a God who reigns over his creation, while also emphasizing the fact that God created human beings with the capacity to live in a vital fellowship with him. For Kuyper this requires that we see all aspects of our lives as

---

[6]Kuyper, *Lectures on Calvinism*, 20.

[7]Kuyper, *Lectures on Calvinism*, 20 (emphasis original).

[8]J. H. Bavinck, "Defining Religious Consciousness: The Five Magnetic Points," in *The J. H. Bavinck Reader,* ed. John Bolt, James D. Bratt, and Paul J. Visser, trans. James A. De Jong (Grand Rapids, MI: Eerdmans, 2013), 181.

taking place before the presence of God. Kuyper regularly uses a wonderful Latin phrase to capture this reality: *coram Deo*, which means "before the face of God." He insists that the genius of Calvinism is that it sets forth a life-system that highlights the inescapable reality of our living every moment before the face of God.

The obvious Christian alternative to Calvinism for Kuyper is the Roman Catholic view, which he likes to label "Romanism." The key defect in Catholicism for him is the way it relies on the church as mediating our relationship to God. For the Calvinist, Kuyper argues, divine grace comes to us directly from God, and nothing must stand in the way of "a direct and immediate communion with the Living God."[9] More broadly, Kuyper also objects to the way the Catholic Church had long seen itself as mediating the relationship between God and the other spheres. For Kuyper, the churchly realm is just one of the areas of collective life—alongside the state, the art guild, the university, and the area of economic activity—that stands directly under God's sovereign rule.

Kuyper sees other Christian traditions—Baptists, Anglicans, Wesleyans, and Lutherans, for example—as lacking the full life-system character of Catholicism and Calvinism. The Anabaptists receive special criticism from him for what he sees as their refusal to engage the larger culture at all.

As my student made clear, the tone of Kuyper's depiction of other Christian groups can strike us today as much too confrontational. Fortunately, we will find him acknowledging, as he moves to his conclusions in the final lecture, the positive lessons he has been learning from Catholics—and even from modernist Protestants.

What we cannot excuse in this opening lecture, however, are the remarks he makes about traditional African culture. Kuyper credits Asia for its cultural development while also criticizing Asians for failing to contribute their cultural riches to the larger world. But Africa, he suggests, simply has not had any significant cultural development to share with the rest of humanity. In offering this assessment, he even mentions

---

[9]Kuyper, *Lectures on Calvinism*, 21.

Noah's sons—alluding to the tradition which has taught that Ham, who was cursed by his father, was the one whose offspring populated the African continent. Such a sentiment, of course, reveals at the very least an unwillingness to expand one's understanding of culture; at its worst, it reveals something much more sinister.

Kuyper's perceptions of African culture were clearly shaped by the views of the Dutch who had settled in Southern Africa—he was closely in touch with them. Those folks would soon establish the racist apartheid structures, and the Dutch Reformed theological system which supported that regime is often thought of as drawing on Kuyperian ideas. Ironically, in this lecture, Kuyper insists that the development of a robust global culture can come only by "the commingling of blood"[10]—a direct challenge to the separation of the races that was foundational to the apartheid regime.

The Black South African theologian Russel Botman has acknowledged that while Kuyper did indeed contribute to apartheid thinking, he also had "a liberative influence on South Africa."[11] This meant, Botman observes, that "it was the task of Black Kuyperianism to select the positive aspects and present their theological relevance to South Africa."[12] He cites the assessment of another prominent Black Reformed theologian, Allan Boesak, who saw positive support in Kuyper's thought for the struggle for racial justice:

> We believe passionately with Abraham Kuyper that there is not a single inch of life that does not fall under the lordship of Christ. . . . Here the Reformed tradition comes so close to the African idea of the wholeness of life that these two should combine to renew the thrust that was brought to Christian life by the followers of Calvin.[13]

---

[10]Kuyper, *Lectures on Calvinism*, 35.

[11]H. Russel Botman, "Is Blood Thicker Than Justice? The Legacy of Abraham Kuyper for Southern Africa," in *Religion, Pluralism, and Public Life: Abraham Kuyper's Legacy for the Twenty-First Century*, ed. Luis E. Lugo (Grand Rapids, MI: Eerdmans, 2000), 343.

[12]Botman, "Is Blood Thicker Than Justice?," 344.

[13]Allan Boesak, *Black and Reformed: Apartheid, Liberation, and the Calvinist Tradition* (New York: Orbis Press, 1984), 87, quoted in Botman, "Is Blood Thicker Than Justice?," 344.

All we can do, says Botman, is to acknowledge that "the real Kuyper was both these things: a praiseworthy Reformed theologian who, regrettably, held to the potentially oppressive core value of separateness."[14]

WHAT DID KUYPERIANS DO?

Kuyper's lectures at Princeton did not have the intended effect on his audience.[15] While he had brought a message about a robust Calvinist vision of life that could motivate believers to take on the intellectual, political, and artistic challenges of the broader North American culture, his Princeton hearers (about forty attended each of his lectures) were preoccupied with other matters. They were feeling under attack by the increasing influence of a liberal theology that denied some of the key traditional doctrines, such as the authority of the Bible and Christ as the heaven-sent Son of God who was born of a virgin and shed his blood on Calvary to pay the penalty for human sin. While the Princeton folks certainly sensed that Kuyper was analyzing the basic threats of the modernist influences they were struggling against in their church life, they were seeing the need to defend specific theological implications of Calvinist theology rather than exploring the fundamental character of Calvinism as a culture-embracing life-system.

To be sure, the Princeton Presbyterians respected Kuyper and gave his visit positive reviews. But they took from his lectures particular ideas that would equip them for the immediate theological debates that preoccupied them in the church world.

To see how Kuyper's influence in North America did eventually grow, we need to mention a terminological matter. In a footnote in this first lecture, he explains briefly why he chose to use the label *life-system* in his Princeton presentations.[16] As we have been seeing, that label plays

---

[14]Botman, "Is Blood Thicker Than Justice?," 354.

[15]For the impact of Kuyper's lectures on his Princeton audience, I am drawing here on observations made by George Harinck in his essay, "A Triumphal Procession? The Reception of Kuyper in the USA (1900–1940)," in *Kuyper Reconsidered: Aspects of His Life and Work*, ed. Cornelis van der Kooi and Jan de Bruijn (Amsterdam: VU Uitgeverij, 1999), 275-77.

[16]Kuyper, *Lectures on Calvinism*, 11n.

an important role in the way he sets up his case for Calvinism, and he sticks with it throughout. But in his final lecture, he changes terms, saying that Calvinism provides "a life- and world-view."[17] Where Kuyper's influence took hold, that new label got shortened to, simply, *worldview* and became the standard way of describing the big-picture approach he was advocating.

Again, however, it took quite a while for this worldview perspective to have a significant influence in North American Christianity. The one place it did take hold rather quickly was in the Dutch Calvinist immigrant community, concentrated primarily in the Midwestern United States. Kuyper's Stone Lectures—which appeared rather soon in book form—were read by the folks in that subculture. They understood Kuyper well, and his approach had a deep and lasting effect in their educational institutions, particularly at Calvin University in Michigan.

Unfortunately, though, the recent immigrants were not prepared to translate Kuyper's ideas into active engagement with the larger North American culture. When Kuyper visited Princeton, they were still conducting most of their own religious activity in the Dutch language. And around the time that they did begin the switch to the English language—two decades after Kuyper's Princeton visit—they became preoccupied with theological debates within their own ranks. One of those debates was about a key Kuyperian teaching, common grace, and the controversy led to a wrenching church split in the 1920s.[18] Ironically, then, instead of using the Kuyperian framework for addressing the larger culture, it served as a point of division within their own community.

But the Dutch American Calvinists did at least keep Kuyper's ideas alive within their own somewhat insulated academic culture. This was brought home to me personally in a rather graphic way when I interviewed for a faculty position in philosophy at Calvin University (then Calvin College) in the late 1960s. The final step in the interviewing

---

[17]Kuyper, *Lectures on Calvinism*, 171.
[18]James D. Bratt, *Dutch Calvinism in Modern America: A History of a Conservative Subculture* (Grand Rapids, MI: Eerdmans, 1984), 93-122.

process was a meeting with the college's president. He was cordial, but he also pushed me hard on worldview issues. I had earned my own undergraduate degree at an evangelical college, and he clearly wanted to be sure that I understood what I was getting into at Calvin. At one point he described Calvin's mission in a striking manner: "We take our Calvinist theology very seriously here—but that by itself is not what makes this a Calvinist school. To put it bluntly: if on the same evening the entire theology faculty died and the chapel also burned to the ground, this would still be a Calvinist school the next morning. It's because we have a worldview that shapes everything we teach. Sociology, Chemistry, History, Literature!"

I got to know that president well, and he had a deep commitment to Calvinist theology, along with a warm piety. But in that statement he was expressing what it meant for a college to be true to the Kuyperian vision. While other schools in the evangelical world had long preserved their Christian identity mainly through required theology courses and regular campus worship, the Kuyperian way was for the curriculum itself to be shaped by a Christian worldview.

Again, we can be grateful that the worldview perspective had been preserved for the next half-century by the intellectuals in the Dutch Calvinist community. Right around the time when I had that conversation with Calvin University's president, though, a new awareness of the Kuyperian vision was emerging in the larger evangelical community. In the late 1960s, for example, the important evangelical theologian Carl Henry founded the Institute for Advanced Christian Scholarship in the hope of establishing a new graduate-level university whose purpose would be "the unification of all the university disciplines in the interest of a Christian world-life view."[19]

Carl Henry was not alone in expressing the need for this more robust approach to evangelical learning. Another important voice in this

---

[19]Quoted by Owen Strachan, *Awakening the Evangelical Mind: An Intellectual History of the Neo-Evangelical Movement* (Grand Rapids, MI: Zondervan, 2015). Strachan is drawing here on materials in the Henry Papers at Trinity Evangelical Divinity School's Rolfing Library.

regard was Arthur Holmes, a philosopher who taught with a strong worldview emphasis at Wheaton College, beginning in 1951, for over four decades. His views eventually became influential in evangelical higher education, when his books—*The Idea of a Christian College* and *All Truth Is God's Truth*, published in 1975 and 1977, respectively—were widely read by evangelical faculty members and administrators.

Ministries on university campuses also began to play an important role in promoting worldview sensitivities. An obvious case in point is the publisher of this volume, InterVarsity Press, which has done much to make worldview writings available to a broad audience. A prominent example is *The Universe Next Door*, by Jim Sire, a book first published in 1976, which became a bestseller that has sold hundreds of thousands of copies over the decades. The book originally contrasted the Christian perspective with deism, Eastern mysticism, existentialism, naturalism, and the like—with other perspectives, such as Marxism, New Age, and secular humanism, added in later editions.

While Sire acknowledged Kuyper's influence on his thinking in an interview not long before he died,[20] he also drew on other sources in setting forth his case. Like Henry and Holmes, he saw the importance of making worldview thinking available to a broad evangelical audience without tying the issues too closely to what might be seen in a North American context as an over-reliance on Dutch Reformed doctrines and themes.

While that awareness was growing, positive things were happening among the Dutch American Calvinists, with a new infusion of active Dutch energies into the Kuyperian cause in North America. The post– World War II period brought a significant number of immigrants from the Netherlands, with most of them settling in Canada. These Calvinists had been shaped by movements in the Netherlands that embodied Kuyper's vision for specific areas of cultural engagement, and they

---

[20]James Sire, interview by Fred Zaspel, Books at a Glance, May 12, 2015, www.booksataglance. com/author-interviews/interview-with-james-sire-author-of-apologetics-beyond-reason-why -seeing-is-really-believing/.

arrived in North America with an enthusiasm for carrying on this task in their new homeland. They soon organized Christian farmer groups, a movement for promoting Christian concerns in labor relations, summer conferences for promoting Kuyperian concerns, and an influential "think tank" organization, the Association for the Advancement of Christian Scholarship (known today as the Institute for Christian Studies, in Toronto). Students from these immigrant communities also brought a new enthusiasm for the Kuyperian vision to Calvin University and other colleges and universities that had recently been established by the North American Dutch Calvinists.

One of the ironic developments in the growing post–World War II enthusiasm for Kuyperian ideas in North America has to do with two influential leaders. One was Francis Schaeffer, an American who established a study center in Switzerland and produced several widely read books promoting worldview thinking. The other was Evan Runner, a professor at Calvin University who played a key role in guiding the recent Dutch immigrants in Canada as they brought their Kuyperian sensitivities to their new cultural environment.

Neither Schaeffer nor Runner was of Dutch ethnic stock, but each was an eloquent articulator of Kuyper's thought. And here is the irony: both of them were trained in—and continued to be shaped by—the "Old Princeton" theology that had ruled the day when Kuyper gave his 1898 lectures. The two of them saw the connections that Kuyper had wanted his Princeton audience to grasp. Kuyper's vision was finally being appropriated among the descendants of those original hearers!

WHAT SHOULD WE DO?

As I noted earlier, early on in his first lecture to his Princeton audience Kuyper said that his concern was to show how the "life-principle" set forth in Calvinism was to meet "the requirements of our own century." He made that observation just as the twentieth century was about to begin, and now we are well into the twenty-first century. So, it is

important for us to ask what we need to do with Kuyper's vision in order
to meet the challenges of our own day.

One obvious thing that needs doing, or so it seems to me, is to get
Christians to understand the central concerns of worldview thinking
without requiring them to grasp and accept all the theological and philosophical issues that Kuyper explores in his first Princeton lecture. The
vast majority of the followers of Christ should be able to wrestle with
worldview topics and challenges today without being able to articulate
the technical issues raised by, for example, pantheism, or the philosophy
of the French Revolution, or the Muslim understanding of divine tran-
scendence. I don't mean to disparage those topics—I think about them
a lot. But for fellow Christians who are farmers or computer programmers
or hair stylists, those technical matters are not of great importance.

Nor do such folks need to grasp all the sophisticated theological aspects of Kuyper's Calvinism—even though here too I take what he says
with utmost seriousness. At the heart of what Kuyper is getting at in his
worldview discussion, though, is that God is the sovereign Ruler over
all of life and that we need to shape our patterns of living and acting in
the light of what God has revealed to us about his purposes in the world.
These are the important central truths, and once we have grasped them
we should be able to resist the ways that alternative worldviews encourage us, for example, to see the human person as the highest authority in the universe or to tempt us to devote our lives to satisfying
religious impulses that require no recognition that we are sinners who
desperately need a heaven-sent Savior.

In suggesting that we simplify our formulations about worldviews, I
do not mean to be "dumbing down" these topics. Wheaton College's
Arthur Holmes, whom I mentioned earlier, nicely distinguished between
what he labeled "theologians' theology" and "philosophers' philosophy,"
on the one hand, and "world-viewish theology" and "world-viewish philosophy," on the other. The first two ways of thinking, he wrote, deal with
the kinds of topics that professional theologians and philosophers talk

about when they discuss matters with their scholarly peers, while the "world-viewish" varieties deal with topics that scholars wrestle with when they address questions that arise out of practical real-life contexts.[21]

Holmes certainly respected the more technical scholarly pursuits in philosophy and theology. But in teaching students who were preparing for many different areas of kingdom service, he wanted to provide careful guidance for intelligent Christians to think clearly about fundamental questions that bear on a variety of vocations and life-situations: topics such as sexuality, technology, work, leisure, friendship, and politics.

Brian Walsh and Richard Middleton did an excellent job of making world-viewish topics available to a general audience in a book they authored together. Their own thinking on the subject is indebted to Kuyper, but they make their case in fairly nontechnical—and quite practical—terms. A worldview, they say, whether Christian or otherwise, is made up of a set of answers to these questions: Who am I? Where am I? What's wrong? What is the remedy?[22] People don't always explicitly ask these questions, but human beings typically approach life with some grasp of how those questions are to be answered. And the answers we take for granted do guide our lives.

The "Who am I?" question has to do with a person's basic understanding of what it means to be a human being. "Where am I?" is about how I view the human person's place in the larger scheme of things. "What's wrong?" gets at the widespread sense that our lives, individually and collectively, are often clearly dysfunctional. And "What is the remedy?" addresses what we look to as the fundamental solution to the problems of our human existence.

Those questions cover the same territory as the life-systems discussed by Kuyper in his first lecture. Take, for example, the ideology of the French Revolution. In that worldview human persons are seen as free

---

[21]Arthur F. Holmes, *Contours of a World View* (Grand Rapids, MI: Eerdmans, 1983), 31-32, 34-40.

[22]Brian J. Walsh and J. Richard Middleton, *The Transforming Vision: Shaping a Christian World View* (Downers Grove, IL: InterVarsity Press, 1984), 35.

and rational beings who exist in a universe that is ultimately fully knowable by the proper exercise of our rational capacities. The fundamental problem of human existence is that we do not trust our reason, but regularly give ourselves over to irrational—even superstitious—beliefs and practices. The remedy, then, is collectively to overthrow the oppressive religious institutions and forces that keep us from following the dictates of reason alone.

That is a bit too quick as a summary, but it does get at the basics of what guided the worldview that shaped the French Revolution. In our own time, however, the perspective that formed those events of the final decades in eighteenth-century Europe shows up in the lives of many people who have no knowledge of French history. "I have to do it my way" and "I've got to be me!" are popular contemporary expressions of the "autonomous self" celebrated in the French Enlightenment philosophy. The same for the conviction that we can solve the pressing problems of humankind if only we would promote better education, or rely on what science teaches us, or be more "attentive" to our deepest rational promptings.

On one level, the Christian worldview's answers to those questions are fairly straightforward. Who we are is children of God, fashioned in the divine image. We live in a universe called into being by the living God who calls us to glorify him in all that we do. The problem is that we are sinners, and we cannot save ourselves. But God has provided the amazing remedy by sending his only Son to redeem and restore the likes of us.

Each of these answers, though, points to a variety of underlying topics. And in some cases we must, in dealing with those concerns, not only go further than Kuyper did in his thinking but even go back and correct some of his views. His racial views are an obvious case in point. Who are we? We are human beings of many races and ethnicities who nonetheless possess a shared dignity that is grounded in our being beloved creatures of God. And we together face cultural forces these days that require us to reflect deeply—and act, urgently—on our convictions about our shared humanness. We have, more than Kuyper did in his day, a global awareness of injustice, religious persecution, the plight of refugees and other homeless persons, the blessings and curses of social media and "artificial intelligence," and much more.

The "Where are we?" question takes on special significance because of environmental concerns. The biblical mandate to human beings to "have dominion" over the rest of creation was not a call to dominate nonhuman reality, but to be caretakers (persons who take care) of the creation. To be properly aware of the scope of our human task in this regard is also to recognize the reality of the larger—the structural and "systemic"—dimensions of the cursedness of our sinfulness. This requires (and here Kuyper sets the right sort of tone for our explorations) that we see Jesus not only as our Savior and our Lord but as the King, the sovereign Ruler over all of created reality.

I realize that in setting forth Kuyper's overall perspective, I have emphasized the challenges and problems he wants us to face. This can easily come across as yet another version of gloomy Calvinism. But that would be misleading. Yes, God calls us—mandates us—to take on the complexities of Christian discipleship. But there are joys to be experienced in doing so. In the lectures to follow, Kuyper clearly wants to commend the Calvinist worldview as promoting human flourishing. He will encourage us to grow in grace as mutually supporting members of the body of Christ. He will tell us about the benefits that we can receive by living in a well-ordered society, where the government encourages and supports a rich variety of cultural spheres. He wants us to engage the world of ideas, actively promoting Christian learning. He points us to the importance of the arts in nurturing human well-being.

In some of my own speaking and writing in recent years I have been emphasizing the importance of an active world*viewing* rather than the more static notion of "having" a worldview. I think Kuyper encourages that more dynamic picture when he tells us that we need a Calvinism that is not just a repetition of past ideas but a reappropriation of the best from the past in articulating an exciting vision for the present. And in our present time we walk new paths on our faith journeys and encounter new realities.

There still is at least one important reason not simply to give up talking about the noun *worldview*, however. As we view the new realities along the way, it is crucial that we be continually aware of the big picture of the world Kuyper was advocating. In the Bible "the world" sometimes refers to the sinful patterns of human thought and practice. It is in this sense that the apostle John rightly warns us not to "love the world or anything in the world" (1 Jn 2:15). But that same apostle tells us in his Gospel account that the God who "so loved the world" sent his Son into the world, not "to condemn the world, but to save the world through him" (Jn 3:16-17). The Greek word for *world* there is *kosmos*, referring to the created order that God originally proclaimed to be good.

That is at the heart of Kuyper's understanding of worldview. God loves his creation and has refused to allow our sinful rebellion to cancel his original designs for all that he has made. The world that God still loves includes the patterns and products of human culture—family life, politics, the arts, business activity, academy, medical research, athletics, and more. God wanted all of that to unfold in his creation, and he calls us to be agents of that continuing work of engaging in that which glorifies him. This certainly means work on our part, of course. But it also means enjoying that which others have accomplished—including what has been produced by persons who do not acknowledge the divine source of the talents they possess.

All of this gives us an exciting way of understanding what the psalmist meant when he wrote that "the earth is the LORD's, and everything it" (Ps 24:1). Kuyper is inviting us into a way of life that allows us to flourish in the creation that is being prepared for the day when all things will be made new in Jesus Christ.

FOR FURTHER READING

Dooyeweerd, Herman. *In the Twilight of Western Thought.* Lewiston, NY: Edwin Mellen Press, 1999.

Heslam, Peter. *Creating a Christian Worldview: Abraham Kuyper's Lectures on Calvinism.* Grand Rapids, MI: Eerdmans, 1998.

Naugle, David K. *Worldview: The History of a Concept.* Grand Rapids, MI: Eerdmans, 2002.

Runner, H. Evan. *The Relation of the Bible to Learning.* Toronto: Wedge Pub. Foundation, 1970.

Spykman, Gordon. *Christian Faith in Focus.* Jordan Station, ON: Paideia Press, 1992.

Van Til, Henry R. *The Calvinistic Concept of Culture.* Grand Rapids, MI: Baker Academic, 2001.

Walsh, Brian J., and J. Richard Middleton, *The Transforming Vision: Shaping a Christian Worldview.* Downers Grove, IL: InterVarsity Press, 1984.

Wolters, Albert M. *Creation Regained: A Biblical Basis for a Reformational Worldview.* 2nd ed. Grand Rapids, MI: Eerdmans, 2005.

Wolterstorff, Nicholas. *Reason Within the Bounds of Religion.* Grand Rapids, MI: Eerdmans, 1984.

2

KUYPER AND RELIGION

JAMES EGLINTON

WHAT DID KUYPER SAY?

Since the mid-twentieth century, the notion of religion has taken quite a battering at the hands of Protestant Christians. In his seminal *Church Dogmatics*, for example, that century's great Protestant dogmatician Karl Barth (1886–1968) proclaimed that religion was an inherently faithless endeavor. Seeing religion as an extension of sinful humanity's aversion to God, Barth set it in direct opposition to the notion of divine self-revelation. In our religion, he claimed, we fashion false gods according to our own fancies. Claiming to make our own path toward God, he argued, we use religion to stray all the further from him. In revelation, Barth believed, God practices self-disclosure through, in, and as Jesus Christ, in whom God has come toward us.[1] In the same period, Barth's former student, the anti-Nazi Lutheran theologian Dietrich Bonhoeffer (1906–1945) began to develop his famous arguments for "religionless Christianity."[2] In their context, of course, this

---

[1] Karl Barth, *Church Dogmatics* I.2, ed. G. W. Bromiley and T. F. Torrance, trans. G. T. Thomson and Harold Knight (Edinburgh: T&T Clark, 1980), §17.3; see also Sven Ensminger, *Karl Barth's Theology as a Resource for a Christian Theology of Religions* (London: T&T Clark, 2016).

[2] Dietrich Bonhoeffer, *Letters and Papers from Prison*, ed. Eberhard Bethge (New York: Touchstone, 1971); see also Jeffrey C. Pugh, *Religionless Christianity: Dietrich Bonhoeffer in Troubled Times* (London: T&T Clark, 2008), 69-95.

desire to free Christianity from religion was motivated by the ease with which Nazism had co-opted the feeble liberal Christian religion of its day. In response to this, Barth and Bonhoeffer were looking for the Christian faith's primordial core, which lay buried beneath the thin religious edifice—clerics, church practices and rites, doctrinal beliefs—that had proved susceptible to Nazi takeover.

As the twentieth century progressed, the anti-authoritarian spirit of the 1960s and the individualism of mass market capitalism combined to produce widely asserted Protestant (evangelical) sentiments that Christianity should be seen as a relationship with God rather than a religion—a view that grew up against a broader backdrop of "spiritual but not religious" self-identification.[3] In the four centuries since the Protestant reformer John Calvin penned *The Institutes of the Christian Religion*, his ecclesiastical descendants had come a long way. Whatever their Christianity had become, it was anything but religious.

In view of the generally low view of religion that would develop across the twentieth century, then, the positive handling of religion offered in Abraham Kuyper's second Stone Lecture is notable. While many noted nineteenth-century theological liberals had made efforts to save religion from the Enlightenment by redefining it—the German theologian Friedrich Schleiermacher's *On Religion: Speeches to Its Cultured Despisers*[4] being perhaps that century's most outstanding example—Kuyper's own defense of religion was made in 1898, just as that century came to a close under the shadow of David Friedrich Strauss's bold declaration that the civilized world stood on the cusp of a new, intentionally post-Christian era. In the impending twentieth century, as suggested by Strauss, the closest thing to a religion would be some form of scientism—the belief that the explanatory power of

---

[3]Christian Smith with Melina Lundquist Denton, *Soul Searching: The Religious and Spiritual Lives of American Teenagers* (Oxford: Oxford University Press, 2005), 81; William B. Parsons, ed., *Being Spiritual but Not Religious: Past, Present, Future(s)* (Abingdon, UK: Routledge, 2018).
[4]Friedrich Schleiermacher, *On Religion: Speeches to Its Cultured Despisers*, ed. Richard Crouter (Cambridge: Cambridge University Press, 1996).

empirical science was sufficient to cover every part of human existence, from the artist's workshop to the factory floor.[5] In that argument, the Christian religion (and especially Jesus himself) was presented as the single greatest obstacle to the progress of civilization: to Strauss, its gospel was in no sense good news for science, art, or culture.

For Kuyper, however, religion—as a general phenomenon, among Christians in particular, and as a subject that encompasses all of everyday life—was certainly no unclean thing or barrier to the flourishing of life in the world. Rather, his instincts were the opposite to those of Strauss: the Christian religion, when refracted through Kuyper's Calvinistic prism, was indeed good news for science, art, and culture. When giving these lectures at the close of the nineteenth century, which were themselves a big-picture advertisement for Calvinism as the hope for the world, Kuyper's argument depended on his ability both to critique and advocate for religion in general, and to promote Calvinism as *the* religion necessary to human flourishing.[6]

As part of that larger argument, Kuyper's lecture "Calvinism and Religion"[7] is structured around four questions on religion, each of which directly addressed the concerns of his own day and remains important a century later: (1) Is religion merely a human phenomenon? (2) Must all people be religious? (3) Does religion concern only private matters of the heart or morality, or is its purview much more capacious? and (4) Can religion be a positive force for good in our world? In crafting his own answers to these questions, Kuyper's lecture developed a narrative that laid out the distinctives of his brand of Calvinism—which would later be styled as "neo-Calvinism"—as an articulation of

---

[5]David Friedrich Strauss, *The Old Faith and the New: A Confession*, trans. Mathilde Blind (New York: Henry Holt and Company, 1873).

[6]And this argument on religion, of course, fit into a broader structure within his Stone Lectures: having already argued for the idea of an organizing, animating "life-system" in which humans participate, his lecture on religion in holistic, all-of-life terms would then serve as a stepping stone into his material on the integration of politics, science, and art, which was then rounded off in his provocative lecture "Calvinism and the Future," which Bruce Ashford covers later in this book.

[7]Abraham Kuyper, *Lectures on Calvinism* (1931; repr., Grand Rapids, MI: Eerdmans, 1999), 41-77.

Christianity as a religion that united God and humanity; the individual and society; and head, heart, and hands. Rather than attempting to save Christianity by extricating it from religion, à la Bonhoeffer, or trying to save Jesus's good name by distancing him from the faithless idolatry that is the Christian religion, à la Barth, Kuyper's lecture aimed to redeem religion by showing it at what he believed to be its very best: in Calvinism as the religion of (all of) life lived in God's presence (*coram Deo*). This kind of religion, he argued, certainly was a positive force for good in the world.

Before exploring these questions, it is worth noting that Kuyper does not offer an abstract definition of religion in this lecture. Rather, the meaning of *religious* becomes clear when Kuyper explains his vision of human life lived well—which is to say, when human life, in all its breadth and depth, individually and collectively, is lived to the glory of God. In that light, for Kuyper, religion becomes an intensely practical matter. It is personal and embodied precisely because God has made us for himself—with the goal that human life will become a beautifully harmonious thing because it finds its starting point and goal in God. Kuyper's view of religion, then, is perhaps most clearly seen in his description of the contrast seen between religious and irreligious lives. "To be irreligious," he argued, "is to forsake the highest aim of our existence."[8] Kuyper's alternative kind of life was one that strives "to covet no other existence than for the sake of God, to long for nothing but for the will of God, and to be wholly absorbed in the glory of the name of the Lord, such is the pith and kernel of all true religion."[9] In the Stone Lectures, religiosity and irreligiosity are best understood as two ways to live.

First question: Who is religion about? According to Kuyper, religion should be seen as part of the warp and weft of human life rather than as an abstraction. It is integral to our humanity, which becomes fractured without religion. Kuyper argues this by drawing on Calvin's

---

[8]Kuyper, *Lectures on Calvinism*, 46.
[9]Kuyper, *Lectures on Calvinism*, 46.

notion that God has implanted an innate sense of himself in every human being:[10]

> God Himself makes man religious by means of the *sensus divinitatis*, i.e. the sense of the Divine, which He causes to strike the chords on the harp of his soul. . . . In its original form, in its natural condition, religion is exclusively a sentiment of *admiration* and *adoration* which elevates and unites, not a feeling of dependence which severs and depresses.[11]

Although he claimed that religion is thoroughly embedded in human life, Kuyper nonetheless bucked one important trend common to his own day—namely, the view that religion is best explained as a human product that reflects human psychological needs.

Some decades before Kuyper's lectures, Schleiermacher (1768–1834) recast religion, in its most elevated form, in the context of human consciousness. Religion, he argued, was a "feeling of absolute dependence" on God (and was found in pristine form only in Jesus himself, as the perfectly God-conscious human). Following this, the German atheist philosopher Ludwig Feuerbach (1804–1872) advanced the assertion that religion was thoroughly human, rather than divine, in character. Feuerbach's (then novel) claim was that religion develops as humans explore their own deep psychological needs. As such, he believed, religion's true secret was atheism. His *The Essence of Christianity* (1841) gained a host of admirers across Kuyper's lifetime. In the Netherlands, Kuyper's contemporary Allard Pierson (1831–1896), a noted art historian, came under Feuerbach's influence and argued that religion stood alongside art and poetry as an extension of human personality.[12]

---

[10]Calvin introduces this concept, the *sensus divinitatis* or the awareness of the divine, early in his *Institutes*. In book one, chapter three, he argues that "there is within the human mind, and indeed by natural instinct, an awareness of divinity. . . . God himself has implanted in all men a certain understanding of his divine majesty." John Calvin, *Institutes of the Christian Religion*, ed. John T. McNeill, trans. Ford Lewis Battles (Philadelphia: Westminster Press, 1960), 1.3.1.

[11]Kuyper, *Lectures on Calvinism*, 41 (emphasis original).

[12]S. A. Naber, *Levensbericht van Allard Pierson* (Amsterdam: Johannes Müller, 1898), 7. Having begun his working life as a pastor, Pierson left the ministry on account of his unbelief in divine revelation and later denied that Jesus had ever existed.

Against all of these, Kuyper's insistence was that while religion is an important part of being human, its "human and subjective side" is the fruit of something else: the God-ward direction of human life as intended by its Creator. Religion "produces a blessing for man," Kuyper wrote, "but it does not exist for man."[13] Stated otherwise, because religion is a particular way of living, religion understood well (in Kuyper's terms, as life lived in God's presence) can enable, direct, and ask us to live for something beyond ourselves. To Kuyper, this means that religion is *from* and *for* something other than the humans whose lives are bound up in it. Religion, he put forward, is primarily about God and only secondarily about humans. In this setting, he made his case for Calvinism as the religion that best equips humans to live *coram Deo* in each part of life.

Second question: Must all people be religious? Kuyper introduces his second question through the terms *direct* and *mediate*: Should religion be experienced—or perhaps better stated, lived out—by every member of society (what Kuyper calls "direct" religion), or is it sufficient that a priestly caste within society experience religion on behalf of the masses in order to "mediate" it to them? At this point in the lecture, Kuyper's positive view of generalized religion turns to critique: "In all non-Christian religions, without any exception, human intercessors are deemed necessary."[14] And even within Christianity, particularly in its Roman Catholic and Lutheran forms, Kuyper argued, the enriching benefits of lived religion lose their immediacy because of stratified, hierarchical models of the church. As an antidote to this, Kuyper turns to the Reformation era, where the direct import of religion was rediscovered in Calvin's preference for the "priesthood of all believers" over a more restrictive view of priesthood as the task only of a special class of Christians:[15]

---

[13]Kuyper, *Lectures on Calvinism*, 45.

[14]Kuyper, *Lectures on Calvinism*, 47.

[15]Building on his understanding of Christ's threefold office (as prophet, priest, and king), Calvin insists that all Christians, not merely some, share in Christ's priesthood. As he discusses the

> Not because of any hatred against priests . . . but solely because Calvin
> felt bound to vindicate the essence of religion and the glory of God in
> that essence, and absolutely devoid of all yielding or wavering, he waged
> war, with holy indignation, against everything that interposed itself be-
> tween the soul and God.[16]

The view that religion was for the ordinary person, as Kuyper now
communicated to his American audience in 1898, had animated his
efforts (and striking political success) in his native Netherlands from
the mid-1870s onward. There, his constant refrain had been an appeal
to the "little people" (*de kleine luyden*). On home turf, Kuyper's target
audience centered on blue-collar Christians who needed to hear how
each part of their lives—factory shifts, farm work, marriage, family life,
political allegiance, access to education, and Sunday worship—could
be orchestrated together as a single, empowering, intentional way of
living. In his efforts to empower the working class, Kuyper railed
against aristocratic rule in government and church alike: the ordinary
person, he believed, must become an active participant in both. This
commitment to egalitarian religion, of course, was a natural extension
of Kuyper's belief that religion was primarily concerned with God
rather than humans:

> Religion *for the sake of man* carries with it the position that man has to
> act as a mediator for his fellow-man. Religion *for the sake of God* inexo-
> rably excludes every human mediatorship. . . . If the demand of religion
> is that *every* human heart must give glory to God, no man can appear
> before God on behalf of another.[17]

"priestly office," he affirms that "Christ plays the priestly role, not only to render the Father favorable and propitious towards us by an eternal law of reconciliation, but also to receive us as
his companions in this great office [Rev 1:6] . . . [we] are priests in him" (Calvin, *Institutes*,
2.15.6). Later, in his treatment of the church and its offices, he continues to affirm the universality
of the priestly calling and task for Christians. "[Christ] once for all offered a sacrifice of eternal
expiation and reconciliation; now, having also entered the sanctuary of heaven, he intercedes
for us. In him we are all priests [Rev 1:6; cf. 1 Pet 2:9], but to offer praises and thanksgiving, in
short, to offer ourselves and ours to God" (Calvin, *Institutes*, 4.19.28).

[16]Kuyper, *Lectures on Calvinism*, 47.

[17]Kuyper, *Lectures on Calvinism*, 48 (emphasis original).

With this, the coherence of the answers to Kuyper's first two questions crystallize in sequence: religion is primarily about (and for) God rather than for humans. It is precisely because religion exists for God, however, that religion thus becomes a direct and pressing concern for every human being, each of whom—in Kuyper's reckoning—must decide whether to move toward or away from God. As a matter that primarily concerns God, then, religion is everyone's business.[18]

Third question: Is religion only about matters of the heart, or morals? Kuyper's third question carries over into the present day with little modification: Is religion best viewed as an inherently private thing? Should it be limited to private opinions or feelings, which can flourish when housed only within that secluded domain, or should it also inform each aspect of an individual believer's life and, even more widely, the very structure and workings of society itself? Is religion only about moral values? Is religion a matter of private or also of public truth? (In real-world terms, for example, is it appropriate for a Christian who is a politician to allow her religion to express itself in her politics?) Or, stated in Kuyper's own words, "Is religion *partial*, or is it all-subduing, and comprehensive,—*universal* in the strict sense of the word?"[19]

Across the nineteenth century, attempts were made to define the scope of religion's utility in ways that Kuyper found restrictive: while its capacity to speak in the realm of science (and as such, to form the life of the mind) was given short shrift by many, some—in following the example of the philosopher Immanuel Kant—argued that it retained a

---

[18]In context, of course, it should be stated that Kuyper held to this striking account of the direct relationship between the individual person and God, alongside his equally firm insistence that other human mediators are unnecessary *because* Jesus, as the God-Man, is the only and perfect mediator between God and humanity. Kuyper's affirmation of the "ray of divine light [that] enters straightway into the depth of our heart" should not be read as a permission to seek union with God without going through Jesus Christ. It is also worth noting, in passing, that while Kuyper believed that religion was a pressing concern for every citizen, he strongly rejected the idea that the state should privilege one religious confession or require the people to express their religiosity in one particular way. Rather, Kuyper argued for a kind of religious pluralism in which religiosity in general was supported, rather than discouraged, by the state, without the state discriminating in how individuals practiced that religiosity.

[19]Kuyper, *Lectures on Calvinism*, 49 (emphasis original).

certain degree of usefulness in considering ethical issues, while others limited its scope to the realm of mystical experience:

> Religion is excluded from science, and its authority from the domain of public life; henceforth the inner chamber, the cell for prayer, and the secrecy of the heart should be its exclusive dwelling place. By his *du Sollst* ["Thou shalt"], Kant limited the sphere of religion to the ethical life. The mystics of our own times banish religion to the retreats of sentiment. And the result is that, in many different ways, religion, once the central force of human life, is now placed alongside of it; and, far from the thriving of the world, is understood to hide itself in a distant and almost private retreat.[20]

For Kuyper, the admission that religion has nothing to say to vast swathes of our human existence—and that much of life is lived appropriately precisely when religion is absent—was deeply problematic. To grasp why, we must understand something about Kuyper's account of the nature and purpose of the cosmos—namely, that it was made *in* and *for* Christ and exists in its entirety, inclusive of its breathtaking diversity, for a single purpose, which is the glory of its Creator. This basic commitment to a "God's-eye-perspective" on the cosmos, and the consequent belief in the possibility of a coherent view of the world, is not unique to Kuyper or his neo-Calvinist tradition. Perhaps slightly more distinctive to his movement—although not its exclusive property—was the insistence that as the Eternal Logos who created the cosmos, Christ remained at work in each part of it, sustaining it and shepherding it toward its eventual re-creation in a yet more glorious form. This idea was articulated by Kuyper and his colleagues as the "Logos doctrine." This doctrine affirmed that the quest to glorify God in each sphere of life was, at heart, an approach to the Eternal Logos who sustains all things: the practice of politics was as much a search for the Logos as the practices of art or theology or law. As such, for Kuyper, the claim that any particular sphere of

---

[20]Kuyper, *Lectures on Calvinism*, 50-51.

life could adequately be handled in an irreligious way was actually a
frank admission about Jesus himself: it meant that the Eternal Logos
was lord of some things, but not all; that the Eternal Logos was
present in some spheres, but not all; and would glorify himself in the
redemption of some parts of life, but not all. Kuyper took issue with
this patchy kind of religiosity on christological grounds. The acceptance of a peripheral, rather than central, religion was, in his words,
"the very denying of the Eternal Logos."[21]

Bearing this commitment in mind, it should hardly be surprising
that Kuyper's great life project was centered on the articulation of a
holistic Christian worldview. His "Logos doctrine" was shared by his
colleagues Herman Bavinck (1854–1921) and Jan Woltjer (1849–1917),
and it played a crucial role in the rationale behind the project to establish the Free University of Amsterdam as a new (and at that time,
meaningfully Christian) university. There, Kuyper's goal was the creation of an institution where the search for the Eternal Logos was made
possible in every branch of academic inquiry rather than simply in the
Faculty of Theology. Kuyper's university would serve its host society
well by enabling the study of law, philosophy, and medicine to be *Chris-
tianized*. "If Christianity is to be a leaven in our national life," he argued,
"then the judge too, the physician too, the statesman too, the person of
letters too, the philosopher too, must let the light of Christ shine on the
substance and tenor of his science."[22] For Abraham Kuyper, everything
was religious, and religion was about everything. Kuyper had opened
the Free University with perhaps his most quoted line: "There's not a
square inch in the whole domain of human existence over which Christ,
who is Lord over *all*, does not exclaim, 'Mine!'"[23] Two decades later, his
thinking on religion continued to reflect that belief.

---

[21]Kuyper, *Lectures on Calvinism*, 52.

[22]Cited in Arie van Deursen, *The Distinctive Character of the Free University in Amsterdam, 1880–
2005* (Grand Rapids, MI: Eerdmans, 2008), 5.

[23]Abraham Kuyper, *Souvereiniteit in eigen kring* (Kampen: Kok, 1930), 33 (emphasis original);
see James D. Bratt, ed., *Abraham Kuyper: A Centennial Reader* (Grand Rapids, MI: Eerdmans,
1998), 488.

Fourth question: Can religion be a positive force for good in the world? Kuyper's final question explores whether religion is "normal" or "abnormal." By this, he did not mean to ask if religion is a familiar feature of human life or something strange. Rather, this question is a variation on the earlier question on whether religion exists for humans or for God: in this case, though, the question on religion as normal or abnormal asks whether religion merely reflects our default way of life (as a human product) or whether it rather directs us toward a new way of living (as something that orients humans beyond themselves). Does religion set up our world in a perpetual status quo—affirming all that is broken in it—or does it aim, rather, to change that world?

> The distinction I have in mind here is concerned with the question, whether in the matter of religion we must reckon *de facto* with man in his present condition as *normal*, or as having fallen into sin, and having therefore become *abnormal*. In the latter case religion must necessarily assume a soteriological character.[24]

In answering this question, Kuyper acknowledged that the majority view in European culture at that time tended toward seeing religion in "normal" terms. How could it be otherwise, as a phenomenon that arises from human psychology to meet human needs? Interestingly, Kuyper's account of the growth of irreligiosity in his day was also tied to this view of "religion as normal," where the intentionally irreligious now judged themselves no longer to be in need of religion. Lurking behind Kuyper's fourth question, we also hear echoes of a view common across the moralistic and self-confident nineteenth century—namely, that the history of human culture had been one of much violence and suffering and that the cacophony of religions had failed to turn that tide. In that view, religion was part of the world's problems rather than part of their solution.

In response, Kuyper argued that Calvinism, as religion at its very best, stood resolutely *against* the "normal" view of religion. Calvinism looks

---

[24]Kuyper, *Lectures on Calvinism*, 52 (emphasis original).

on this world and declares its wounds and wailings to be utterly abnormal. Rather than accepting human fallenness, Calvinism prized the notion of positive world transformation as beginning with the "regeneration" of the individual—the act of inner renewal "by which God, as it were, sets right again the crooked wheel of life."[25]

> God regenerates us,—that is to say, He rekindles in our heart the lamp sin had blown out. The necessary consequence of this regeneration is an irreconcilable conflict between the inner world of our heart and the world outside, and this conflict is ever the more intensified the more the regenerative principle pervades our consciousness. Now, in the Bible, God reveals, to the regenerate, a world of thought, a world of energies, a world of full and beautiful life, which stands in direct opposition to his ordinary world, but which proves to agree in a wonderful way with the new life that has sprung up in his heart.[26]

In Kuyper's argument, Calvinism produces "wide awake" people who then find themselves unsatisfied with the world under the conditions of sin and who strive to live within it—in each sphere of their lives—to the glory of God. Kuyper's Calvinism was geared toward renewal. In theological parlance, Kuyper draws on the doctrine of salvation to describe Calvinism's basic posture toward the world: its approach to the world is "soteriological."[27] It presupposes the lostness of humans and the cultures they produce and aims to bring light in their darkness.

The church and religion. Having set out this four-part apology for religion (generally, but with regular nods in a Calvinistic direction) against the backdrop of his own increasingly irreligious age, Kuyper's lecture then went on to deal with the specifics of the Christian church as a manifestation of religion in the real world. In his account of the church as a real-world institution, however, Kuyper begins by arguing that the church's center point is in heaven—where the resurrected Jesus Christ is locally present—rather than on earth. As it exists on earth,

---

[25]Kuyper, *Lectures on Calvinism*, 56.
[26]Kuyper, *Lectures on Calvinism*, 58.
[27]Kuyper, *Lectures on Calvinism*, 58.

then, the Christian church is an echo. It is the earthly ripple of a splash made in heaven's glassy sea (Rev 4:6). Drawing on the language of the Old Testament, Kuyper argued that the church on earth was the "outer court" of a temple whose most holy place was certainly not on this earth. In his retelling of the heavenly Christian church's reach into our world's history, however, Kuyper claimed that the church's true center point had been forgotten in the medieval era, when

> the Church had more and more lost sight of this celestial character,—she had become worldly in her nature. The Sanctuary was again brought back to earth, the altar was rebuilt of stone, and a priestly hierarchy had reconstituted itself for the ministrations of the altar. Next of course it was necessary to renew the tangible sacrifice on earth, and this at last brought the church to create the unbloody offering of the Mass.[28]

In this lecture, the workings and consequences of seemingly obscure theological distinctions—such as the difference between the Roman Catholic doctrine of the Lord's Supper (transubstantiation) and Calvin's Protestant account of Christ's spiritual presence in the Lord's Supper—have profound consequences for how we understand the church's relationship to the world. In the Roman Catholic doctrine of transubstantiation, the bread and wine *become* Jesus' physical flesh and blood, through which Christ is constantly present in this world and is continually being sacrificed within it. In Calvin's alternative account of the sacrament, Christ remains locally (i.e., fully, physically and spiritually) present in heaven while also being spiritually present *with* his people in the Supper, albeit not in a physical sense *as* the bread and wine. In noting this doctrinal difference, Kuyper traces a line into the profoundly contrasting ways he argues the Roman Catholic and Calvinistic churches inhabit the world. Because of its Christology, he argues, the Catholic Church's center point remains very much *within* this world, as the scene of its tangible sacrifice. By contrast, Calvinism "dared to put away [this earthly altar] entirely" because of its view of

---

[28]Kuyper, *Lectures on Calvinism*, 60.

Christ's atoning sacrifice as complete and of Christ as now locally present—in his glorified body, and soul—only in heaven. The Calvinistic churches' center point, then, is entirely external to this world.

In Kuyper's argument, these different centerpoints orient the Roman Catholic and Calvinistic churches in different directions: the former, he argues, is prone simply to appropriating, rather than confronting, the idolatries that riddle our world, whereas Calvinism's heavenly center of gravity challenges this world's ever-present corruption.

At this point, Kuyper's keenness to defend Calvinism as a historical Christian tradition required him to respond to the criticisms most commonly leveled at it in his day. In the first place, he had to respond to the fragmented (and fracturing) nature of Calvinistic churches from the Reformation era onward. In an argument shared in near-identical form by his colleague Herman Bavinck, Kuyper claimed that in this world, utter uniformity of religious belief and practice was possible only by strained imposition or coercion.[29] Bearing in mind his wholehearted liberal ideals on the freedom of religious expression (which reject the state as tasked with imposing religious beliefs or practices on the people) and his lack of support for the authority of bishops and popes, it is hard to imagine how Kuyper might have supported anything other than a pluralistic religious landscape—even one in which different groups of Calvinists failed to see eye to eye on every issue.[30] While this landscape was not ideal for Kuyper or Bavinck, both regarded it as the best option given the circumstances: a society in which the state acted to force religious uniformity might gain a united church, but that church would be an association of the obliged rather than Kuyper's ideal "congregation of believers."[31] And a church in which an elite class of authority figures (bishops), or even a single individual (the pope), ensured unity was wholly unacceptable, given Kuyper's combination of Protestantism,

---

[29]Kuyper, *Lectures on Calvinism*, 63-65.
[30]Herman Bavinck, *Reformed Dogmatics: Holy Spirit, Church, and New Creation*, ed. John Bolt, trans. John Vriend (Grand Rapids, MI: Baker Academic, 2008), 411-34.
[31]Kuyper, *Lectures on Calvinism*, 63.

grassroots Romanticism (which aimed at empowering the "little people" to stand against elites), and liberal democratic values tying human flourishing to their religious freedom. In searching for ways to make Christianity uniform here on earth, Kuyper believed, any hypothetical solutions immediately generated far more profound problems.

Following this, Kuyper offered a simultaneous response to two other prominent criticisms of Calvinism: that Calvinists are prone to moral laxity because of their belief in predestination and, conversely, that Calvinists are uptight moralistic prudes. These criticisms, Kuyper perceived, are not easily made compatible: it is hard to see how the same Christian tradition can be at fault for being both immoral and too stringent on morals. Kuyper's choice to respond to them in the same breath, then, was quite intentional, and afforded him the space to make his case for Calvinism as a form of Christianity that teaches believers that they are not saved by rule-keeping[32] but that their love for God creates within them a new desire for holiness in each part of their lives: "Love and adoration are, to Calvin, themselves the motives of every spiritual activity, and thus the fear of God is imparted to the whole of life as a reality— into the family, and into society, into science and art, into personal life, and into the political career."[33]

That desire for the purification of life—which, Kuyper notes, is the reason for the original designation of some Calvinists as "Puritans"— has given Calvinism its distinctive historical character: unlike Lutheranism (which, he believed, tended toward world conformity) and Anabaptism (which held the fallen world at arm's length to avoid its corrupting influence), Calvinism aimed to find its feet on earth while always being subject to a heavenly gravitational pull. Kuyper believed that the kind of Calvinistic participation in culture that emerged from this—neither fleeing from the world, nor conforming to it but rather positioning itself as that world's most loving critic—had been deeply

---

[32]Kuyper, *Lectures on Calvinism*, 69.
[33]Kuyper, *Lectures on Calvinism*, 72.

misunderstood by many: hence the oft-heard view that Calvinism was a repressive cultural force, as demonstrated, apparently, by Calvinistic opposition to card playing, dancing, and the theater at various points in its history. In responding to these particular red herrings, Kuyper set out that in each case, Calvinist opposition to games of blind fortune, forms of dance that objectify women, and artistic forms that glorify human depravity did not mean that Calvinism was inherently anti-culture. To the contrary, he argued, Calvinism is compatible with entertainment, human sexuality, and the arts more generally. Specific instances of cultural objection did not mean that Calvinism glowered in disapproval at all culture simply because it was the work of sinners. "How highly did Milton appreciate Shakespeare's Drama, and did not he himself write in dramatic form? Nor did the evil lie in public theatrical representations, as such. Public performances were given for all the people at Geneva, in the Market Place, in Calvin's time, and with his approval."[34]

WHAT DID KUYPERIANS DO?

Kuyper's lecture on religion ends with a victory claim: Calvinism changes the world. Calvinism works:

> What censor among you will deny the palm of moral victory to Calvinism, which in one generation, though hunted from the battlefield to the scaffold, created, throughout five nations at once [i.e., the Netherlands, Scotland, England, Switzerland, and the United States of America], wide serious groups of noble men, and still nobler women, hitherto unsurpassed in the loftiness of their ideal conceptions and unequalled in the power of the moral self-control.[35]

This was, indeed, quite a claim to make about the contribution of the Protestant Reformation to the development of culture in the nations that followed its Calvinist, rather than Lutheran, stream. Reread a

---

[34]Kuyper, *Lectures on Calvinism*, 74.
[35]Kuyper, *Lectures on Calvinism*, 77.

century after Kuyper's death, it perhaps seems a jarring and bombastic claim—particularly to those who recognize the broad brushes often used by Kuyper when painting pictures of the past. In making these claims, was Kuyper merely calling for the continuation of some older mythical Calvinist utopia at odds with the general flow of traffic in the late nineteenth century? While it is certainly true that the nineteenth century witnessed the ongoing validity of the Christian religion challenged like never before, in the Netherlands, the remarkable neo-Calvinist revival that took place between the 1870s and 1890s saw the century end on something of a high note for that country's Reformed Christians—led by Abraham Kuyper, whose efforts to promote a resurgent modern form of Calvinism had taken him from village pastor to the cusp of his appointment in 1901 as prime minister of the Netherlands (as representative of the country's first modern democratic political party, the Anti-Revolutionary Party).

Those decades had seen Kuyper work tirelessly to promote a holistic Christian worldview in response to the fragmentation of Dutch culture in the late nineteenth century and had led to historically striking real-world consequences. Alongside the foundation of the Anti-Revolutionary Party, these decades witnessed the beginnings of new Christian national newspapers (*De Heraut* and *De Standaard*), a new Reformed university (the Vrije Universiteit in Amsterdam), a growth of interest among Calvinists in poetry and art,[36] and the application of Christianity to grassroots politics among blue-collar workers.[37] And as has been noted, it led to Abraham Kuyper's election to the Dutch premiership three years after giving these lectures in Princeton. They were decades in which a worldview was built—and that in concrete, rather than merely theoretical, terms. To Kuyper, the notion of worldview required the

---

[36]Both Bavinck and Kuyper wrote substantial works on poetry: Herman Bavinck, *Bilderdijk als denker en dichter* (Kampen: Kok, 1906); Abraham Kuyper, *Bilderdijk en zijn nationale beteekenis* (Amsterdam: Höveker & Wormer, 1906).

[37]See, for example, Abraham Kuyper, "The Social Question and the Christian Religion," in *Makers of Modern Christian Social Thought: Leo XIII and Abraham Kuyper on the Social Question*, ed. Jordan J. Ballor (Grand Rapids, MI: Acton Institute, 2016), 45-118.

active participation of the ordinary citizens and led to the transformation of real-world social institutions. The real backdrop to Kuyper's call for Calvinistic religion in 1898, then, was not some seventeenth-century mythical utopia: it was, rather, quite real. His backdrop was the capacious push for the Christianization of Dutch culture that had turned his own country on its head across the previous three decades. In arguing that Calvinism works, Kuyper did not see himself as dealing in hypotheticals or sketchy historiography. His own immediate experience told him that it was indeed possible for the Christian religion to bring all of life together under Christ's lordship in the modern age—life *coram Deo* was indeed possible in the church pew, classroom, theater, poetry recital, sports field, news desk, and dinner table.

WHAT SHOULD WE DO?

A century on, the world has become a very different place—as has Kuyper's own country. While the Netherlands has undergone secularization to a degree that Kuyper could scarcely have imagined, its culture remains profoundly influenced by his arguments on religion and liberty: in 2021, the Netherlands is a country where one can choose from a selection of national daily Christian newspapers, where parents choose their children's education from a selection of state-funded schools run along explicit worldview-lines (Christian, Hindu, Muslim, or secular), and where voters of whatever worldview persuasion can usually find a political party that represents their own core beliefs in a more-or-less coherent way (and for whom they can vote without holding their noses). In historical terms, none of this would be the case were it not for Abraham Kuyper's arguments on religion.

Further afield, Kuyper's influence can be traced along diasporic lines: where the Dutch Reformed went, the importance of holistic Christian thinking and living often went with them. For that reason, his views on all-of-life Christianity continue to wield considerable influence in Christian liberal arts institutions with historic Dutch roots—Redeemer

University (Hamilton, Ontario), Calvin University and Kuyper College (both Grand Rapids, Michigan), and Dordt University (Sioux Center, Iowa) being prime examples.[38] The extent of his influence, however, is not limited to the Dutch diaspora: scholars at liberal arts Christian colleges often turn to Kuyper when looking for resources that might undergird their own ambitions to join the disciplinary dots in their pursuit of integrated Christian thinking. For the most part though, viewed in line with Kuyper's own reasoning, the Protestants of 2021—certainly the bulk of today's evangelicals—live out a strangely irreligious kind of Christianity. Theirs is a faith that informs some, but certainly not all, spheres of their lives—teaching them how to get to heaven but saying far less about how to think and live Christianly on the shop floor, the classroom, the supermarket, or the counselor's office. A century on from its first airing, Kuyper's insistence that "one supreme calling must impress the stamp of *one-ness* upon *all* human life, because one God upholds and preserves it, just as He created it all" sounds as ripe with upheaval as it did on that October evening in Princeton.[39]

FOR FURTHER READING

Audi, Robert, and Nicholas Wolterstorff. *Religion in the Public Square: The Place of Religious Convictions in Public Debate*. Lanham, MD: Rowman & Littlefield, 1997.

Bavinck, Herman. *Philosophy of Revelation*. Edited by Cory Brock and Nathaniel Gray Sutanto. Peabody, MA: Hendrickson, 2018.

Bratt, James D., ed. *Abraham Kuyper: A Centennial Reader*. Grand Rapids, MI: Eerdmans, 1998.

Kuyper, Abraham. *On the Church*. Edited by John Halsey Wood Jr. and Andrew M. McGinnis. Bellingham, WA: Lexham Press, 2016.

———. *Scholarship: Two Convocation Addresses on University Life*. Translated by Harry Van Dyke. Grand Rapids, MI: Christian's Library Press, 2014.

———. *Wisdom and Wonder: Common Grace in Science and Art*. Edited by Jordan J. Ballor and Stephen J. Grabill. Translated by Nelson D. Kloosterman. Grand Rapids, MI: Christian's Library Press, 2011.

---

[38]See, for example, Cornelius Plantinga Jr., *Engaging God's World: A Christian Vision of Faith, Learning, and Living* (Grand Rapids, MI: Eerdmans, 2002), xiii.

[39]Kuyper, *Lectures on Calvinism*, 54 (emphasis original).

Lugo, Luis E., ed. *Religion, Pluralism, and Public Life: Abraham Kuyper's Legacy for the Twenty-First Century*. Grand Rapids, MI: Eerdmans, 2000.

Rasmussen, Joel D. S., Judith Wolfe, and Johannes Zachhuber, eds. *The Oxford Handbook of Nineteenth-Century Christian Thought*. Oxford: Oxford University Press, 2019.

Van Deursen, Arie. *The Distinctive Character of the Free University in Amsterdam, 1880–2005*. Grand Rapids, MI: Eerdmans, 2008.

Wood, John Halsey. *Going Dutch in the Modern Age: Abraham Kuyper's Struggle for a Free Church in the Nineteenth-Century Netherlands*. Oxford: Oxford University Press, 2013.

3

KUYPER AND POLITICS

JONATHAN CHAPLIN

NORTH AMERICANS TODAY ARE increasingly troubled by two deeply divisive questions: How can citizens and governments find ways to overcome the glaring inequalities of wealth, power, and status that blight their societies? And how can citizens find ways to live together peacefully and respectfully amid their increasingly deep and clashing differences of belief, practice, and identity? In this chapter I'll show how the political thought of Abraham Kuyper can offer surprising shafts of wisdom on both challenges. The first section introduces the basic principles of Kuyper's political thought as expressed in the lecture "Calvinism and Politics."[1] The second builds on that account while also tracing how his ideas have been applied by North American Christians. The third assesses his legacy and suggests ways to correct and improve it.

WHAT DID KUYPER SAY?

Among North American Christians interested in politics, Kuyper is known mainly for his concept of sphere sovereignty.[2] This is the idea

---

[1]Abraham Kuyper, *Lectures on Calvinism* (1931; repr., Grand Rapids, MI: Eerdmans, 1999), 78-109.

[2]Kuyper's fullest statement of the idea is his 1880 lecture "Sphere Sovereignty," in *Abraham Kuyper: A Centennial Reader*, ed. James D. Bratt (Grand Rapids, MI: Eerdmans, 1998), 461-90.

that many different social institutions—families, schools, trade unions, hospitals, businesses, arts associations, charities, churches—have their own God-given nature and purpose and possess a corresponding right to self-governance (sovereignty) free from intrusive control from government or other institutions. Today we call many of these the institutions of civil society.[3] This idea of a free and robust civil society is at the heart of Kuyper's political project and proved to have powerful appeal among Calvinist Christians in the Netherlands in the late nineteenth and early twentieth centuries. Kuyper himself put it to work in founding several institutions: a church, a newspaper, a university, a political party, and more. His first major public campaign sought to defend the rights of orthodox Protestant schools to govern themselves without excessive government control so that they could determine their own ethos and not be forced into the mold of the dominant, secularizing liberalism of his day.[4]

Sphere sovereignty actually covers two distinct but related ideas (which Kuyper sometimes conflates): the general freedom of social institutions from excessive state control and the specific freedom of those institutions to adopt and live by a religious vision, leading to a condition of religious pluralism. The former is primary in Kuyper's thought and will be my focus in this section. I introduce the issue of religious pluralism in the second section. But it should be borne in mind that Kuyper's political thought ranged much more widely than sphere sovereignty, which was the idea most enthusiastically taken up by North American sympathizers.[5]

---

[3]In academic discussions, "civil society" is usually seen as consisting of the realm of free voluntary associations in contrast to the state, the market, and the family or household. For "Kuyperian" analyses, see Jonathan Chaplin, "Civil Society and the State: The Neo-Calvinist Perspective," in *Christianity and Civil Society: Catholic and Neo-Calvinist Perspectives*, ed. Jeanne Heffernan Schindler (Lanham, MD: Lexington, 2008), 67-96; James W. Skillen, "Civil Society and Human Development," in *In Pursuit of Justice: Christian-Democratic Explorations* (Lanham, MD: Rowman & Littlefield, 2004), 19-40.

[4]On Kuyper's political career, see James D. Bratt, *Abraham Kuyper: Modern Calvinist, Christian Democrat* (Grand Rapids, MI: Eerdmans, 2013).

[5]The wide range of his thought is evident in his extended commentary on the program of the political party he founded. Titled "Our Program" (*Ons Program*), it appeared in 1878, and his

Sphere sovereignty. To understand sphere sovereignty we must see it in the context of Kuyper's wider Christian political theory.[6] In "Calvinism and Politics," the first thing Kuyper asserts is that no political tradition gains real traction in history unless it is grounded in a "faith"— either religious or anti-religious, as James Eglinton argues earlier.[7] The realm of politics can never be religiously neutral but reflects the power of underlying, if unrecognized, faith commitments. There is, he claims, a specific political tradition rooted in distinctly Calvinist convictions, one that has profoundly shaped the political histories of nations like the Netherlands, the United States, and England.[8]

The heartbeat of this tradition is "liberty."[9] That, of course, will have gone down well with his American audience. But he is not simply flattering his hosts. For he goes on to argue that true liberty is not secured primarily through the assertion of autonomous individual rights, as was claimed by the secular liberalism that was already dominant in the United States when he delivered his lectures. Instead, true liberty is secured

commentary followed the next year: Abraham Kuyper, *Guidance for Christian Engagement in Government*, trans. and ed. Harry Van Dyke (Grand Rapids, MI: Christian's Library Press, 2013).
[6]See Peter S. Heslam, "Third Lecture: Calvinism and Politics," chap. 6 in *Creating a Christian Worldview: Abraham Kuyper's Lectures on Calvinism* (Grand Rapids, MI: Eerdmans, 1998), 142-66; Bratt, "Political Theorist," chap. 7 in *Abraham Kuyper: Modern Calvinist*, 130-48; Vincent E. Bacote, *The Spirit in Public Theology: Appropriating the Legacy of Abraham Kuyper* (Grand Rapids, MI: Baker Academic, 2005); Craig Bartholomew, "Sphere Sovereignty: Kuyper's Philosophy of Society" and "Politics, the Poor, and Pluralism," chaps. 5 and 7 in *Contours of the Kuyperian Tradition: A Systematic Introduction* (Downers Grove, IL: IVP Academic, 2017), 131-60, 191-212. For comparisons between Kuyperian and other strands of contemporary Christian political thought, see P. C. Kemeny, ed., *Church, State, and Public Justice: Five Views* (Downers Grove, IL: InterVarsity Press, 2007); James W. Skillen and Rockne M. McCarthy, eds., *Political Order and the Plural Structure of Society* (Atlanta, GA: Scholars Press, 1991). See also Paul Marshall, *God and the Constitution: Christianity and American Politics* (Lanham, MD: Rowman & Littlefield, 2002).
[7]Kuyper, *Lectures on Calvinism*, 78.
[8]He might have added Scotland. He suggests that countries shaped mainly by the Lutheran tradition have not displayed the same commitment to liberty, but that is not borne out by history. In fact, the United States could not be said by the late nineteenth century to be largely shaped by Calvinism any longer. Also, England was as much shaped by Anglicanism as Calvinism, depending on how one understands those distinctions.
[9]See Abraham Kuyper, "Calvinism: Source and Stronghold of Our Constitutional Liberties," in Bratt, *Abraham Kuyper: A Centennial Reader*, 279-322. See also John Witte Jr., "The Biography and Biology of Liberty: Abraham Kuyper and the American Experiment," in Luis E. Lugo, ed., *Religion, Pluralism and Public Life: Abraham Kuyper's Legacy for the Twenty-First Century* (Grand Rapids, MI: Eerdmans, 2000), 243-62.

through what I will call *constitutional pluralism*, a political system in which authority (sovereignty) is shared across both individuals and the many institutions of civil society. In such an arrangement, individual and institutional rights are both respected, each serves to protect and limit the other, and both put clear limits on government. In turn, government is tasked with protecting and supporting the free exercise of these rights in civil society while also protecting the wider public good.

Thus, Kuyper's political thought begins not with *individuals* but *institutions*. This is in striking contrast to the individualistic liberalism that now dominates American—and much Canadian—political thinking. North Americans shaped by that individualism—and many North American *Christians* who have unwittingly succumbed to it—will need to work hard to make the paradigm shift Kuyper calls for. Kuyper asks us to start not with "my rights" and "my interests" (or those of people like me, such as those who share "my identity") but with what binds me to my fellow human beings in all kinds of shared social and institutional settings.

Kuyper's argument is that constitutional pluralism is the political application of the fundamental Calvinist belief in the comprehensive scope of God's authority over all creation. He affirms "the sovereignty of the Triune God over the whole cosmos, in all its spheres and kingdoms, visible and invisible."[10] But then divine sovereignty issues forth in three "deduced" (i.e., delegated) expressions of sovereignty in the human realm: in the state, in society, and in the church. God is the ultimate source of all human authority—we don't conjure it up ourselves from our autonomous wills. But God entrusts portions of his authority to humans for specific purposes. We are therefore to use it responsibly and reverently, knowing that we are mere trustees of a power we did not create. Authority of any kind in human life is a "calling" that we must exercise as those accountable to God for its proper use.[11]

---

[10]Kuyper, *Lectures on Calvinism*, 79.
[11]For a "Kuyperian" account of authority, see David T. Koyzis, *We Answer to Another: Authority, Office, and the Image of God* (Eugene, OR: Pickwick Publications, 2014).

In "Calvinism and Politics" Kuyper begins by discussing the state, but the shape of his thought becomes clearer if we begin with society. I will not address his conception of the church, as that is discussed by both James Eglinton and Bruce Ashford in this volume. I will, however, comment on his views on church and state.

Sovereignty in society. Kuyper speaks of "sovereignty in the sphere of society," or "sphere sovereignty."[12] As already indicated, he has in mind many distinct spheres, each possessing a distinct kind of sovereignty or authority corresponding to the particular nature or purpose of the entity in question. In various writings he offers different classifications of spheres, but here he lists four types:[13]

1. personal sovereignty

2. institutional sovereignty

3. family sovereignty

4. local sovereignty

Kuyper uses the term *sphere* in a rather loose way, so let me offer some clarifications of the territory these types cover. First, the examples I have so far given fall into either categories 2 or 3, which refer to definite social structures like family, business, or school having a specific purpose. Second, the state (or government) is also an example of this institutional sovereignty, and, as we'll see below, that turns out to be a crucial point: the state is just one social institution among many. Third, the fourth category, which he calls "communal autonomy,"[14] refers to the authority possessed by local governments. This is better seen as governmental sovereignty expressed at the local (or state or provincial) levels. Fourth, in the lecture Kuyper also speaks of science and art as spheres.[15] But these are really broad social *practices*, which then give

---

[12]Kuyper, *Lectures on Calvinism*, 90. These are renditions of the Dutch phrase "souvereiniteit in eigen kring," which literally translates as "sovereignty in one's own sphere."

[13]Kuyper, *Lectures on Calvinism*, 96.

[14]Kuyper, *Lectures on Calvinism*, 96.

[15]Kuyper, *Lectures on Calvinism*, 90.

rise to particular institutions or associations devoted to pursuing them, such as universities or research institutes for science, or theater companies or museums for the arts (as he notes).[16] Fifth, Kuyper's account of personal sovereignty refers to the influence that individuals exercise on a culture in virtue of their talents or capacities.[17] This is not essential to his political thought, and I won't consider it here.[18] In what follows, I will concentrate on institutional sovereignty: first in society, then in the state.

Kuyper makes the striking claim that social institutions in these categories are not mere human inventions but arise out of our God-given created nature. He conveys this idea by describing such institutions as organic, drawing a sharp distinction between "the *organic* life of society" and "the *mechanical* character of the government."[19] Things that develop directly out of God's original creation order are organic. They grow from what God has already placed within creation, emerging over time in human history, appearing in different forms, but reflecting God's original "ordinances" for that institution.[20] This is seen most clearly in the way that families spontaneously—by which he means naturally—emerge from marriage, but it is true for all other social institutions as well.[21]

Of course, as a Calvinist, Kuyper asserts that social institutions reflect not only the goodness of creation but also the corrupting effects of the fall. They often turn what was a blessing into a curse[22]—families into emotional prisons, or businesses into destroyers of the environment, for

---

[16]Kuyper, *Lectures on Calvinism*, 96-97.

[17]Kuyper, *Lectures on Calvinism*, 94-95.

[18]His basic point about the cultural influence of prominent individuals seems valid enough, but the way he frames it strikes us as archaic. The superior power of some "men" over others is evident in every area of society, Kuyper claims. That may be so as a matter of fact, but it is problematic to claim that this arises "organically" from "life's sovereignty itself." Kuyper, *Lectures on Calvinism*, 95.

[19]Kuyper, *Lectures on Calvinism*, 91 (emphasis original).

[20]"Whatever among men originates directly from creation is possessed of all the data for its development, in human nature as such." Kuyper, *Lectures on Calvinism*, 91.

[21]Together, all social institutions "form the life of creation, in accord with the ordinances of creation, and therefore are *organically* developed." Kuyper, *Lectures on Calvinism*, 92 (emphasis original).

[22]Kuyper, *Lectures on Calvinism*, 91.

example. But these effects have been restrained by common grace.[23] This is not the *redeeming* grace of the gospel but the *preserving* grace by which God sustains the original creation so that the damage done to human society by sin is contained, allowing human life to continue with at least a measure of peace and order.[24]

Kuyper's language here reflects an organic theory of society.[25] A society or nation was seen as an interconnected, developing whole—like a biological organism—of which particular institutions were subordinate organs or parts. Not surprisingly, North American sympathizers have dropped such language because it has so little resonance there. But Kuyper also distances himself from the theory. He asserts that social institutions grow out of what is given in creation but also that what has thus grown must be respected for its own sake. Social institutions are fully independent and self-governing wholes with their own unique purpose, not mere parts of some larger social reality such as society, the nation, or worse, the state.

It is precisely because diverse social spheres ultimately derive from creation and so stand directly under God's authority that Kuyper insisted they are not creatures or instruments of the state.[26] That's a

---

[23]Kuyper, *Lectures on Calvinism*, 92.

[24]See Abraham Kuyper, "Common Grace," in Bratt, *Abraham Kuyper: A Centennial Reader*, 165-201. For a discussion of the theme, see Richard Mouw, *He Shines in All That's Fair: Culture and Common Grace* (Grand Rapids, MI: Eerdmans, 2001). For another biblical and systematic introduction to this theme, see Abraham Kuyper's contemporary Herman Bavinck in his 1894 rectoral address, "Common Grace." Herman Bavinck, "Herman Bavinck's 'Common Grace,'" trans. Raymond C. Van Leeuwen, *Calvin Theological Journal* 24, no. 1 (1989): 35-65.

[25]Kuyper's use of "organic" language raises important questions. In his use of such language, is Kuyper's meaning consistent with that of broader society, where it was popular? Or is he drawing on theological concepts and methodology from his own Calvinist roots? In his important work, *Trinity and Organism: Towards a New Reading of Herman Bavinck's Organic Motif* (London: T&T Clark, 2012), James Eglinton convincingly argues that Bavinck's use of the same organic language is grounded in "a richly Trinitarian doctrine of God as received by the Patristic and Reformation traditions"—not modern theology (Eglinton, *Trinity and Organism*, 54). While Eglinton's work focuses on Bavinck, it does not ignore Kuyper, whose use of the language is similar. Certainly, Kuyper's use of the term *organic* is much more consistent with Calvin's understandings than the broader Hegelian understanding of the time.

[26]"[These spheres] do not owe their existence to the state, and . . . do not derive the law of their life from the superiority of the state, but obey a high authority within their own bosom; an authority which rules by the grace of God, just as the sovereignty of the state does. [Such

warning against what states should *not* do. Let us now turn, then, to what they *should* do—to the unique calling, the sphere sovereignty, of the state.

Sovereignty in the state. Over against the organic character of the spheres of society stands the mechanical character of the state. This contrast was familiar within the organic social theory I just mentioned. But Kuyper frames it within a biblical view of government. That which is organic arises naturally out creation, while that which is mechanical arises as a result of the fall. By *state* (or *government*) Kuyper here means the coercive state,[27] governing through enforceable law and backed by "the sword."[28] He claims that the state *in this sense* is not original with creation but is instituted by God after the fall to restrain the disruptive and violent effects of sin.[29] It is another example of common or preserving grace.[30] On account of its use of coercion, the state in this sense is experienced by humans as "unnatural"[31]—we instinctively resent being ordered around. And on account of its possession of coercion, states are prone to a "dreadful abuse of power"[32] and to "all manner of despotic ambitions," so we must remain ever vigilant against the threat these abuses pose to our liberties.[33]

But what might have happened without sin? Kuyper proposes that a noncoercive, organic form of political order would have evolved out of the family, perhaps even developing into a world government embracing

---

spheres] *have nothing above themselves but God*, and . . . the state cannot intrude here, and has nothing to command in their domain." Kuyper, *Lectures on Calvinism*, 90 (emphasis original).

[27]Kuyper, *Lectures on Calvinism*, 79-81.

[28]Kuyper, *Lectures on Calvinism*, 93. This includes the sword of "justice" (criminal law), the sword of "war" (resistance against foreign threats), and the sword of "order" (resistance against domestic threats) (93). None of this would have been necessary without sin (80). Without law and government, life in a fallen world would be "a veritable hell on earth" (81).

[29]This view goes back as far as St. Augustine and was held by Luther and Calvin.

[30]Kuyper, *Lectures on Calvinism*, 81, 82-83.

[31]Kuyper, *Lectures on Calvinism*, 80.

[32]Kuyper, *Lectures on Calvinism*, 80.

[33]Kuyper, *Lectures on Calvinism*, 81. He did, however, defend the idea that the state should have a "monopoly" of physical coercion. This was its unique, God-given prerogative. He would not have accepted the idea that the US Constitution's mention of a "right to bear arms" implied a general right of individuals to own lethal weapons.

all of humanity.[34] Such an order would be rooted in creation, not merely a postlapsarian necessity. In that case there would have been no territorial nation-states. But the disintegrating force of sin has broken the human race up into distinct nations each needing their own government.[35]

This is not to say that *nations themselves* are the result of sin. On the contrary: "God created the nations. They exist for Him. They are His own. And therefore, all these nations, and in them humanity, must exist for his glory and . . . after his ordinances, in order that in their well-being . . . His divine wisdom may shine forth."[36] I'll come back to the idea of a "God-glorifying nation" later.

On account of sin, then, states need to exercise coercive authority over their citizens. But without a legitimate right to do so, such power becomes merely "the right of the strongest." Only God can create such a right.[37] Political authority, then, derives from a divine act of providential authorization.

Kuyper highlights the stark contrast between his claim and two very powerful secular theories that were dominant in the Europe of his time: "popular sovereignty" and "state sovereignty."[38] His targets were not abstract theories. The former was the creed of the dominant Dutch political and economic elites of his day, meshing neatly with the individualistic capitalism from which they profited. The latter was the doctrine behind the centralizing and domineering states in neighboring France and Germany, and parallel ideas were gaining ground in the Netherlands.[39]

---

[34]He adds that this would have occurred "after a patriarchal fashion," by which he seems to mean that male family heads would have been the basis of an emerging system of governance. Kuyper, *Lectures on Calvinism*, 80.

[35]Kuyper, *Lectures on Calvinism*, 79-80.

[36]Kuyper, *Lectures on Calvinism*, 81.

[37]Kuyper, *Lectures on Calvinism*, 82. In a world without sin, presumably government would have held an organic right to exercise authority. He implies that this right would have arisen from creation, not from a special post-fall intervention by God.

[38]For a "Kuyperian" analysis of a range of modern political ideologies, see David T. Koyzis, *Political Visions & Illusions: A Survey and Christian Critique of Contemporary Ideologies*, 2nd ed. (Downers Grove, IL: InterVarsity Press, 2019).

[39]Kuyper also sees socialism (he refers to it in this lecture as "social democracy") as another example of state sovereignty, though it derived from Marxism rather than from the tradition he

According to popular sovereignty, political authority derives from a social contract (real or imagined) between individuals, by which the right to rule is generated.[40] This is the classical liberal account that was becoming dominant in the Netherlands in his day and which was already dominant in the United States (and remains so today in both the United States and Canada). Kuyper sets himself so strongly against this view because it is the theory that motivated the atheistic French Revolution that arrogantly cast aside the authority of God and led to tyranny across much of Europe.[41] By contrast, the three Calvinistic revolutions—in the Netherlands, England, and the United States—were examples of God-fearing resistance to tyranny.[42]

According to state sovereignty, political authority derives not from a contract but from the historical tradition of a nation. The state emerges as a "mysterious being" to embody the nation's unique identity and will. Because it claims to represent the whole people in itself, it asserts complete authority to govern them and all their social institutions.[43] This flies in the face of sphere sovereignty since it holds that the authority of

---

has in his sights here (which he terms "German philosophical pantheism"). Kuyper, *Lectures on Calvinism*, 88.

[40] Kuyper, *Lectures on Calvinism*, 82.

[41] Kuyper, *Lectures on Calvinism*, 87-88. On this view, "The sovereignty of God is dethroned and man with his free will is placed on the vacant seat. It is the will of man which determines all things. . . . [In the] people . . . is thus hidden the deepest fountain of all sovereignty" (87).

[42] Kuyper, *Lectures on Calvinism*, 86-87. This strong anti-revolutionary impulse leads him to oversimplify and caricature the classical liberal tradition, which also had powerful Christian influences behind it—not least in those three countries. When Kuyper established a Calvinist political party in 1879, he called it the "Anti-Revolutionary Party." The name conveys opposition to the atheistic spirit of the French Revolution rather than a stance of political reaction. His campaign against intrusive liberal legislation for schools mobilized the largest number of citizens the Netherlands had ever seen. The party was formed in a breach with the aristocratic conservative movement with which those who called themselves anti-revolutionaries had initially been allied. It was the first Christian Democratic party to be established in Europe, indeed one of the first European mass membership parties. Just as original Calvinism inspired democratizing movements in the seventeenth century, so Dutch neo-Calvinism under Kuyper's leadership did in the nineteenth. See John Bowlin, ed., *The Kuyper Center Review, Volume 4: Calvinism and Democracy* (Grand Rapids, MI: Eerdmans, 2014).

[43] As he puts the theory, "That which exists is good, because it exists; and it is no longer the will of God, of Him Who created us and knows us, but it becomes the ever-changing will of the State which, having no one above itself, actually becomes God" (Kuyper, *Lectures on Calvinism*, 89). Again, Kuyper is here oversimplifying a complex set of theories, not all of which "deified" the state in this way.

such institutions is derived directly from the state—a classic example of statism.

Calvinism, however, is radically antistatist because it grounds the rights of social institutions (and persons) in the creation ordinances of God.[44] Kuyper claims, in fact, that Calvinism made a decisive contribution to the modern idea of constitutional government—government limited by laws that are themselves rooted in justice. It affirmed the coercive authority of government as necessary, even if mechanical, while also championing the independent authority of organic social spheres.[45]

But this does not mean that the state cannot exercise its own proper authority over other social spheres. Kuyper is not advocating a libertarian-style minimal state, popular in influential strands of American conservatism. The state has three duties toward these spheres. The first is to ensure that, when spheres get into conflict, they are made to respect each other's proper boundaries. A contemporary example would be intervening to set some ground rules when a trade union clashes with a business. Elsewhere, Kuyper offered intriguing proposals for how the state should encourage a Code of Labor to protect workers' rights and on how to address the larger *social question*—the term used to refer to the widespread exploitation and impoverishment suffered by the industrial working classes of late nineteenth-century Europe.[46] The second duty of the state is to protect vulnerable individuals against abuses of power by social institutions themselves. Just as the state's authority is limited, so is that of the social spheres, and it is the duty of the state to

---

[44]It "teaches us to look upwards from the existing law to the source of the eternal Right in God" and "creates in us the indomitable courage incessantly to protest against the unrighteousness of the law in the name of this highest Right." Kuyper, *Lectures on Calvinism*, 90.

[45]Kuyper, *Lectures on Calvinism*, 93-94. Just as Calvinism "honored the authority of the magistrate, instituted by God," so it equally honored "that *second sovereignty*, which had been implanted by God in the social spheres." (94, emphasis original). Thus the state "may neither ignore nor modify nor disrupt the divine mandate under which these spheres stand. . . . [It] must never become an octopus, which stifles the whole of life. It must occupy its own place, on its own root, among all the other trees of the forest, and this it has to honor and maintain every form of life which grows independently in its own sacred authority" (96-97).

[46]See Abraham Kuyper, "Manual Labor," in Bratt, *Abraham Kuyper: A Centennial Reader*, 231-54; and Abraham Kuyper, *The Problem of Poverty*, ed. James W. Skillen (Grand Rapids, MI: Baker, 1991).

intervene (by civil rights legislation, for instance) to protect individuals against injustices (such as race discrimination) committed by the institutions that have authority over them.[47] The third duty of the state is to ensure that the people make their own contribution to good government, such as by paying fair taxes and taking part in the democratic process.[48]

The larger goal is to promote what I earlier termed constitutional pluralism, in which the state cooperates constructively with social institutions and individual citizens to create a proper balance of rights and duties for the public good.[49] In his day, Kuyper as public theologian and statesman made a decisively important contribution to that project in the Netherlands.

WHAT DID KUYPERIANS DO?

Earlier I distinguished between the two senses in which Kuyper uses the term *sphere sovereignty*. The first refers to the *general* freedom of social institutions from intrusive state control, while the second refers to the *specific* freedom of such institutions to adopt and live by a religious vision. The latter concerns just one of the many kinds of freedom that nonstate social institutions would want to protect, albeit a very important one. American Christian political thinker James Skillen has termed these two senses *structural pluralism* and *confessional*

---

[47] I use the contemporary example of race discrimination here for the sake of clarity rather than as an example from Kuyper's own time. On Kuyper's problematic views of race, see chapter seven in this volume.

[48] Kuyper's views on democracy evolved over time and were not always consistent. He certainly favored the prevailing system of representative, parliamentary democracy that existed in the Netherlands in his day and supported an extension of the franchise to all men (not yet women). In this lecture, he also entertains the idea of "corporative franchise" in which social institutions as well as individuals would also be allowed to vote (Kuyper, *Lectures on Calvinism*, 98). Elsewhere he expressed support for the idea that social institutions be represented in a second chamber of parliament. Neither idea was successful. See George Harinck, "Neo-Calvinism and Democracy: An Overview from the Mid-Nineteenth Century till the Second World War," in Bowlin, *Kuyper Center Review*, 1-20; Henk E. S. Woldring, "Kuyper's Formal and Comprehensive Conceptions of Democracy," in *Kuyper Reconsidered: Aspects of His Life and Work*, ed. Cornelius van der Kooi and Jan de Bruijn (Amsterdam: VU Uitgeverij, 1999), 206-17.

[49] Kuyper, *Lectures on Calvinism*, 97.

pluralism.[50] In this section I move back and forth between Kuyper's own work and that of those who have been inspired by him in North America.

Structural and confessional pluralism were equally important in Kuyper's own work. But it is striking that it is the second sense that has attracted by far the most interest among those who have sought to apply his ideas in North America. There are rather few examples of North American Christians trying to promote justice via structural pluralism where the main issue at stake was not also confessional pluralism. Almost invariably, it has been a concern about restrictions on the public manifestation of religion in one or other area of social life that has been the impetus for Kuyper-inspired initiatives. If we were to ask for the biography of the first sense of sphere sovereignty in North America—sphere sovereignty where faith was not the issue—we would not have all that much to report (a point I'll come back to). There is, however, a good deal to report on the biography of the second sense.

Let me begin with a brief summary of how Kuyper understood confessional pluralism. In Kuyper's time, three main "confessional" visions were contending for public recognition: Calvinism, Catholicism, and secular humanism. Secular humanism was, he claimed, the religion of the political liberalism dominant in his day. Such liberalism was unwilling to grant proportionate public space—as distinct from private religious freedom—to Calvinism and Catholicism. Secular liberals claimed that their prescriptions for public life offered a neutral space in which every confessional group could flourish freely. Exactly the same claim is made today by North American secularists who seek to promote equal liberty among citizens by establishing a public realm free from the "divisive" influence of religion.

Kuyper countered, however, that secular liberals were actually in the business of imposing a confining set of public norms—in education or

---

[50]See James W. Skillen, *Recharging the American Experiment: Principled Pluralism for Genuine Civic Community* (Grand Rapids, MI: Baker Books, 1994). Both are examples of what Skillen calls "principled pluralism," or what I have termed *constitutional pluralism.*

industrial relations, for example—that kept Calvinists and Catholics on the margins of the public realm and stifled the public expression of their faith. He launched his career defending the rights of Calvinists, and later Christians generally, with the aim of liberating them from the heel of secular liberalism. But quite quickly he came to adopt a much larger goal: the creation of an open public space in which *all* confessional communities—religious and secular—would be equally free to live out their convictions, not only in church life but also in education, business, labor, journalism, politics, and more.

As I noted, confessional pluralism champions the religious liberty claims of structurally plural institutions and the duty of states to respect those claims. The state was not to try to create confessional institutions. These could be established only by the voluntary initiative of free persons following their consciences. But the state should, through various means, protect their legal freedom to exist and to govern themselves. In some cases it should also allow them to share in the delivery of public services such as education or health (for which public funding might be required) according to their own convictions and, where appropriate, enable them to contribute to the shaping of public policy by giving them rights to be consulted on major changes.

Kuyper therefore argued that Christians should not seek a position of political or legal privilege in their public squares but rather one of parity. Their aim should be to enjoy equal rights alongside other confessional communities, within a state marked by wide freedom of expression and fair democratic representation. At the height of his struggle for equal treatment for Christian schools, Kuyper asserted that "our unremitting intent should be to demand *justice for all*, justice for every life-expression."[51] This implies neither a sacred public square nor a naked (neutral) public square but a plural public square.[52]

---

[51]Quoted in Bratt, *Abraham Kuyper: Modern Calvinist*, 73 (emphasis added).
[52]See Os Guinness, *The Global Public Square: Religious Freedom and the Making of a World Safe for Diversity* (Downers Grove, IL: InterVarsity Press, 2013). Guinness speaks of a civic as well as a plural public square.

By the end of his career he could look back with some satisfaction at the emergence of pluralistic arrangements in at least some spheres of society, notably education. These were significant achievements of the neo-Calvinist movement he led, often working in close cooperation with Catholics. More were to be established after his death. In the Netherlands, this eventually led to the emergence of what political scientists have called pillarization—the existence of diverse confessional pillars, each serving their own supporting communities and recognized by the state. Catholic-inspired Christian Democrats promoted parallel arrangements elsewhere in Europe.

But, given his commitment to confessional pluralism, in what sense did Kuyper still entertain the idea of a Christian nation? On the one hand, he rejected the model of Christendom that had prevailed in the Middle Ages. This amounted to the granting by the state of exclusive public primacy to the Christian faith or Christian churches. In spite of the Reformation, such a model survived in some European states until the eighteenth and nineteenth centuries. In his own day, Kuyper had to face down traditionalists in his own Calvinist constituency who wanted to cling onto such primacy.

Yet, on the other hand, he continued to speak of the Netherlands as a Christian nation. By this he was referring mainly to the deep historical imprint of Calvinism on Dutch culture and politics. He gave thanks to God for that legacy but did not appeal to it in order to mount a contemporary claim for a confessionally Christian state (the Dutch Reformed Church had been disestablished in the Liberal revolution of the mid-nineteenth century). He reminded his followers that orthodox Calvinism, however decisive it had been to the historical formation of the nation's core, now represented only a tenth of its population. Defending the Christian character of the nation could now only take place democratically from the bottom up—such as through the influence of the Christian political party he founded—and could no longer rely on inherited constitutional advantage. As James Bratt puts it, for Kuyper

"Calvinism was not an erstwhile establishment, but a philosophy of diversity."[53]

This had immediate implications for church-state relations, some of which were taken up by his North American sympathizers. Kuyper's motto was "a free church in a free state"[54]—an aspiration his American audience would have readily affirmed. The church should not seek any legal privileges denied to other confessional communities nor tolerate any legal burdens on its ability to govern itself. Here Kuyper takes explicit distance from Calvin and much of the early Calvinist tradition which had defended the medieval idea that the state was bound to protect, even enforce, "true religion" and oppose, even persecute, rival faith traditions.[55]

But states must inevitably interact with religion and so need some ground rules for how they should do so. Kuyper defines the duties of the state to religion as threefold. First, toward the church, the state must, first of all, do nothing: it must refrain from taking a view on what is the true church, allowing all churches equal legal freedom to exist and proclaim their message in public. This is both because the state itself lacks any access to religious truth (such truth is beyond its God-given mandate) and because to rule on what is true religion would infringe the sphere sovereignty of the church, where only Christ rules.[56] Second, toward the individual, the state must uphold freedom of conscience, in two senses: first, in the public realm, since such freedom is the

---

[53]Bratt, *Abraham Kuyper: Modern Calvinist*, 70. See also John Bolt, "Tyranny by Another Name? Theocrats and Pluralists," chap. 7 in *A Free Church, a Holy Nation: Abraham Kuyper's Public Theology* (Grand Rapids, MI: Eerdmans, 2001), 303-50.

[54]Kuyper, *Lectures on Calvinism*, 99.

[55]Kuyper, *Lectures on Calvinism*, 99-101. In "Calvinism and Politics" Kuyper suggests that this practice followed directly from the view that there should be only one institutional form of the church and that once that view is abandoned, freedom for all churches follows (101). He also argues that the splitting up of religious unity is "natural" (105). These are not very convincing arguments. Elsewhere he offers better defenses of religious freedom and pluralism. He also claims, rightly, that the Netherlands was a relatively religiously tolerant nation already in the seventeenth century, ahead of other European states. He might have noticed that the first powerful case for religious toleration in the English-speaking world was made by the radical seventeenth-century English-American Puritan Roger Williams.

[56]Kuyper, *Lectures on Calvinism*, 105.

"primordial and inalienable right of all men";[57] second, where necessary against the church so that it does not seek to compel people to remain within it against their conscience or try to disadvantage them politically if they leave. From the standpoint of the state, the church must be treated as a voluntary association where members are legally free to join and leave at will.

These two duties of the state will immediately resonate with North American Christians, and they have been robustly defended by those taking their cue from Kuyper. Indeed, Kuyperians have joined with other Christians who readily sought to extend the scope of these duties to believers both in non-Christian religions and in secular faiths. Kuyperians in North America have been keen defenders of the principle of the religious impartiality of the state.[58] This does not imply the state's *moral* neutrality; Kuyper himself saw that this is impossible. But it does imply a stance of even-handedness or equitable treatment on the part of the state in its dealings with diverse confessional communities, both religious and secular. Kuyper's twentieth-century successors in the Netherlands had little difficulty in seeing that the principle must also extend to the large number of Muslims arriving from former Dutch colonies or other Muslim nations. They have also recognized that the Netherlands is less and less a Christian nation in the sense Kuyper understood it. And they have concluded that, by implication, the principle of state religious impartiality implies equitable treatment in public policy by, for example, faith-based organizations such as a Jewish school, an Islamic bank, or a Buddhist health-care association. Such ideas have been taken up by many North American Kuyperians (and, of course, others).

But Kuyper also proposes a third duty of the state that, to our ears, appears to stand in tension with the first two—namely, a duty toward

---

[57]Kuyper, *Lectures on Calvinism*, 108.

[58]For a sympathetic critique of Kuyperian confessional pluralism, see James K. A. Smith, "The City of God and the City We're In: Augustinian Principles for Public Participation," chap. 7 in *Awaiting the King: Reforming Public Theology* (Grand Rapids, MI: Baker Academic, 2017), 209-24.

God (in fact, in his lecture he begins with this duty). States must recognize God as "Supreme Ruler" and rule "according to His ordinances."
That includes, for example, outlawing blasphemy, confessing God's name
in the constitution,[59] protecting the sabbath, proclaiming days of prayer
and thanksgiving, and "invoking His Divine blessing."[60] This does sound
like a throwback to Christendom.[61] Certainly, most of these duties
seem to be ruled out by the US Constitution's First Amendment establishment clause. Suffice it to say here that most North American Kuyperians reject such explicit duties toward God on the part of the state as
inconsistent with the basic thrust of confessional pluralism.[62]

Kuyper here adds an important qualification. The principal way in
which God is to be honored in the state is not by an official acknowledgment of God or by deferring to a church for advice but rather by
individual officeholders reaching their own conscientious judgments
as to the will of God for the state.[63] Nations can be governed in a
Christian way only "through the subjective convictions of those in authority, according to their personal views of the demands [of Christian
political principles]."[64]

That qualification has helped confirm what most of Kuyper's North
American followers already knew. Not only have they dispensed with
Kuyper's official "duties of the state towards God"; they have democra-
tized his claim about God ruling via the consciences of officials by ex-
tending it to every believing citizen. Under confessional pluralism, they
have argued, Christian influence on the state can only ever be channeled
through the conscience-led democratic work of individual Christian

---

[59] As, by the way, does Canada, in the Preamble to its 1982 constitution. However, in 1999 a senior
judge pronounced it a "dead letter."

[60] Kuyper, *Lectures on Calvinism*, 103.

[61] Kuyper defines the duty to impose a blasphemy law carefully, however. He argues that such a
law would not take a view on the religious truths being defended but only defends against the
"attack on the foundation of public law" implied in blasphemy (Kuyper, *Lectures on Calvinism*,
103). Secular humanists were not persuaded on the point.

[62] Such "duties" seem to breach Kuyper's ideas that states lack access to the knowledge of religious
truth and that they should treat all confessional communities—including atheists—equally.

[63] Kuyper, *Lectures on Calvinism*, 104.

[64] Kuyper, *Lectures on Calvinism*, 104.

citizens and their organizations, alongside that of officeholders. They have therefore opposed those Christians who have argued for some form of official state recognition of Christianity or God.[65]

I mentioned citizens and their organizations. Kuyper's public theology has inspired the creation of several new Christian organizations in various spheres of life. The editors suggest in the introduction that Kuyper's was "the worldview that has launched a thousand Christian institutions." I have not done a strict count, but certainly in North America one could identify scores of institutions, many of them educational, that to some degree have been founded on a Kuyperian vision. There are also many that existed before Kuyper's influence crossed the Atlantic but have been subsequently shaped by his thinking (Calvin University, for example). Associations of Christian schools, and of colleges, have been formed in the United States and Canada, partly under Kuyperian influence. Initiatives beyond education have also appeared. In Canada, followers of Kuyper (mostly postwar Dutch immigrants) established the Christian Labour Association of Canada (CLAC) in 1952 with the aim of bringing to bear a Christian view of work and economics to the field of industrial relations. It now represents sixty thousand workers across a range of industries and services.[66] The same community also birthed the Christian Farmers Federation of Ontario, which has the goal of applying Christian wisdom to the field of agriculture and now represents four thousand farmers.[67]

Kuyperians have also created several significant political organizations. In Canada, Citizens for Public Justice was set up in 1963 to offer resources of political education for members.[68] Initially—as the

---

[65]Kuyperian pluralism is contrasted with various "Christian nation" positions in Gary Scott Smith, ed., *God and Politics: Four Views of the Reformation of Civil Government* (Phillipsburg, NJ: P&R Publishing, 1989).

[66]"CLAC: Better Together," CLAC, accessed April 6, 2020, www.clac.ca/. See Edward Vanderkloet, ed., *A Christian Union in Labour's Wasteland* (Toronto: Wedge Publishing, 1978).

[67]"Christian Farmers Federation of Ontario," Christian Farmers Federation of Ontario, accessed April 6, 2020, www.christianfarmers.org/.

[68]"Citizens for Public Justice," Citizens for Public Justice, accessed April 6, 2020, https://cpj.ca/. See Gerald Vandezande, *Justice, Not Just Us: Faith Perspectives and National Priorities*, ed. Mark R. Vander Vennen (Toronto: Public Justice Resource Centre, 1999).

Committee for Justice and Liberty—it was primarily concerned with protecting the rights of Christian schools and those of the fledgling CLAC (which had to fight long and hard against a secular establishment to win public recognition). Later it widened its brief to lobby governments on other key issues of justice such as child poverty, homelessness, and the rights of aboriginal (First Nations) people. Generated from within the CLAC itself in the late 1990s, the Work Research Foundation, later renamed Cardus, has become perhaps the most influential Christian think tank in Canada, increasingly well known for its work in the United States as well. Its in-house publication, *Comment* magazine, has become a leading Christian contribution to cultural and political debates on a wide range of contemporary issues, and drawing on authors within and well beyond the Kuyperian tradition.[69]

In the United States, what is today named the Center for Public Justice (CPJ) was launched in 1977.[70] Based in Washington, DC, it was led for many years by political thinker James Skillen, who has published widely on Kuyperian approaches to public affairs.[71] CPJ has educated, advised, and lobbied on a wide range of issues including religious freedom for faith-based schools and other social organizations, fair political representation (through proportional representation), welfare reform and family policy, immigration reform, and many more.[72]

These organizations were both founded on a commitment to structural and confessional pluralism (though, as noted, it was the latter that initially motivated their establishment). While they have from time to time focused on specific issues, they have deliberately not set out to be

---

[69]"Comment Magazine," Cardus, accessed April 6, 2020, www.cardus.ca/comment/.

[70]"The Center for Public Justice," Center for Public Justice, accessed April 6, 2020, www.cpjustice.org.

[71]In addition to his works cited above, see also James Skillen, *The Good of Politics: A Biblical, Historical, and Contemporary Introduction* (Grand Rapids, MI: Baker Academic, 2014); and *With or Against the World? America's Role Among the Nations* (Lanham, MD: Rowman & Littlefield, 2005).

[72]See the breadth of issues covered by CPJ's journal, *Public Justice Review*: "Public Justice Review: A publication of the Center for Public Justice," Center for Public Justice, accessed April 6, 2020, www.cpjustice.org/public/public_justice_review. On welfare, see Stanley Carlson-Thies and James W. Skillen, eds., *Welfare in America: Christian Perspectives on a Policy in Crisis* (Grand Rapids, MI: Eerdmans, 1996).

single-issue organizations but have tried to represent a broader, integrated Christian political vision that was originally inspired by Kuyper's own. Albeit small in resources and staff, they have often been looked to as pioneers of a distinctive and credible form of Christian political engagement, striking out their own paths and resisting accommodation to prevailing secular ideologies or political parties. Today they work alongside many other kindred organizations shaped by different theological and secular perspectives.[73]

WHAT SHOULD WE DO?

One way to assess Kuyper's legacy is to ask what light his ideas, suitably recast, might shed on the two basic sources of division in North American societies I mentioned at the start of this chapter. I'll suggest that confessional pluralism points to promising ways of making sense of our clashing public identities, while structural pluralism points to ways to analyze the deep economic inequalities that blight those societies.

The growing conflict between different identities in the public realm is giving rise to an identity politics in which citizens identify themselves first by what distinguishes them from their fellow citizens rather than by what unites them as Americans, Canadians, and so forth.

We can distinguish three categories of identity currently bidding for public recognition. The first is traditional religions such as Christianity, Judaism, Islam, or Buddhism (each with its own internal diversities). Migration is adding to religious diversity every day, bringing to North American shores new variants of faith previously thought of as foreign (Nigerian Pentecostalism, Hispanic Catholicism, Arabic Islam). The second is secular faiths such as secular humanism, radical postmodernism, or radical ecologism.[74] These faiths are increasingly claiming the same equal treatment long afforded to traditional religions.

---

[73]In addition, many individuals who are shaped by Kuyper's vision also work within various faith-based and secular organizations, and some have held political office or engaged in public service at different levels of government.

[74]This is the belief that humans are merely one of nature's species among others.

The third includes a cluster of given characteristics such as gender, race, ethnicity, sexual orientation, or disability. Some of these already have substantial legal protection, while advocates of others are actively campaigning for it.

Conflicts of identity are not new—traumatic clashes over race, ethnicity, and religion are as old as the founding of both the United States and Canada. But newer forms of identity are appearing all the time. What is more, they are increasingly intersecting—such as when people of color suffer both racial discrimination and economic marginalization—creating a bewildering and acrimonious identity landscape. As contending identities each make their distinctive claims on the public realm, the task of government to promote justice among them all gets more and more complicated. I offer three comments on how the legacy of Kuyper might be enlisted to speak to this issue.

First, the vision behind Kuyper's defense of confessional pluralism in the nineteenth-century Netherlands still demands extensive work across North America in the face of continuing secular liberal attempts to thwart its advance or roll it back where it exists. This work will involve advocating a robust and comprehensive assertion of personal and institutional religious freedom. It will require rebutting the false assertion that faith-based claims are incompatible with liberal democracy or that faith-based organizations cannot deliver truly public services. It will involve showing—by both argument and example—how citizens of faith can and do make valuable contributions to public life while also training Christians to ensure that their contributions are constructive and not merely narrow identity assertions made without regard to the claims of others or the public good.[75]

---

[75]See, for example, the following works on these themes inspired directly or indirectly by Kuyperian ideas: John Inazu, *Confident Pluralism: Surviving and Thriving Through Deep Difference* (Chicago: University of Chicago Press, 2016); Stephen V. Monsma and Stanley W. Carlson-Thies, *Free to Serve: Protecting the Religious Freedom of Faith-Based Organizations* (Grand Rapids, MI: Brazos Press, 2015); Stephen V. Monsma, *Pluralism and Freedom: Faith-Based Organizations in a Democratic Society* (Lanham, MD: Rowman & Littlefield, 2012); Dave Donaldson and Stanley Carlson-Thies, *A Revolution of Compassion: Faith-Based Groups as Full Partners in Fighting America's Social Problems* (Grand Rapids, MI: Baker Books, 2003); Charles L. Glenn, *The Ambiguous Embrace:*

Second, what Kuyper meant by *pluralism* needs to be expanded to take account of identities he himself did not adequately recognize and which some of his North American followers have been slow, or reluctant, to acknowledge. For example, Richard Mouw and Sander Griffioen have proposed adding a third category alongside structural and confessional pluralism—namely, *contextual* pluralism. This refers to particular cultural (or ethnic) characteristics that shape the other two types and that may need public recognition.[76] One key challenge facing Christians in both Europe and North America is to develop this idea into a positive and critical Christian account of multiculturalism. This should be understood not as a celebration of every form of ethnic or cultural difference (for all ethnicities and cultures are tainted by sin) but as a targeted public policy approach that respects specific cultural or ethnic claims when these are threatened by discrimination or exclusion in the political sphere.[77] It's worth noting that one way in which the state can do justice to such cultural plurality is, simply, also to respect structural pluralism. For example, when an ethnic association (such as a social enterprise designed to assist Hispanic immigrants to start businesses) is accorded equal treatment with other voluntary associations for the purposes of recognition or funding, that is simply respecting it as a distinct structure with its own purpose. Such an association will also contribute in a small way to mitigating economic inequality.

Third, while Kuyper's ideas help us map and respond to some of the third kinds of identity noted above (I've so far discussed culture and

---

Government and Faith-Based Schools and Social Agencies (Princeton, NJ: Princeton University Press, 2000); Stephen V. Monsma and J. Christopher Soper, eds., *Equal Treatment of Religion in a Pluralistic Society* (Grand Rapids, MI: Eerdmans, 1998); Stephen V. Monsma, *Positive Neutrality: Letting Religious Freedom Ring* (Grand Rapids, MI: Baker Books, 1993).

[76]Richard J. Mouw and Sander Griffioen, *Pluralisms and Horizons: An Essay in Christian Public Philosophy* (Grand Rapids, MI: Eerdmans, 1993). Instead of structural and confessional pluralism, they speak of associational and directional pluralism.

[77]See Jonathan Chaplin, *Multiculturalism: A Christian Retrieval* (London: Theos, 2011); Matthew Kaemingk, *Christian Hospitality and Muslim Immigration in an Age of Fear* (Grand Rapids, MI: Eerdmans, 2018).

ethnicity), they leave us a lot of work to do on others. These cover a wide range of human characteristics and circumstances. Most are given, but some, such as gender identity or even race, are increasingly (and problematically) being seen as chosen. They can also imply very different kinds of public treatment. Consider two examples. First, claims of disability concern physical and financial support in overcoming the exclusions experienced by disabled people; some of these can be provided by the state, others by non-governmental providers. But they also require the overcoming of deep-seated social prejudices that states are ill-equipped to secure. Second, nondiscrimination claims made by LGBT people require, first, the protection of equal legal rights in areas such as employment and housing. Yet such rights need to be balanced fairly with, for example, the religious freedom claims of traditional religious believers. These complex questions demand a lot of hard, new work by Christians.[78]

It quickly becomes clear that sphere sovereignty is of limited use here since we are talking about fundamental questions of human nature rather than social structure. Kuyper, and many of his first heirs in North America, took for granted a widely shared Christian-humanist understanding of human nature that is now rapidly breaking down in the face of radical individualism and advancing biotechnology. That is a major challenge facing Christian cultural action: here the task is to articulate a compelling vision of human beings as embodied, relational, communal, dependent but capable persons and oppose reductionist views that strip us of our human dignity as those made in the image of God. A major challenge facing Christian political action is entering the increasingly acrimonious debates over which kinds of identity really do merit public recognition or protection. The state cannot simply defer to any subjective identity claim but has to seek a democratic consensus as to what justice requires. Approaching such a consensus is that much

---

[78]See, e.g., Stephanie Summers, ed., "Fairness for All: Does Supporting Religious Freedom Require Opposition to LGBT Civil Rights?," *Public Justice Review* 9, no. 3 (2019), www.cpjustice.org /public/public_justice_review/volume/9-3.

more complex precisely because the meaning of justice itself is profoundly contested due to escalating confessional diversity. Even getting
constructive public debates started on such issues is a daunting task
today, but Christians should not shrink from it.

Confessional pluralism, then, can suggest ways to engage with the
challenges of identity politics—though it promises no easy solutions.
Structural pluralism, I now want to suggest, can help us reckon with
the challenges of deep economic inequality. This question has been
dominated by a polarized and increasingly fruitless contest between
conservatives and liberals (as Americans call them). Conservatives
often argue that the economy is most efficient and productive when
government regulation is reduced to a minimum and markets are left
free to operate according to their own devices. Inequality is best
overcome by liberating markets to generate wealth. Liberals counter
that markets don't reliably deliver efficiency or productivity unless government prevents them from exploitation or corporate failure, supports investment, and adopts interventionist fiscal and monetary
policies. Inequality is best overcome by actively managing the economy
and distributing its fruits to the economically deprived.

Kuyper's rich account of many diverse social institutions, each offering a specific form of service to the flourishing of society, cuts
through this simple-minded standoff between the market and the state.
He shows how no independent-minded Christian can simply identify
as conservative or liberal in these impoverished senses. In his late
nineteenth-century context, Kuyper himself did not think that the
state could or should take a leading role in reducing economic inequality, and on that point we need to correct his limited expectations.[79]
But his larger political theory helps us to see that what we call the
market is in fact a highly complex network of business enterprises and
consumers, each of which needs to act responsibly if the fruits of economic activity are to be enjoyed fairly. For example, businesses can help

---

[79]See, e.g., his otherwise powerful essay *The Problem of Poverty*.

address economic inequality in numerous ways, such as by creating jobs, offering training, or engaging in just employment and trading practices. Trade unions can contribute by building worker solidarity and robustly representing just worker interests. Consumers can contribute by choosing responsibly produced and fairly traded products, not consuming to excess, and staying loyal to local producers and retailers on which their neighborhoods depend.

But the state has a unique and potentially extensive responsibility as well. Markets, even in so-called free market economies like the United States, are already extensively regulated by law, and necessarily so. The scope and functioning of markets are actually constituted by states that set the parameters of economic exchange. And it is the state's unique task to establish terms that promote just economic activity and to help compensate for the serious inequalities that even fairly regulated markets inevitably generate—such as by breaking up monopoly power, reining in exploitative corporations, supporting vulnerable business sectors (perhaps those exposed to unfair competition), devising taxation and public spending policies that serve to offer a minimum level of economic security to those suffering sustained economic exclusion, or acting to protect the environment. On such a model, every economic actor—individuals, families and households, voluntary and charitable bodies, businesses, banks, governments at all levels including international regulatory bodies—has distinct, sphere-specific responsibilities to act in ways that redress deep economic inequalities, overcome economic exclusion and exploitation, protect nature, and empower every member of society to live a responsible economic life and enjoy its fruits.[80]

---

[80]In the Netherlands, prominent economist and politician Bob Goudzwaard has pioneered a powerful approach to economics inspired by a Kuyperian vision. See, e.g., Bob Goudzwaard, *Globalization and the Kingdom of God* (Grand Rapids, MI: Baker Books, 2001); *Capitalism and Progress: A Diagnosis of Western Society* (Grand Rapids, MI: Eerdmans/Toronto: Wedge Publishing, 1979); Bob Goudzwaard and Harry de Lange, *Beyond Poverty and Affluence: Towards a Canadian Economy of Care* (Toronto: University of Toronto Press, 1994). A Dutch economist working in the same vein is Roelf Haan. See his *The Economics of Honour: Biblical Reflections on Money and Property* (Grand Rapids, MI: Eerdmans, 2009). In North America, Christian

North American Christians have made decent progress in applying Kuyperian insights into confessional pluralism, although they still have much work to do in that area. They have, however, only just begun to explore how a Kuyperian model of structural pluralism might shed light on the deep economic injustices of our societies and suggest steps toward remedying it.

FOR FURTHER READING

Bacote, Vincent. *The Political Disciple: A Theology of Public Life*. Grand Rapids, MI: Zondervan, 2015.

Bratt, James D. *Abraham Kuyper: Modern Calvinist, Christian Democrat*. Grand Rapids, MI: Eerdmans, 2013.

Chaplin, Jonathan. *Faith in Democracy: Framing a Politics of Deep Diversity*. London: SCM, 2021.

Goudzwaard, Bob. *Capitalism and Progress: A Diagnosis of Western Society*. Grand Rapids, MI: Eerdmans; Toronto: Wedge Publishing, 1979.

Hoang, Bethany H., and Kristen Deede Johnson. *The Justice Calling*. Grand Rapids, MI: Brazos Press, 2017.

Inazu, John. *Confident Pluralism: Surviving and Thriving Through Deep Difference*. Chicago: University of Chicago Press, 2016.

Kemeny, P. C., ed. *Church, State, and Public Justice: Five Views*. Downers Grove, IL: InterVarsity Press, 2007.

Koyzis, David T. *Political Visions & Illusions: A Survey and Christian Critique of Contemporary Ideologies,* 2nd edition. Downers Grove, IL: InterVarsity Press, 2019.

Kuyper, Abraham. *The Problem of Poverty*. Edited by James W. Skillen. Grand Rapids, MI: Baker Books, 1991.

---

economists such as John Tiemstra and George Monsma (both formerly of Calvin University) and Elwil Beukes (The Kings University, Edmonton) have utilized the work of Goudzwaard and other Kuyperian thinkers. See, e.g., John Tiemstra, *Stories Economists Tell* (Eugene, OR: Pickwick Publications, 2012); and John Tiemstra, ed., *Reforming Economics: Calvinist Studies on Methods and Institutions* (Lewiston, NY: Edwin Mellen Press, 1990). Kuyperian ideas are influential on the think tank Cardus, such as its "Work and Economics" program: "Work & Economics—Cardus," Cardus, accessed April 6, 2020, www.cardus.ca/research/work-economics/. See also Nicholas Wolterstorff, "Lima or Amsterdam: Liberation or Disclosure?" and "The Rich and the Poor," chaps. 3 and 4 in *Until Justice and Peace Embrace* (Grand Rapids, MI: Eerdmans, 1983), 42-68, 73-98; Lambert Zuidervaart, "Macrostructures and Societal Principles," in *Religion, Truth, and Social Transformation: Essays in Reformational Philosophy* (Montreal: McGill-Queens University Press, 2016), 252-76.

Monsma, Stephen V., and Stanley W. Carlson-Thies. *Free to Serve: Protecting the Religious Freedom of Faith-Based Organizations.* Grand Rapids, MI: Brazos Press, 2015.

Mouw, Richard J., and Sander Griffioen. *Pluralism and Horizons: An Essay in Christian Public Philosophy.* Grand Rapids, MI: Eerdmans, 1993.

Skillen, James W. *The Good of Politics: A Biblical, Historical, and Contemporary Introduction.* Grand Rapids, MI: Baker Academic, 2014.

4

KUYPER AND SCIENCE

DEBORAH B. HAARSMA

I KNEW NOTHING OF KUYPER as a child. I grew up in a wonderful church in the evangelical tradition. The adults all encouraged me to do well in school, and the parents of my church friends included a math professor and an engineer, so I didn't see my interests in school and science as divorced from my faith. Yet this tradition emphasized evangelism in a way that gave me the impression that to fully follow God, I should work in missions or ministry. How did science fit in?

In the late 1980s, I landed at Bethel College (now Bethel University) in Minnesota and discovered the "Kuyperian tradition." I don't recall the term being used, but the power of Kuyper's thought had certainly spread to this Baptist college. After my public-school experience, I was delighted to have Christian professors leading devotions before each lecture. But it was more than that. The phrase *integrating faith and learning* echoed through the hallways and the curriculum. Suddenly my faith was engaged on an intellectual level that it never had been before. I heard John Calvin's phrase "all truth is God's truth," and it transformed my thinking: I felt less fear and more freedom to study every area I could. I discovered there was a Christian way to think about history, about physics, and about music as they flowed out of a "Christian worldview." I learned that a science career could be a

Christian vocation, because science was the study of the very handiwork of God. I eventually became an astronomer, studying galaxies
and the expanding universe.

It wasn't until I became a professor at Calvin College (now Calvin
University) that I read Kuyper's 1898 lecture "Calvinism and Science"
and learned about the origins of the Kuyperian tradition.[1] In this essay,
I will summarize the key points of Kuyper's lecture that have fostered
my vocation as a Christian astronomer and have influenced Christian
colleges and institutions in the decades since. Many of these points are
more relevant than ever in the twenty-first century, for the church and
our science-dominated culture.

WHAT DID KUYPER SAY?

In the years I taught physics and astronomy at Calvin, I enjoyed my
responsibility to bring a Christian perspective to every science course.
Here I will present the gems of Kuyper's lecture as I would to my students, focusing on the points that endure today, updating the termi-
nology, and shifting the outline. While Kuyper frames much of the
lecture as an argument for Calvinism over and against other traditions
of Christianity, in other work he reasoned from Christianity broadly,[2]
and I will follow that approach here. I'll postpone discussion of Kuyper's
views of evolution till later in the essay.

First, some definitions. Kuyper uses the word *science* differently than
is typical in English, even in 1898 English. He uses it to refer to scholarly
thinking in all fields—not just the natural sciences such as astronomy
and medicine, but law, history, and philosophy. And Kuyper means
more than a list of disciplines; he uses *science* to refer to overarching

---

[1]Abraham Kuyper, *Lectures on Calvinism* (1931; repr., Grand Rapids, MI: Eerdmans, 1999), 110-41.
In this article I focus on Kuyper's 1898 Princeton lecture, but occasionally refer to "Common
Grace in Science and Art," published in 1905. For a recent translation, see *Wisdom and Wonder:
Common Grace in Science and Art*, ed. Jordan J. Ballor and Stephen J. Grabill, trans. Nelson D.
Kloosterman (Grand Rapids, MI: Christian's Library Press, 2011).
[2]E.g., Abraham Kuyper, "Evolution," in *Abraham Kuyper: A Centennial Reader*, ed. James D. Bratt
(Grand Rapids, MI: Eerdmans, 1998), 405-40.

unity of thought in all fields, the "unity in our cognizance of the entire cosmos."[3] He speaks of what we might today call the big questions, "questions of the origin, interconnection, and destiny of everything."[4] Since other essays in this volume address other academic fields, I will focus my attention on the natural sciences (physics, chemistry, biology, astronomy, etc.) and use *science* to refer to these. When I refer to Kuyper's larger meaning, I will use the word *scholarship*.

Yet even *science* can refer to many aspects of the natural sciences. I will distinguish four aspects:

1. The presuppositions of science. Science is based on key assumptions that all scientists share. These include beliefs that the natural world has regular, repeatable patterns, that people have the ability to investigate it, and that science is a worthwhile activity. These assumptions are not provable by science alone.

2. The methods of science. Science is a structured human activity, with agreed-on behaviors and methods. These include observations, experiments, mathematical models, hypothesis testing, and peer review. Each subfield of science has developed its own particular methods, to give consistent and useful results in its own area.

3. The findings of science. Science is a body of knowledge about the natural world. This body of knowledge includes particular observations (e.g., Galileo's observations of planetary motion) and well-tested models to explain those observations (e.g., the heliocentric model of the solar system in which planets orbit the sun, not the earth).

4. The implications of science. The findings of science have implications well beyond the natural world that science investigates. For example, if the earth isn't the center of the solar system, what does that mean for our understanding of Scripture? For the significance

[3]Kuyper, *Lectures on Calvinism*, 113.
[4]Kuyper, *Lectures on Calvinism*, 113.

of human beings? The sun-centered universe led to many larger questions that science couldn't answer.

Most people think of science as mainly a body of knowledge (3), the findings that you learn about in school and on nature documentaries. Most scientists, however, think of science mainly as the practice and methods of doing science (2). Kuyper goes beyond both of these, helping us think deeply and carefully about the presuppositions (1) and the larger implications (4) of science.

Called to study Christ's handiwork. Kuyper's first point is that a Christian worldview fosters a love of science. Christianity leads to "an impulse, an inclination, and an incentive" for scholarly investigation.[5] The motivations of the scientist are an important part of the presuppositions of science. Should (or even can) we do science, and if so, why? The worth of science seems obvious today, but it has not always been so. In early cultures that believed nature was inhabited by multiple spirits or warring gods, a scientific study of nature would seem like nonsense, a waste of time, or even profane. In the medieval church, Kuyper argues, the pursuit of heavenly life and the eternal became so one-sided that the church "neglected to give due attention to the world of God's creation."[6] In today's church, we also see challenges of Christians neglecting or rejecting science. While most Christians have positive views of science in general,[7] many also reject some key scientific findings,[8] often out of

---

[5]Kuyper, *Lectures on Calvinism*, 110.

[6]Kuyper, *Lectures on Calvinism*, 118.

[7]Among (American) evangelical Protestants, 48 percent believe science and religion can work in collaboration, 21 percent see them as referring to different aspects of reality, and only 31 percent see them in conflict. Elaine Howard Ecklund and Christopher Scheitle, "Religious Communities, Science, Scientists, and Perceptions: A Comprehensive Survey," February 16, 2014, paper prepared for presentation at the Annual Meetings of the American Association for the Advancement of Science, www.aaas.org/sites/default/files/content_files/RU_AAASPresentation Notes_2014_0219%20%281%29.pdf.

[8]"Public's Views on Human Evolution," Pew Research Center, December 30, 2013, www.pewforum .org/2013/12/30/publics-views-on-human-evolution/. Among White evangelicals, only 27 percent agree that humans and other living things have evolved over time, while among those unaffiliated with a religion, 78 percent agree. Other Christian groups are more likely to accept that humans evolved: 44 percent of Black Protestants, 53 percent of Hispanic Catholics, 68 percent of White Catholics, and 76 percent of White Mainline Protestants.

concern for the implications of science.[9] Unfortunately, many scientists believe that the church has rejected science.[10] Sadly, our own young people have also absorbed this impression, with 49 percent of church-going teenagers today agreeing that "the church seems to reject much of what science tells us about the world."[11]

Kuyper argues that a Christian worldview gives us the appropriate presuppositions for doing science. God's sovereignty gives us "the certainty that the existence and course of all things, i.e. of the entire cosmos, instead of being a plaything of caprice and chance, obeys law and order, and that there exists a firm will which carries out its design, both in nature and in history."[12] The universe did not arise on its own or from an impersonal force. Rather, the universe was created by a Person, a Person who is still intimately involved. The entire natural world was ordained by God from the beginning with a firm will and a clear design, and it continues to be governed by God to accomplish his intention: a universe of wonders, a planet thriving with life, and humans created in his image. God's faithful character in governing this universe gives the Christian confidence that the universe is not capricious but has a "stability and regularity ruling everything."[13] Kuyper will return to the topic of presuppositions later in the lecture, but from the beginning he is clear about the Christian motivations for science. Christianity does not lead to "contempt for the world, neglect of the temporal and the undervaluation of cosmical things."[14] Rather, study of the natural world can "regain its worth, not at the expense of things eternal, but by virtue of its capacity as God's handiwork and as a revelation of God's attributes."[15]

---

[9]Elaine Howard Ecklund, *Religion vs. Science: What Religious People Really Think* (Oxford: Oxford University Press, 2018).

[10]Elaine Howard Ecklund, *Science vs. Religion: What Scientists Really Think* (Oxford: Oxford University Press, 2012).

[11]Barna Group, *Gen Z: The Culture, Beliefs, and Motivations Shaping the Next Generation* (Ventura, CA: Barna Group, 2018), 71.

[12]Kuyper, *Lectures on Calvinism*, 114.

[13]Kuyper, *Lectures on Calvinism*, 114.

[14]Kuyper, *Lectures on Calvinism*, 119-20.

[15]Kuyper, *Lectures on Calvinism*, 119-20.

Here, for the Christian, is the ultimate motivation for science: to study the handiwork of God and to learn more of his attributes.

Kuyper quickly makes clear that the study of creation is not something apart from Christ; rather, it flows from Christ. Too often, discussions of science and faith have been watered down to a discussion of mere theism—Is there a God? Is there a designer?—with little definition of what is meant by "God." Not so for Kuyper! His argument is fully centered on Christ. One of Kuyper's most famous lines comes from his 1880 address on sphere sovereignty: "There is not a square inch in the whole domain of our human existence over which Christ, who is Sovereign over all, does not cry, Mine!"[16] In the present lecture, Kuyper critiques the error of "mystic worshipping of Christ alone, to the exclusion of God and Father Almighty, Maker of heaven and earth," critiquing those for whom "Christ was conceived exclusively as the Savior, and His cosmological significance was lost out of sight."[17] The cosmological character of Christ is clear in Scripture. In Colossians 1:15-17 and John 1:1-3, Christ is proclaimed as the Creator, not just of a part but of all things. Christ is also cosmic in his redemption. The "work of redemption is not limited to the salvation of individual sinners, but extends itself to the redemption *of the world*, and to the organic reunion of all things in heaven and earth to Christ as their original head."[18] This is not a mere intellectual argument. Kuyper describes it as a wide, cosmic gospel that we apprehend with our souls, as we are overwhelmed with a deep impression of God's majesty that molds our lives.[19]

Kuyper offers two beautiful metaphors here. One is the metaphor of "two books," as used in the Belgic Confession (Article 2)[20] and elsewhere,

---

[16]Abraham Kuyper, "Sphere Sovereignty," in *Abraham Kuyper: A Centennial Reader*, ed. James D. Bratt (Grand Rapids, MI: Eerdmans, 1998), 488.

[17]Kuyper, *Lectures on Calvinism*, 118.

[18]Kuyper, *Lectures on Calvinism*, 119 (emphasis original).

[19]Kuyper, *Lectures on Calvinism*, 119.

[20]Guido de Brès, *The Belgic Confession*, 1561. English translation available in *Our Faith: Ecumenical Creeds, Reformed Confessions, and Other Resources* (Grand Rapids, MI: Faith Alive Christian Resources, 2013), 25-68.

in which nature is a second "book" alongside Scripture. Both books are revelations from God and means by which we may know God and his attributes. The other metaphor compares Scripture to a lens, to eyeglasses that bring the natural world into focus and allow us to decipher the divine thoughts revealed in nature. Both metaphors make clear that nature is a fundamental part of God's revelation, not a mere "accessorial item." Kuyper tells the story of Peter Plancius, a preacher in the 1600s who was also a scientist that advised seafarers with his extensive geographical knowledge. "The investigation of the lines of longitude and latitude of the terrestrial globe formed in his estimation one whole with the investigation of the length and breadth of the love of Christ. He saw himself placed between two works of God, the one in creation, the other in Christ, and in both he adored that majesty of Almighty God, which transported his soul to ecstasy."[21]

Kuyper is clear that any individual area of scholarship is incomplete on its own. He affirms the "study of nature"[22] and the "empirical investigation of special phenomena,"[23] but within a larger context that goes beyond science itself. Indeed, the methods and findings of science, while reliable and powerful in their own sphere, simply are not equipped to address the broader implications of science for the big questions of life. The natural sciences alone cannot give us meaning, explain personhood, determine ethics, or reveal the character of God. Kuyper argues that we all have a thirst for something more, a higher level of thought and knowledge that brings all the particular fields into a unified whole. He rails against those who limit us to being agnostic or ignorant on such higher questions or who claim that our thirst for this highest form of knowledge can never be satisfied, calling this "spiritual vandalism."[24] In recent decades, we've seen a new kind of vandalism, that of militant atheist scientists such as Richard Dawkins and Jerry Coyne. These

---

[21]Kuyper, *Lectures on Calvinism*, 120.
[22]Kuyper, *Lectures on Calvinism*, 114.
[23]Kuyper, *Lectures on Calvinism*, 115.
[24]Kuyper, *Lectures on Calvinism*, 113.

atheists elevate the methods and findings of science as the best, or perhaps only, valid form of knowledge, mocking religion as mere superstition. Both then and know, Christianity offers an all-encompassing picture that goes beyond science alone to satisfy our thirst for wholeness. God's sovereignty over all things—the natural world, human existence, the destiny of everything—brings "a deep conviction of the unity, stability, and order of things" and assurance of an "organic interconnection of the universe."[25]

Seeing the natural world as God's creation more than validates science: Christianity commands that we know God through his handiwork. "Thus vanishes every dread possibility that he who occupied himself with nature has wasted his capacities in pursuit of vain and idle things. It was perceived, on the contrary, that for God's sake, our attention may not be withdrawn from the life of nature and creation."[26] This vision finally answered the question of my childhood—how does the pursuit of science fit with my faith? Science does not distract from faith, nor somehow diminish faith, but rather is a vital part of a wholehearted faith. Following Christ is about more than making a one-time decision for Christ; it is about how we follow him in our lives thereafter. As Kuyper argues later in the lecture, while we are on a spiritual pilgrimage, we yet have important tasks to perform on earth, where the wealth of nature is "spread out before, under, and above" us. This "entire limitless field" must be worked, and to this labor we must consecrate ourselves "with enthusiasm and energy."[27]

A distinctively Christian approach to science. When I reached graduate school, new questions loomed for me. If doing science was an expression of my Christian faith, how is it that the non-Christian scientists around me were able to do such great science? In my research lab I worked alongside people of many faiths and no faith, yet we all did the same work. The great scientists I studied in class and heard at

---

[25]Kuyper, *Lectures on Calvinism*, 115.
[26]Kuyper, *Lectures on Calvinism*, 120-21.
[27]Kuyper, *Lectures on Calvinism*, 130.

conferences were clearly smarter than me! It felt strange to be learning so much from people who did not know Jesus Christ.

Kuyper addressed this issue directly in his teaching about common grace. He argues that if sin were left unbridled and unfettered, it would destroy everything. Instead, God gives common grace to all, to prevent evil from coming fully to the surface.[28] In common grace, God gives gifts to people regardless of their beliefs; as Jesus taught, God "sends rain on the just and on the unjust" (Mt 5:45 ESV). For Kuyper, "it was the 'common grace' of God which had produced in ancient Greece and Rome the treasures of philosophic light, and disclosed to us treasures of art and justice, which kindled the love for classical studies."[29] In a key article a few years later on common grace in science, Kuyper fleshed out this point: "In modern times as well, no one can deny that in the disciplines of astronomy, botany, zoology, physics, and so on, a rich science is blossoming. Although being conducted almost exclusively by people who are strangers to the fear of the Lord, this science has nevertheless produced a treasury of knowledge that we as Christians admire and gratefully use."[30] Scientists of all religious stripes are studying the handiwork of God, even if they do not acknowledge it as such. "God created in human beings, as his image-bearers, the capacity to understand, to grasp, to reflect, and to arrange within a totality these thoughts expressed in the creation."[31] Thus, we do not need to be suspicious of every scientific discovery made by a non-Christian. If the discovery is grounded in evidence in God's creation and in the skills of reason given through common grace, it is of God. Because of God's common grace, we can learn from one another in a pluralistic society and collaborate on scientific research across worldviews, cultures, and nations.

Yet common grace does not resolve all conflicts. In our culture, we see many tensions around the intersection between faith and science.

---

[28]Kuyper, *Lectures on Calvinism*, 123.
[29]Kuyper, *Lectures on Calvinism*, 125.
[30]Kuyper, *Wisdom and Wonder*, 53.
[31]Kuyper, *Wisdom and Wonder*, 41-42.

This is where Kuyper emphasizes a critical distinction: the conflict is not between *science* and faith. Rather, the fundamental conflict is between differing worldviews. Science is not separate from faith, to be in conflict with it; rather, science is a component of many faiths and worldviews. Each worldview has its own beliefs, each claims the whole domain of human knowledge, and each has its own views of God. Now, Kuyper's description of the worldview conflict in academia of his day is quite strong: an "antithesis, which separates the thinking minds . . . into two opposite battle-arrays" with both sides in earnest and the ideas encompassing one's entire world- and life-view.[32] Although this picture doesn't describe today's university (which includes scientists of many worldviews, not just two, and in which most have not thought deeply about what a fully consistent world- and life-view would mean for them), the strength of Kuyper's approach is reframing the discussion in terms of worldviews rather than autonomous reason.[33] The conflict is not facts versus values or reason versus religious experience. Rather, every worldview incorporates evidence, reason, religious experience, and faith.

Granting that science is part of one's larger worldview, we must ask, how exactly does worldview make a difference in science? What does a distinctly Christian approach to astronomy look like? The antithesis picture suggests that our fundamentally different starting point should lead to dramatically different conclusions. Yet the common grace picture suggests much commonality—surely math is math the world over! We need to find the right balance between the antithesis and common grace. Kuyper notes that Christians are opposed to humanists when they endeavor to substitute life in the world for the eternal, but Christians are allies to the humanist who merely requests proper acknowledgment of secular life,[34] a distinction between presuppositions and shared methods.

---

[32]Kuyper, *Lectures on Calvinism*, 131-33.
[33]Craig Bartholomew, *Contours of the Kuyperian Tradition: A Systematic Introduction* (Downers Grove, IL: IVP Academic, 2017), 113.
[34]Kuyper, *Lectures on Calvinism*, 121.

Kuyper also distinguishes between findings and larger implications, saying that findings from every field of scholarship (astronomy, chemistry, history, etc.) should be respected but can be separated from the conclusions drawn from them.[35] In a later article, he writes, "We have not ceased on account of sin to be rational creatures. . . . No, the actual darkening of sin lies in something else entirely . . . that we lost the gift of grasping the true context, the proper coherence, the systematic integration of all things."[36] Thus, there is a broad and practical commonality across worldviews in the methods and findings of science due to the common grace of reason and God's general revelation in nature. The differences in worldview show up primarily in the presuppositions and implications of science, sometimes quite strongly as an antithesis.

Kuyper focuses on the presuppositions (see below for more discussion of implications). Worldviews give fundamentally different starting points for the presuppositions of science. Kuyper lists some of these presuppositions: that we are self-conscious, that our senses are working accurately, and that universal patterns underlie the particular phenomena we observe.[37] For the sciences, we can add presuppositions that the natural world is comprehensible by humans, that science is a worthwhile activity, that natural phenomena are regular and repeatable, and that conclusions must be supported by observations and experiments (armchair theories are not science).[38] All of these presuppositions are necessary for the methods of science, yet these presuppositions "do not come to us by proof, but are established in our judgment by our inner conception."[39]

For the Christian, the presuppositions needed for science flow naturally from biblical teaching about human nature and God's work in

---

[35]Kuyper, *Lectures on Calvinism*, 139.

[36]Kuyper, *Wisdom and Wonder*, 54-55.

[37]Kuyper, *Lectures on Calvinism*, 131.

[38]Kuyper makes several of these points in a later article, arguing that the universe is the expression of God's thought and therefore, as God's image bearers, humanity has the capacity and calling to do scholarship (*Wisdom & Wonder*, 36-43).

[39]Kuyper, *Lectures on Calvinism*, 131.

creation. In no sense does a Christian set aside her faith in order to do science. The Christian does not need to adopt a "neutral" posture when he enters the lab. Rather, scientific methods and human reasoning are fully Christian activities. The Christian believes that humans have reliable senses and the ability to comprehend the natural world for biblical reasons: humans are made in God's image (Gen 1:27) and gifted by God to name and study his handiwork (Gen 1:28; 2:19-20; Prov 25:2). The Christian believes that experiments are necessary because we know that mere armchair theories are susceptible to human limitations and fallenness (Job 38). The Christian believes that nature operates with universal, repeatable patterns, because Scripture teaches that nature is not filled with capricious gods, but ruled by one God in a faithful, consistent manner (Gen 1; Ps 119:89-90; Jer 33:19-26). It is because of God's faithfulness that physical processes like gravity and electricity behave consistently across all time and the entire universe, with incredible mathematical precision. For the Christian, the beauty and symmetry of these laws is clearly an expression of the beauty of the Creator. This Christian worldview strongly influenced many of the leaders of the scientific revolution, such as Galileo, Newton, Boyle, and Kepler. Although Christianity cannot take full credit for the scientific revolution (many factors contributed to the rise of science in seventeenth-century Europe), it is certainly true that Christian thinking had a profound and positive influence on the rise of science. Those who claim that Christian doctrine is fundamentally opposed to science are sorely mistaken.

For those of other worldviews, the presuppositions needed for science come from other directions. For Jewish and Muslim scientists, many of the scriptures regarding creation are shared with Christianity, leading to a similar basis for the presuppositions. For militant atheist scientists, the belief in the regular functioning of nature is based on an explicit rejection of the erratic behavior and superstitious reasoning that they (mistakenly) expect from religion. Many scientists do not have an internally consistent worldview. Most common in my experience is the scientist for whom the presuppositions seem self-evident, as principles taught in science class and continually affirmed by the fact that scientific methods are so powerful and reliable. Yet philosophers of science remind us that past performance is no guarantee of future results—on what basis can such a scientist believe that the natural world will continue to behave as it has? As the editors of this book write in the opening chapter, such scientists don't realize they are "busy trading off the religious past of the great scientific minds of history, who bequeathed to us a scientific method charged with trust in a kind of universe suspiciously laden with wonder, goodness, and discoverability." As Christians, we need not fear that we are adopting atheistic methods when doing science. Rather, we can celebrate the positive influence the Christian worldview has had on establishing the presuppositions and methods of science that are now shared by all scientists.

But we should not get comfortable. Although Christian worldviews overlap with atheist worldviews in the methods and findings of science, we must never forget our radically different starting points. In the public square, we must not concede to an atheistic framing of science. Kuyper calls us from resignation to action: "If we console ourselves with the thought that we may without danger leave secular science in the hands of our opponents if we only succeed in saving theology, ours will be the tactics of the ostrich."[40] Every Christian scholar should feel this as "a sharp incentive" to go back to his own principles, to renew scientific investigation on the lines of these principles, and to speak boldly about it in the university and public square.[41] "We do not assail the liberty of the [atheist] to build a well-construed science from the premises of his own consciousness, but our right and liberty to do the same thing we are determined to defend, if needs be, at any cost."[42]

---

[40]Kuyper, *Lectures on Calvinism*, 139.
[41]Kuyper, *Lectures on Calvinism*, 139.
[42]Kuyper, *Lectures on Calvinism*, 138.

WHAT DID KUYPERIANS DO?

Kuyper's approach to science and worldviews has had an important influence in the last 120 years, although not as large an influence as it should have. Again, I'll focus on the natural sciences rather than all areas of scholarship. I'm not a historian, but I can offer a few historical trends and personal reflections. Several of these trends refer to evolution, the most prominent faith/science topic of the last 160 years; see the following section for more discussion of the findings and implications of evolution.

When Kuyper lectured at Princeton in 1898, Princeton scholars were actively engaged in discussions of science, faith, and worldview, and had been for decades. Historian Bradley Grundlach describes how the language of warfare against evolutionary science had decreased, so that by the 1890s the scientists at Princeton college had "a wide latitude in their explorations of evolution's mechanisms and effects under the general concept of theism."[43] Princeton theologian B. B. Warfield (1851–1921), an early defender of biblical inerrancy, wrote substantially on evolution as a possible (and even likely) explanation of natural development under God's governance.[44] The debate was instead focused in the same general direction that Kuyper took, on how to combat the worldviews of evolutionary philosophy and "the emerging liberal theological views that took such evolutionary notions as a guide or an excuse for making alterations to the faith."[45] The Princetonians had a major recognized influence on the twentieth-century discussion of faith and science, yet Kuyper himself has not been seen as a prominent figure. He is not mentioned by name in several recent handbooks and histories of science and Christianity.[46]

---

[43]Bradley J. Grundlach, "Protestant Evangelicals," in *The Warfare Between Science and Religion: The Idea That Wouldn't Die*, ed. Jeff Hardin, Ronald L. Numbers, and Ronald A. Binzley (Baltimore, MD: Johns Hopkins University Press, 2018), 170-71.

[44]Mark Noll, "Jesus Christ: Guidance for Serious Learning," chap. 3 in *Jesus Christ and the Life of the Mind* (Grand Rapids, MI: Eerdmans, 2011), 43-64.

[45]Grundlach, "Protestant Evangelicals," 171.

[46]Kuyper does not appear in the indexes of any of the following works: Ronald Numbers, *The Creationists: The Evolution of Scientific Creationism* (New York: Knopf, 1992); Paul Copan et al., eds., *The Dictionary of Christianity and Science: The Definitive Reference for the Intersection of*

But over the decades, the inheritors of the Kuyperian tradition have gradually risen to a larger level of influence.

In the early decades of the twentieth century, it was likely practical considerations that prevented a full implementation of Kuyper's vision for the sciences in the United States. Kuyper ends his lecture with a call to found separate Christian institutions to pursue scholarship with a Christian worldview from the ground up, and he himself founded the Free University of Amsterdam. Catholics had the capacity to grow institutions that engaged in scientific research such as the Vatican Observatory and the University of Notre Dame. But the Dutch Americans were a small immigrant community. They founded Christian schools, colleges, seminaries, and publishers, but it took decades to develop the resources to offer degrees in science, and even longer to engage in full scientific research.

Meanwhile, fundamentalism was on the rise, in both the United States and the Netherlands. The writings of George McCready Price led the way to the modern young-earth creationist movement, with the publication in 1923 of *The New Geology*. At the Free University in Amsterdam, neo-Calvinist theologians of the 1920s and 1930s had become less open to the findings of evolutionary science; Abraham Filpse, in his historical overview, writes they "were inclined to reject the outcomes of scientific research and they also had stricter views about the authority of Scripture and the interpretation of the first chapters of Genesis."[47] By the postwar period, however, Kuyperian scientists were beginning to weigh in, both in the United States and the Netherlands. These included books by Jan Lever, professor of zoology at the Free University of

---

Christian Faith and Contemporary Science (Grand Rapids, MI: Zondervan, 2017); James Stump and Alan Padgett, eds., *The Blackwell Companion to Science and Christianity* (Chichester, UK: Wiley-Blackwell, 2012); Heidi A. Campbell and Heather Looy, eds., *A Science and Religion Primer* (Grand Rapids, MI: Baker Academic, 2009); Ian G. Barbour, *Religion and Science: Historical and Contemporary Issues*, rev. ed. (San Francisco: HarperSanFrancisco, 1997).

[47] Abraham C. Flipse, "Creation and Evolution: History of the Debate in the Netherlands," BioLogos, November 17, 2014, https://biologos.org/articles/creation-and-evolution-history-of-the-debate -in-the-netherlands.

Amsterdam,[48] and John De Vries, professor of chemistry at Calvin University in Michigan.[49] They followed Kuyper's thinking on the worldview basis for science but showed that scientific findings, including evolution, could be framed in a Christian worldview. At such Kuyperian institutions, the young-earth creationist views of Henry Morris (including his *The Genesis Flood*, published in 1961) rarely took hold.

Of larger influence than the books of Lever and De Vries was the publication of *The Christian View of Science and Scripture* in 1954 by theologian Bernard Ramm. Although Ramm was Baptist, the book was published by Eerdmans and mentions Kuyper briefly. Ramm shared Kuyper's view that the conflict was centered on worldview, on scientism rather than science itself. He called evangelicals to reject the "ignoble tradition" prevalent among fundamentalists of the time and to "call evangelicals back to the noble tradition of the closing years of the nineteenth century."[50] It was Ramm's work that influenced several of the new evangelical institutions of the mid-twentieth century: Billy Graham in founding *Christianity Today* in 1956 and the early leaders of the American Scientific Affiliation (a professional organization for Christians in the sciences, founded in 1941).[51] The Au Sable Institute (an environmental education and conservation group) was founded in 1961, but not by Dutch American Kuyperians. Why were Kuyperians not more prominent in these movements? It is not clear. James Bratt, in *Dutch Calvinism in Modern America*,[52] offers a hint, describing Dutch American Calvinists as fully promoting Kuyper's vision of worldview presuppositions influencing science but having a posture of responding to threats such as secular scientism on a more theoretical level than a practical one. I wonder too if this insular immigrant community simply

[48]Jan Lever, *Creation and Evolution*, trans. Peter G. Berkhout (Grand Rapids, MI: Grand Rapids International Press, 1958).

[49]John De Vries, *Beyond the Atom: An Appraisal of Our Christian Faith in This Age of Atomic Science*, 2nd ed. (Grand Rapids, MI: Eerdmans, 1950).

[50]Bernard Ramm, *The Christian View of Science and Scripture* (Grand Rapids, MI: Eerdmans, 1954), 9.

[51]Grundlach, "Protestant Evangelicals," 177-79.

[52]James D. Bratt, *Dutch Calvinism in Modern America: A History of a Conservative Subculture* (Grand Rapids, MI: Eerdmans, 1984), 146.

did not see the larger tides of American evangelicalism to be their problem and thus did not see a need to create more institutions or to share the wealth of the Kuyperian tradition more broadly.

But eventually the Dutch Americans developed a deeper engagement in the sciences as resources became available. Calvin geologist Clarence Menninga recalls Tymen Hofman, who earned a geology degree from the University of Alberta in 1946, then decided to pursue a career in ministry. While Hofman was a Calvin Theological Seminary student, he and his fellow students wrote a letter to the Calvin administration to urge the offering of a geology course, which was approved in 1950.[53] Worldviews also played a role in the launch of astronomy at Calvin. I personally recall a conversation with William Spoelhof, president of Calvin from 1951 to 1976, in which Spoelhof described the construction of the new science building in the 1960s. He personally insisted that the building include a rooftop astronomical observatory, even though the college did not yet offer courses in astronomy, because of the importance of students studying God's creation and to better engage the post-Sputnik scientific culture. Ecological sciences received a Kuyperian framing from Calvin De Witt, Calvin class of 1957 and ecology professor at the University of Wisconsin–Madison, who took over leadership of the Au Sable Institute in 1979.

By the 1980s and 1990s, Kuyperian approaches to the sciences were becoming more widely implemented in evangelical colleges, publishers, and other institutions. I personally learned it at my Baptist college in the 1980s, then was exposed to more authors and speakers through InterVarsity Christian Fellowship in the 1990s. Among Christian graduate students, there was a clear difference between those who graduated from Christian colleges with some Kuyperian grounding and those who had not. I recall others wrestling with questions like "I enjoy studying physics, but doesn't God want me to be working full time at a

---

[53]Clarence Menninga, "History of Geology at Calvin College," April 10, 2001, https://studylib .net/doc/14496792.

homeless shelter?" It was a joy to share with them how scientific study can be a fully Christian calling. I later saw the Kuyperian tradition in the sciences being developed in detail at Calvin University, both before and after my arrival on the faculty, by scientists such as Howard Van Till, Clarence Menninga, Davis Young, Arie Leegwater, and Ralph Stearley, and by philosophers such as Alvin Plantinga, Richard Mouw, and Del Ratzsch.

In 2009, BioLogos was founded to engage rigorous science from a Christian perspective, at first focusing on evolution and later more topics. The first leaders did not have close ties to the Kuyperian tradition, but the organization quickly attracted many Kuyperians along with a broader coalition of Christian traditions around a mission of celebrating the harmony between God's Word and God's world.[54] Today, ideas like "all truth is God's truth" and the two books metaphor continue to have profound effects in the broader evangelical conversation on science, where such insights are still brand new for many audiences. In the further reading section at the end of this chapter, I list some recent books on science and Christianity, including those coming out of the Kuyperian tradition.

WHAT SHOULD WE DO?

What can we do with Kuyper's rich insights for science today? The insights I discussed above are as relevant as ever and ripe for application. Here I'll address three areas where Kuyper's thinking benefits from revision or expansion, particularly in light of the needs of today's world and the last 120 years of scientific findings.[55]

---

[54]"BioLogos," BioLogos, accessed October 19, 2019, https://biologos.org/.

[55]Other aspects of Kuyper's writing are best left in the dust of history. In some places he writes in ways that today are clearly racist (e.g., *Lectures on Calvinism*, 124); see the chapter by Vincent Bacote in this volume for a wise response to Kuyper's racism. Also, in his zeal for Calvinism, he uses derogatory language against other Christian traditions (e.g., against Arminians in *Lectures on Calvinism*, 114). Contemporary voices in the Kuyperian tradition are quick to affirm the value of other traditions. See, e.g., Bartholomew, *Contours of the Kuyperian Tradition*, 52; and Cornelius Plantinga Jr., *Engaging God's World: A Christian Vision of Faith, Learning, and Living* (Grand Rapids, MI: Eerdmans, 2002), xvi.

Beyond Christian universities. In both this lecture and later work,[56] Kuyper sees only limited value in the role of Christian scholars embedded in larger secular institutions, and advocates strongly for separate Christian research institutions. I believe a hybrid approach is needed. Christian institutions continue to be important for both education and scholarship. The Christian university is the proper home for the in-depth interdisciplinary scholarship that Kuyper called us to, bringing together scholars of multiple disciplines to address the big questions from a fully Christian perspective. However, Christian universities are not enough. On their own, they are at risk of insular conversation and tribalist tendencies. Their excellent Christian scholarship would not reach the larger church of all traditions. And other channels are needed to fully engage the public square and counteract the atheistic presuppositions and implications so often attached to science.

For these goals, Kuyperian thinking needs to spread from the Christian college incubators to the larger world. Christian publishers continue to bring the work of these scholars to broad Christian audiences. Christian parachurch organizations, like BioLogos, the American Scientific Affiliation, the Canadian Scientific and Christian Affiliation, and the Au Sable Institute, reach Christians of many other traditions with the message that modern science and biblical faith can walk hand in hand. And to fully and effectively engage the public square, the biggest need continues to be for believing scientists to serve as top research scientists, embedded in research universities and other secular institutions. Such scientific leaders can shape the tone of the conversation at their institutions, dispel many misconceptions about Christianity and science, serve as role models for Christian students at the university, and be a living witness to the gospel in the secular scientific culture. The common ground we share in the methods and findings of

---

[56]Kuyper, *Wisdom and Wonder,* 92-95. This seems in contrast with his argument earlier in that work (43-46) that a multitude of diverse people from many nations are necessary to do scholarship, and that, even if working separately, they will achieve stability because God is the ultimate architect of scholarship.

science give us a strong basis for Christian witness, and we have so much to offer in the rich, beautiful Christian presuppositions of science, based in the cosmic Christ.

Called to address ethics. Kuyper's discussion of the implications of the natural sciences almost always focuses on evolutionary science (discussed below).[57] Today we see multiple areas of science and technology leading to many questions of personhood, ethics, and public policy for which the world needs to hear a robust and clear Christian voice. The first gene-edited babies were born in China in 2018 under an ethical cloud; while illegal in the United States, the technology now exists to edit our children and to pass those changes on to all of their children. How will Christians respond? Environmental issues, from land use to species extinction to climate change, are an urgent call to care not only for God's creation but for the people most impacted by environmental change, often the poor and powerless. In astronomy, what would it mean for Christian theology if we were to discover intelligent life on other planets? In these areas and more, the world needs to hear the full-orbed understanding of Christian scholarship that Kuyper envisioned. We need to bring together knowledge and wisdom from many fields of study to understand the truths of the natural world, of human nature, and of the big questions, and to promote wise public policies on challenging ethical issues and human needs. Such Christian scholarship brings light to a dark world.

Understanding evolution. Kuyper spends a significant portion of the lecture discussing evolution,[58] so I will spend the rest of this section in response. Kuyper rejects evolution in the strongest terms. His objections, however, are not focused on the scientific findings of evolution.[59]

---

[57] An exception is a comment on the practice of medicine if it ignores the spiritual dimension, *Wisdom and Wonder*, 99

[58] In 1899, a year after his Princeton lecture, Kuyper expanded his argument in the lecture "Evolution" (*Centennial Reader*, 405-40). It includes a description of the scientific evidence available at the time, and expands his critique of social Darwinism and other spreading of evolutionary thought into the social sciences and humanities.

[59] This key distinction is clouded by Kuyper's frequent use, especially in the 1899 lecture, of the terms *evolution* and *theory of evolution* to refer to the larger implications that some draw from

In fact, he seems to refer to "the laws of heredity and variation which control the whole organization of nature" as a positive example of the cosmos developing according to a firm order.[60] Rather, he sees evolution as a marker in a larger battle between two opposing worldviews in which the differences are their presuppositions.[61] On the question of evolution, the antithesis is paramount for Kuyper. He defines two worldviews: one that I'll call atheistic evolutionism and the other a Christian position.

In atheistic evolutionism, the presuppositions of this worldview lead to a complete rejection of miracles and supernatural activity, allowing only logical inferences of cause and effect. Atheistic evolutionism does accept the findings of evolution, that all species developed out of lower and preceding forms of life. Yet from this, atheistic evolutionism draws implications that go well beyond the findings and that directly contradict Christian faith. In atheistic evolutionism, there is no such thing as sin and no need for redemption, but merely an evolution from a lower to a higher moral position. In atheistic evolutionism, Scripture is only a human production, Christ is only a man, and any supreme being is conceived based on some human ideal.[62] Clearly all Christians must reject atheistic evolutionism! Kuyper's call to action in countering this worldview is as relevant as ever.[63]

The problem is in how Kuyper defines his Christian position on evolution. In his passion to reject atheistic evolutionism, he does not follow his own principles regarding common grace and general revelation. He paints himself into a corner by defining a Christian position that is opposed not only to the atheistic implications but to the scientific findings

---

evolutionary science (such as atheism and social Darwinism). Scientists use *evolution* and *theory of evolution* to refer to the scientific findings of evolutionary biology.

[60]Kuyper, *Lectures on Calvinism*, 115.

[61]Kuyper, *Lectures on Calvinism*, 138.

[62]Kuyper, *Lectures on Calvinism*, 132.

[63]A prime example of a modern treatment is *Where the Conflict Really Lies* by leading philosopher Alvin Plantinga (Oxford University Press, 2011). Plantinga shows the deep concord between science and Christian belief, rebuts militant atheists who try to frame the conflict as science vs. theism, and rejects atheistic accounts of evolution.

themselves and even to the methods of studying natural mechanisms. Unfortunately, he allows no other Christian positions, particularly none that incorporate the scientific findings of evolution, and ridicules such views as amphibious.[64]

Yet many Kuyperian scientists today accept a position that combines acceptance of evolutionary findings with Christian presuppositions and implications, which I'll call evolutionary creation (EC).[65] These Kuyperians believe EC is more in line with Kuyper's core vision, including his emphases on the Christian basis of doing science, on common grace, and on the natural world as God's revelation. I would make four broad points:

First, the search for natural explanations in the created order, including the origin of species, is a fully Christian endeavor. Kuyper is inconsistent when he casts the search for natural explanations in the methods of evolutionary science as inherently atheistic. Like other fields of science, the methods of evolutionary science flow naturally from Christian presuppositions. God calls us to investigate natural mechanisms in natural history, whether the development of a star from a gas cloud, an oak tree from an acorn, or a complex species from a simpler species. Such investigation is not a denial of God's action or creative power but rather a recognition of God's faithfulness and providential power in upholding the natural world.

Second, scientific findings do not determine spiritual implications. The findings of evolutionary science can inform our theological thinking, but science is not equipped to *determine* theology. The worldview of atheistic evolutionism goes beyond science when it claims that humans do not have a unique identity, that sin isn't real, or that God is not at work in the universe. Whatever mechanism God used to create *Homo sapiens*, whether miraculously from dust or using the natural mechanisms of evolution, God created us in his image. God is

---

[64]Kuyper, *Lectures on Calvinism*, 133.
[65]See "For Further Reading" for examples.

the source of our capabilities and our calling to represent him on earth in a way unique and distinct from all other species. While science can document bad behavior, it cannot perceive the spiritual reality of our rebellion against God or offer a cure. Common grace limits the effects of sin, but full salvation and regeneration are found only in Christ. The mechanisms God used to create *Homo sapiens* do not change these spiritual realities.

Third, presuppositions for science, including evolutionary science, do not require the rejection of miracles in natural history. The methods of science are designed to investigate patterns and regularities in the natural world, but these are just methods, not an absolute law eliminating the possibility of miracles. For the Christian, the patterns in nature are due to the faithful manner in which God typically governs creation, and thus there is no problem recognizing that God can and does occasionally step outside of those patterns for his kingdom purposes. In any given instance, we can determine which type of action God chose to take by studying the evidence. However, this is a place where Kuyperians disagree; some see evidence for gaps or additions in natural history that indicate supernatural action, while evolutionary creationists see evidence for God working consistently through natural mechanisms.

Fourth, the scientific findings for evolutionary history and processes are strong and growing. At Kuyper's time, the evidence was weaker and acceptance of Darwin's ideas in mainstream universities was at an ebb. In the decades since, the evidence has grown by leaps and bounds. Unfortunately, misinformation regarding evolution has led 49 percent of White evangelical Christians today to believe that there is a debate among mainstream scientists about the reality of evolution;[66] in fact, there is not. Among biologists of all worldviews, Christians and all others, 91 percent affirm the evidence for gradual development of life

---

[66]"Strong Role of Religion in Views About Evolution and Perceptions of Scientific Consensus," Pew Research Center, October 22, 2015, www.pewresearch.org/science/2015/10/22/strong-role-of-religion-in-views-about-evolution-and-perceptions-of-scientific-consensus/.

forms over billions of years through evolutionary mechanisms.[67] Although scientific questions remain, many past mysteries have been solved and gaps in evidence are being steadily filled in. The evidence shows that God chose not to use miracles to create the species. Rather, God chose to create the species using natural processes that generate diversity of life and modification over time, accomplishing his intention of a world of rich, abundant life and humans capable of bearing his image.

We must continue to resist atheistic evolutionism. We cannot let the theme of common grace become so strong that we allow other worldviews to set the story in the public square about the nature of science or the larger implications for humankind and religion. But there is also a danger in framing the antithesis in a way that denies the Christian call to study natural mechanisms or denies the truths revealed in God's creation. Christians will provide a much stronger rejection of atheistic evolutionism by addressing it directly at the level of worldview while still affirming the scientific findings. The evolutionary creation view is such an example that brings together science, theology, and philosophy in a comprehensive picture that upholds Christian theology and God's revelation in nature.

The Kuyperian tradition is more important than ever. Many things in the science and faith arena have changed since Abraham Kuyper lectured in 1898. Scientific findings in all fields have exploded. The portrayal of science as an atheistic endeavor has become widespread. Some believing scientists have tacitly accepted an atheistic framing, living compartmentalized lives and not seeing their science as part of their faith. Other Christians, in their passion to reject atheistic framings of science, have gone too far and rejected the findings of science that are clear in God's creation. All of this has left many Christian young people today in a crisis of faith, believing that the

---

[67]"Elaborating on the Views of AAAS Scientists, Issue by Issue," Pew Research Center, July 23, 2015, www.pewresearch.org/science/2015/07/23/elaborating-on-the-views-of-aaas-scientists -issue-by-issue/.

church has rejected science and that Christianity is not relevant for our modern scientific world.

For all of these groups, the Kuyperian tradition offers a rich, compelling alternative: a full-bodied Christian faith, centered on Christ and Scripture, that encompasses all of life, including science. Humans are made in God's image, called to study his handiwork, and equipped by God to engage in scientific investigation. Thus, the Christian worldview provides the presuppositions needed to engage the methods of science. The methods and findings of science, by God's common grace, are shared among all peoples, filling all with wonder at the regularity, variety, and abundance of God's world, even when they do not acknowledge it as such. Those who know *both* books, God's Word as well as God's world, perceive a cosmos created by Christ with firm purpose—a rich, living world and humans capable of loving God and one another. As believers we are called to address the challenging implications of modern science and technology, following Kuyper's call to bringing together Scripture, theology, philosophy, and science in a unified vision that offers a compelling and constructive voice to the university and the public square.

FOR FURTHER READING

Bancewicz, Ruth. *God in the Lab: How Science Enhances Faith*. Oxford: Lion Hudson, 2014.

Bishop, Robert C., Larry L. Funck, Raymond J. Lewis, Stephen O. Moshier, and John H. Walton. *Understanding Scientific Theories of Origins: Cosmology, Geology, and Biology in Christian Perspective*. Downers Grove, IL: InterVarsity Press, 2018.

Collins, Francis. *The Language of God: A Scientist Presents Evidence for Belief*. New York: Free Press, 2006.

Ecklund, Elaine Howard. *Religion vs. Science: What Religious People Really Think*. Oxford: Oxford University Press, 2018.

Flipse, Abraham C. "Creation and Evolution: History of the Debate in the Netherlands." BioLogos, November 17, 2014. https://biologos.org/articles/creation-and -evolution-history-of-the-debate-in-the-netherlands.

Haarsma, Deborah B., and Loren D. Haarsma. *Origins: Christian Perspectives on Creation, Evolution, and Intelligent Design*. Grand Rapids, MI: Faith Alive Christian Resources, 2011.

Hardin, Jeff, Ronald L. Numbers, and Ronald A. Binzley, eds. *The Warfare Between Science and Religion: The Idea That Wouldn't Die*. Baltimore, MD: Johns Hopkins University Press, 2018.

Hoezee, Scott. *Proclaim the Wonder: Engaging Science on Sunday*. Grand Rapids, MI: Baker Books, 2003.

Kinnaman, David, and Aly Hawkins. *You Lost Me: Why Young Christians Are Leaving Church . . . and Rethinking Faith*. Grand Rapids, MI: Baker Books, 2011.

McGrath, Alister. *Enriching Our Vision of Reality: Theology and the Natural Sciences in Dialogue*. West Conshohocken: Templeton Press, 2017.

Plantinga, Alvin. *Where the Conflict Really Lies: Science, Religion, and Naturalism*. Oxford: Oxford University Press, 2011.

Van den Brink, Gijsbert. *Reformed Theology and Evolutionary Theory*. Grand Rapids, MI: Eerdmans, 2020.

Young, Davis, and Ralph Stearley. *The Bible, Rocks, and Time: Geological Evidence for the Age of the Earth*. Downers Grove, IL: InterVarsity Press, 2008.

5

KUYPER AND ART

ADRIENNE DENGERINK CHAPLIN

IT MAY COME AS a bit of a surprise for some to hear that Kuyper devoted one of his six lectures to Calvinism and the arts.[1] After all, Calvin and his iconoclastic followers are not best known for their art-friendliness. Yet for Kuyper it was precisely the popular myth that Calvin was anti-art which prompted him to tackle the subject. He had used a similar opportunity a decade earlier when, at his appointment as the first rector of the Free University of Amsterdam in 1888, he had chosen art and Calvinism as the main topic for his inaugural address. In doing so he wanted to make clear that Calvinism was not just a theological or ecclesiastical movement but an all-embracing worldview that had implications for both sacred and secular life. That worldview was relevant not only to politics and education, the areas for which he had become best known, but also for the whole realm of human endeavors, including culture and the arts. His lecture at Princeton provided him with another occasion to bring those points home, this time for an American audience.

WHAT DID KUYPER SAY?

The fact that Kuyper took the arts seriously at all was an important development itself. Although, as we will see, Calvinism itself was not

---

[1]Abraham Kuyper, *Lectures on Calvinism* (1931; repr., Grand Rapids, MI: Eerdmans, 1999), 142-70.

in fact as anti-art as it is customarily portrayed, at the time of Kuyper's writing, very few Protestants concerned themselves with art. Notwithstanding a budding fascination with the visual and performing arts among the Dutch rising middle class in general, Protestants tended to feel more at home with matters of the word and mind. They knew little about the world of art and regarded it with some suspicion, especially the "frivolous" worlds of theater, dance, and film. At the beginning of his lecture, Kuyper himself warned against excessive adulation of the arts and any indulgence in their sensuous pleasures. Yet he recognizes as few before him that art is a central force in society and human existence: "Art is not fringe that is attached to the garment, and no amusement that is added to life, but a most serious power in our present existence."[2]

Critics often pointed out that Calvinism had never produced any major works of art or architecture comparable to, say, the masterpieces of classical Greece or, indeed, the Catholic Church. By banning all visual imagery from their places of worship, Protestant churches had become bare and austere. In that context, Kuyper's decision to address the arts and to defend its place in Calvinism against its detractors was as bold as it was surprising.

To argue his case, Kuyper sets out to answer three questions: First, why was Calvinism not allowed to develop an art style of its own? Second, what implications does the lack of a Calvinist art style have for understanding the nature of art? And, third, what has Calvinism done in practice for the advancement of art?

In response to the first question, Kuyper goes back to the origins of both art and religion. He notes that, in their respective origins, art and religion were closely intertwined. There is hardly any major artistic style or movement the origins of which cannot be traced back to some form of worship practice, whether in a temple, a pagoda, a cathedral, or a mosque. However, he argued, for religion to grow properly and mature fully, it

---

[2]Kuyper, *Lectures on Calvinism*, 151.

needed to get rid of the "crutches" of visual imagery and statues. Grown-up religion operated at a purely "spiritual" level, in people's hearts and minds, undistracted by the physical appearances of concrete works of art.[3]

This loosening of the ties between religion and art, Kuyper argued, was not only important for the proper development of religion but also for that of art. Art needed to be freed from its bondage to religion and its service to the church.[4] This enabled it to spread its wings and explore other kinds of subject matter such as landscapes, portraits, or domestic life. In principle, anything in creation can be a worthy subject matter for the arts, no matter how big or small. And there are many different ways in which such subject matter can be depicted. Calvinism does not prescribe any particular medium or style. On the contrary, it specifically avoids any imposition of a uniform art style on a nation. This explains why Calvinism never sought to create an art style of its own. It aimed to promote a rich diversity of styles. In other words, far from taking Calvinism's lack of its own art style and tradition as a sign of its poverty or failure, it should be seen as its strength. It enabled art to develop in different directions and, as such, come into its own.[5]

Kuyper did not deny that periods in the past in which art and religion were closely intertwined had produced some major masterpieces—the Parthenon in Athens, the Hagia Sophia in Istanbul, or Saint Peter's Basilica in Rome, just to mention a few. He particularly admired the art of ancient Greece with its emphasis on order, harmony, and beauty. Classical art, for Kuyper, had set the standard for all subsequent art. But he also points out that such large projects relied heavily on major funding from a wealthy state or national religion and that this inevitably created a dependence relation that risked curtailing an artist's independence and freedom of expression.[6]

---

[3]Kuyper, *Lectures on Calvinism*, 145-49. Kuyper draws explicitly on the philosophers G. W. F. Hegel (1770–1831) and Eduard von Hartmann (1842–1906) to make this point. Both Hegel and Von Hartmann taught that only the lower stages of religion needed visual and symbolic imagery.
[4]Kuyper, *Lectures on Calvinism*, 146-49.
[5]Kuyper, *Lectures on Calvinism*, 151-52.
[6]Kuyper, *Lectures on Calvinism*, 145-47.

The importance of the independence of and differentiation between different "spheres" in life is a recurrent theme in Kuyper.
Whether education, religion, politics, or the economy, it is essential
that one sphere does not dominate the other or, alternatively, become
subsumed by it. Each needs to be granted its own "sphere sovereignty,"
its distinctive space to develop properly. This also applies to the
sphere of art or "the aesthetic," a topic he addresses in relation to his
second question.

In his response to the second question, that of understanding the
nature of art, Kuyper focuses not on any particular art form or style,
whether classical or other, but on the role and nature of art as such. In
doing so he appeals directly to Calvin. For Calvin all the arts—and in
Calvin's time this would have included all the so-called liberal and
mechanical arts, from astronomy and music to shoemaking and
weaving—are gifts of the Holy Spirit given to humans for their comfort
and for the praise of God. Together they form distinct responses to
the general cultural calling in Genesis to develop the earth and make
it fruitful.[7]

When Kuyper talks about the arts, he uses the term in a narrower
sense than Calvin, more in the sense we use it today. This is clear from
his references to the issues that were debated in aesthetics during his
time. One of these debates consisted of the quarrel between "realists"
and "idealists": Is art meant to copy or "imitate" the world as realistically as possible, or is it supposed to transcend and "idealize" it?
Kuyper's position is somewhere in the middle: art should always be
rooted in nature as God-given creation but should not slavishly copy
its appearance. Instead, it should seek to "reveal a higher reality than is
offered to us by this sinful world."[8] It is the task of painting to produce
"a beautiful world that transcends the beauty of nature."[9] Music,
moreover, has the power to move hearts and ennoble character.

---

[7]Kuyper, *Lectures on Calvinism*, 152-53.
[8]Kuyper, *Lectures on Calvinism*, 154.
[9]Kuyper, *Lectures on Calvinism*, 154.

For Kuyper, as for Calvin, art is an expression of beauty defined in classical terms of harmony and order.[10] Beauty is "the expression of a Divine perfection" and, as such, is rooted in an objective reality.[11] Although marred by sin and brokenness, art has the "mystical task" of reminding people of the beauty of the world before the fall and of providing glimpses of what it would be like in the world to come.[12] As Kuyper puts it,

> Standing by the ruins of this once so wonderfully beautiful creation, art points out to the Calvinist both the still visible lines of the original plan, and what is even more, the splendid restoration by which the Supreme Artist and Master-Builder will one day renew and enhance even the beauty of his original creation.[13]

For Kuyper, the highest ideal of beauty was achieved by the ancient Greeks. Even though the Greeks were unbelievers, they had achieved the highest expression of order and harmony. The reason Kuyper did not hesitate to attribute this honor to the pagan Greeks was Calvin's doctrine of common grace: "Calvinism . . . has taught us that all liberal arts are gifts which God imparts *promiscuously* to believers and unbelievers."[14] He even added that unbelievers were often more skilled in art than believers: "As art history shows, these gifts have flourished even in a larger measure outside the holy circle."[15] He illustrates this with the building of the temple in Jerusalem, which required outside help and skills from craftsmen from pagan nations. Although Israel possessed the truth in matters of religion, it lagged behind in terms of the sciences, politics, commerce, and the arts.

---

[10]Kuyper, *Lectures on Calvinism*, 156.

[11]Kuyper, *Lectures on Calvinism*, 156.

[12]Kuyper, *Lectures on Calvinism*, 155.

[13]Kuyper, *Lectures on Calvinism*, 155.

[14]Kuyper, *Lectures on Calvinism*, 160 (emphasis added). We may hear echoes of the Canons of Dort, which call for "the promise of the gospel" to be declared to "all persons promiscuously and without distinction." Synod of Dort, *Decision of the Synod of Dort on the Five Main Points of Doctrine in Dispute in the Netherlands*, Second Head of Doctrine, Article 5. English translation available in "Synod of Dort," Christian Classics Ethereal Library, accessed May 16, 2020, https://ccel.org/ccel/anonymous/canonsofdort/canonsofdort.iii.i.html.

[15]Kuyper, *Lectures on Calvinism*, 160.

Calvinism's separation of art and religion also meant that art was no longer able to express God's perfection in visual images. By its own principle Calvinism forbade religion "the symbolical expression of its religion in sensuous and sensual forms."[16] This meant that, although various external forms of beauty can still point to the eternal beauty of the infinite, it cannot rely on visual images for its communion with God. In its highest expression, Calvinism is a religion of the word and inner heart.[17]

Kuyper argues that, even though Calvinism did not create an art form that expressed divine perfection or an important style of its own, it nevertheless *"actually and in a concrete sense advanced the development of the arts."*[18] Kuyper explains this in his response to the third question, what Calvinism had done in practice for the advancement of art. Having argued, in response to the first question, that it was good for religion to develop on its own, Kuyper now shows how this separation from religion was also good for art. No longer bound to religious subject matter, art had become free to explore nature and human life in all their rich variety. Kuyper proceeds to illustrate this point with reference to the successful Dutch School of painting in the seventeenth century with its tradition of landscapes, domestic scenes, and portraits. Unlike the medieval and Renaissance paintings that limited themselves to religious or mythological topics, Dutch painters had begun to depict day-to-day life with people from different social classes and backgrounds. They depicted the "common man," including his expressions of feelings such as joy and excitement or sorrow and calm.[19]

Kuyper explained this new trend by pointing to the Calvinist principle of election. This principle entails that it is God's will to save some but not others for eternal life on the new earth.[20] While, in our modern sensibilities,

---

[16] Kuyper, *Lectures on Calvinism*, 152.

[17] The centrality of the heart in the life of the believer is a recurrent feature in the Heidelberg Catechism (1563). See, for instance, Q&A 21, 58, 60, 65, 76, 94, 102, 108, 113, and 117.

[18] Kuyper, *Lectures on Calvinism*, 163 (emphasis original).

[19] Kuyper, *Lectures on Calvinism*, 165-67.

[20] John Calvin, *Institutes of the Christian Religion*, vol. 2, ed. John McNeill, trans. Ford Lewis Battles (Philadelphia: Westminster Press, 1960), 3.21.5.

this doctrine is often felt to be unfair with respect to the doomed, Kuyper, by contrast, highlights God's impartiality by saving not only those of importance by worldly standards but, at least in principle, anyone:

> If an ordinary man to whom the world pays no special attention, is valued and even chosen by God as one of his elect, this must lead the artist also to find a motive for his artistic studies in what is common and of every-day occurrence, to pay attention to the emotions and the issues of the human heart in it, to grasp with his artistic instinct their ideal impulse, and, lastly, by his pencil to interpret for the world at large the precious discovery he has made.[21]

This new attention for the common man and his inner feelings also applied to religious painting. Previously idealized prophets, apostles, and saints were being humanized by being depicted realistically, in their full human condition. This was particularly evident in the religious paintings of Rembrandt van Rijn. Although Kuyper acknowledged that Rembrandt himself did not self-identify as a Calvinist—indeed, Rembrandt often crossed denominational boundaries—he nevertheless held that his paintings and that of many of his contemporaries were influenced by the Calvinist principles that had shaped Dutch culture and society more generally.[22]

Kuyper argues that the development of art in a particular nation always depends on a wide range of factors that include available resources and national character and talent: "That the Italian has a more tuneful voice than the Scot, and that the German is carried away by a more passionate impulse of song than the Netherlander, are simply data with which art had to reckon, under Roman supremacy, as well as under that of Calvinism."[23]

As regards resources, Kuyper reminds us that the Netherlands did not have the same supply of stone and marble for building as, say, Italy.

---

[21]Kuyper, *Lectures on Calvinism*, 166.
[22]Kuyper, *Lectures on Calvinism*, 165-67.
[23]Kuyper, *Lectures on Calvinism*, 164.

The fact that the Netherlands excelled in painting, music, and literature was in part due to the fact that these arts were less dependent on vast natural resources or wealthy patronage. Kuyper writes that he would have liked to discuss "the treasures of Dutch Literature" as a product of the influence of Calvinism but that, since these works could never be expected to gain international fame due to the limited range of the Dutch language, he will focus on music instead, which is "heard by the ear [and] understood by the heart."[24]

In line with this intention, Kuyper concludes his lecture by drawing attention to Calvinism's contribution to religious music. Until the Reformation, religious music was performed almost exclusively by professional musicians, with people in the congregation merely listening. Any music outside the church, such as the folk tunes played in taverns and on the streets, was usually frowned on by churchgoing people. All this changed under Calvin's Reformation. Calvin wanted to involve the congregation in the singing of the psalms as well as to encourage believers to sing at home among the family. Two composers in particular, Loys Bourgeois and Claude Goudimel, started to arrange the psalms on tunes from popular folksongs that could be easily sung along with. The professional choir was abandoned, and the congregation was encouraged to sing the new psalms with heartfelt enthusiasm. Goudimel transformed the music of his time by giving the leading part to the high soprano voice instead of to the tenor, which, until then, had functioned as the *cantus firmus*.[25]

Bourgeois transformed traditional Gregorian chant by adding rhythm to it and by reducing its modal scales to two main keys, major and minor. Kuyper points out that Bourgeois had worked with Calvin in Geneva and claims that he was directly influenced by his thinking.[26]

Looking back over Kuyper's lecture as a whole, we can thus identify three core Calvinist principles that informed his thought: first, the

---

[24]Kuyper, *Lectures on Calvinism*, 165.
[25]Kuyper, *Lectures on Calvinism*, 167-70.
[26]Kuyper, *Lectures on Calvinism*, 168-69.

principle of sphere sovereignty that inspired him to free art from the service of the church and to branch out as an independent human endeavor with its own irreducible task; second, the principle of common grace, which allowed him to appreciate the art of unbelievers, whether the pagan classical art of the ancient Greeks or the secular folk tunes of musicians in Calvin's time, and incorporate and transform them into a new art form; and third, the principle of election, which provided the impetus to consider ordinary people and scenes a worthy subject matter of art.

As we will see in the next section, the first two principles continue to play an important role in Reformed aesthetics after Kuyper. The third principle, however, that of election, has all but disappeared in current Reformed thinking about the arts. Even so, artistic attention for the "every-day occurrence" and the "common man" has continued. Today it would be more common to argue this theologically on the grounds that every human being is created equally in the image of God.

WHAT DID KUYPERIANS DO?

Although Kuyper did not initiate any major art institutions or art projects in the Netherlands comparable to, for example, the Free University, the national newspaper *Trouw*, or the Anti-Revolutionary Party, his overall worldview nevertheless significantly shaped the thought of a handful of Christian art historians and philosophers whose works, in turn, inspired several generations of Protestant evangelical artists. This group of thinkers includes art historian Hans Rookmaaker, philosophers of art Calvin Seerveld and Nicholas Wolterstorff, and social philosopher Lambert Zuidervaart. Together they produced a body of work in aesthetics and philosophy of art that is variously referred to as "Kuyperian," "neo-Calvinist," or "reformational."

For some of the above thinkers, Kuyper's influence came filtered through the work of Dutch philosopher Herman Dooyeweerd, who had expanded Kuyper's doctrine of sphere sovereignty for social life into a broader philosophy of life and the world viewed as a kaleidoscope of different dimensions or "modal aspects," none of which could be reduced to the other. One of these he called the aesthetic aspect. For Rookmaaker, Dooyeweerd's "modal theory" was a key inspiration underlying his short book *Art Needs No Justification*,[27] a public letter to a Christian art student. Most evangelical Protestants in Rookmaaker's time got involved with art only for the purposes of evangelism or biblical illustration. In his book, as suggested in the title, Rookmaaker argued that there was a place for art *as such* that needed no further justification by external purposes. This insight liberated many Christians to embark on a career in the arts, something they might previously have avoided as irrelevant to the gospel.

Following both Dooyeweerd and Kuyper, Rookmaaker characterized the core aspect of the aesthetic in classical terms of beauty—more specifically, "beautiful harmony." Even so, that did not mean to imply that all art had to follow classical rules or be beautiful in the conventional sense of being pleasing or pretty. Rookmaaker strongly believed that art also had a role to play in exposing the brokenness of the world and human suffering. In the end he became best known for his book *Modern Art and the Death of a Culture*,[28] which shows how art both *reflects* and *reflects on* the culture in which it finds itself. The book is sometimes read as if it condemned modern art as such. But that would not do Rookmaaker justice. Instead, it is a critique of the spirit of modernism as captured and depicted, often critically, *in* modern art.

One of the most fertile and influential neo-Calvinist philosophers of art and the aesthetic is Calvin Seerveld, who taught for many years at the Institute for Christian Studies in Toronto, a graduate school founded in the neo-Calvinist tradition. Inspired by Dooyeweerd's modal theory,

---

[27]Hans Rookmaaker, *Art Needs No Justification* (Leicester, UK: Inter-Varsity Press, 1978; repr., Vancouver: Regent College, 2010). Also published in *Western Art and the Meanderings of a Culture*, vol. 4 of *The Complete Works of Hans Rookmaaker*, ed. Marleen Hengelaar-Rookmaaker (Carlisle, UK: Piquant, 2001–2002), 315-49.

[28]Hans Rookmaaker, *Modern Art and the Death of a Culture* (London: Inter-Varsity Press, 1970). Reprinted as *Modern Art and the Death of a Culture*, vol. 5 of *The Complete Works of Hans Rookmaaker*, 3-166.

Seerveld developed an elaborate and sophisticated account of the nature of art and the aesthetic. Unlike Kuyper, Dooyeweerd, and Rookmaaker, Seerveld does not consider beauty or harmony as the defining feature of the aesthetic. He even claims that the idea of beauty has clouded our understanding of art to the point that it became a curse. Instead, he proposes the notion of "allusivity," sometimes also referred to as "suggestiveness" or "imaginativity."[29] This notion applies not only to art but to a wide range of phenomena and everyday activities such as playing games and telling stories.

When the aesthetic dimension of life becomes a focus of special attention and training, a transition takes place from playful aesthetic engagement to professional artistic expertise. At that point art becomes a dedicated skill practiced by professional people.

Seerveld draws attention to the fact that, although prior to 1800 most professional artistry and music was linked to the needs of day-to-day living—woven rugs, decorated pottery, lullabies, and so on—there was no conscious recognition of the distinct character of the artistic aspect as such. Most skilled art and music had to abide by the requirements of some commissioning body or institution. It was with the emergence of separate museums and concert halls, and a growing recognition of the unique nature of the artist's task, that we encounter the first instances of so-called autonomous art—that is, art valued on its own artistic terms.[30]

For Seerveld the key task of art is the imaginative articulation or capturing in some form—visually, musically, literarily, and so on—of particular aspects of the world and lived human existence.[31] Art thus enables us to convey nuanced, prereflective meanings about the world that are otherwise typically overlooked and ignored. Because of that, art

---

[29]Calvin Seerveld, *A Christian Critique of Art and Literature* (Toronto: Tuppence Press, 1995), 42-47; *Rainbows for the Fallen World* (Toronto: Tuppence Press, 1980), 125-35.

[30]Seerveld, *Rainbows for the Fallen World*, 109-14. See also Calvin Seerveld, *Redemptive Art in Society* (Sioux Center, IA: Dordt College Press, 2014), 12 and further.

[31]Seerveld defines art as "'the symbolical objectification of certain meaning realities, subject to the law of allusiveness." *Rainbows for the Fallen World*, 132.

is not just an optional extra when everything else has been said and done, but an integral part of what it means to be human.

Central to Seerveld's aesthetics is the recognition that the human sphere of the aesthetic contains norms which can be respected or violated. He frequently uses the phrase "aesthetic obedience" or "aesthetic health," something rarely heard in the world of art.[32] The fact that art needs no justification and has its own irreducible sphere does not mean that it cannot also serve some external purpose. Some art, for instance, serves to commemorate or celebrate or is used for the purpose of worship or political action. Seerveld refers to art that is embedded in other practices as "double-duty" art.[33] A good hymn, for instance, should not only be theologically sound and singable by a congregation but also musically excellent and interesting so that it could be sung repeatedly without becoming repetitive. Seerveld is especially interested in public art that has a socially critical, prophetic voice yet without this turning it into a message board or propaganda. He often refers to the murals of Mexican painters Diego Rivera to illustrate how their unique style can give a voice to the downtrodden and make it heard evocatively and imaginatively. Attention for the common man and for life in all its breadth is a central feature in Seerveld's aesthetics, as it is in all neo-Calvinist philosophers of art. For Seerveld it represents one of Kuyper's most decisive insights.[34]

The same interest in art outside the gallery and other established art institutions can be seen in the writings of Nicholas Wolterstorff. One of Wolterstorff's enduring criticisms of modern philosophies of art, including those in the neo-Calvinist tradition, is that they buy into the idea of what he calls "the Grand Narrative."[35] This idea entails that art came into its own only in the eighteenth century with the emergence of its

---

[32]Seerveld, *Rainbows for the Fallen World*, 42-77.
[33]Seerveld, *Redemptive Art in Society*, 22-23.
[34]Seerveld, *Christian Critique of Art and Literature*, 55.
[35]Nicholas Wolterstorff, *Art Rethought: The Social Practices of Art* (Oxford: Oxford University Press, 2015), 25-33.

separate galleries and music venues and that the only proper way of engaging with art is by means of detached aesthetic contemplation. Echoing Seerveld's "double-duty art," he argues that art is a social practice that can perform multiple social functions.[36] In 1980, Wolterstorff and Seerveld engaged in a fascinating exchange on whether the emergence of art as an autonomous realm should be seen as a positive or a negative development.[37] Whereas Seerveld argued that it gave art a space to grow and experiment on its own terms, Wolterstorff took the opposite view and argued that it removed art from daily life and contributed to its elitism.

Despite their differences in this respect, both Seerveld and Wolterstorff call on the arts to be agents of cultural renewal and social transformation. Part of a Christian artist's vocation or "ministry of reconciliation" is to produce culturally transformative art both within and outside the church.[38] Art can bring healing to the world, even as it highlights human suffering and the world's brokenness. Indeed, it is part of its prophetic calling to expose the world's pain and corruption as part of its fallen condition.

The social role of art is also a dominant theme in the work of philosopher Lambert Zuidervaart, himself a former student of Seerveld and colleague of Wolterstorff at Calvin University. Although his Kuyperian roots are not as much on the surface as in some other thinkers in the tradition, by his own account they are central to his own work in the reformational tradition in aesthetics.[39] For Zuidervaart the arts play an essential role in civil society as they are to keep both the state and the economy in check. As such they are a vital condition for a healthy democratic culture.

---

[36]Wolterstorff, *Art Rethought*, 83-106.

[37]Calvin Seerveld and Nicholas Wolterstorff, "Two Writers Engage in Rainbow Action: Nick Looks at Cal; Cal Looks at Nick," *Vanguard* 10, no. 6 (November–December 1980): 4-5, 18. Seerveld's piece is reprinted in Craig Bartholomew, ed., *In the Fields of the Lord: A Calvin Seerveld Reader* (Carlisle, UK: Piquant, 2000; Toronto: Tuppence Press, 2000), 360-64.

[38]Seerveld, *Rainbows for the Fallen World*, 156-201; *Redemptive Art in Society*; Nicholas Wolterstorff, *Art in Action: Toward a Christian Aesthetic* (Grand Rapids, MI: Eerdmans, 1980), 65-174.

[39]Lambert Zuidervaart, *Art, Education, and Cultural Renewal: Essays in Reformational Philosophy* (Montreal: McGill-Queen's University Press, 2017), 103.

This independence of art from, on the one hand, the state and, on the other, the free market, reflects Kuyper and Dooyeweerd's principle of sphere sovereignty, which calls for a proper distinction not only between art and religion but also between art, the state, and the world of commerce.

On Zuidervaart's view, all Western societies typically contain three "macrostructures": the administrative state, the for-profit economic sector, and civil society.[40] Of these three, civil society is the space for the social interaction and debate that shape the culture we live in. It is also the space for creativity and the arts but only if these are not dictated by the demands of the market or prescribed by a propagandist state. The arts simultaneously depend on and contribute to healthy political and economic structures because they can hold both the state and the market to account and prevent either from becoming overbearing. By nurturing open and critical dialogue on issues of shared human concern, they are able to help shape the way the state and the market are meant to operate. Seemingly paradoxically, this makes the nonprofit public arts sector a worthy candidate for public funding. Unless the arts in public are supported, Zuidervaart argues, our society and culture will fall prey to disempowering and soul-destroying global market forces.

Kuyper's emphasis on the importance of the separation between art, religious institutions, and the state sounds remarkably contemporary. Warning of the dangers of art's dependence on the church, he writes, "Our fathers broke with the *splendor ecclesiae*, with her outward glitter, and so also with her vast possessions, by which art was financially held in bondage."[41]

Although today it is not the church but an overheated market that holds art in "financial bondage," Kuyper highlights the need for a social infrastructure and a robust civic society that can provide a potential

---

[40]For Zuidervaart's ideas on the place of art in society, see Lambert Zuidervaart, *Art in Public: Politics, Economics, and a Democratic Culture* (Cambridge: Cambridge University Press, 2011); and "Art in Public: An Alternative Case for Governments Arts Funding," *The Other Journal*, January 3, 2009, http://theotherjournal.com/2009/01/03/art-in-public-an-alternative-case-for -government-arts-funding/.

[41]Kuyper, *Lectures on Calvinism*, 159-60.

buffer from both state and market pressures. People turn to the arts for orientation and reflection on important questions of life. For Zuidervaart, as for Seerveld, art has the capacity to articulate elusive and nuanced insights and perceptions that do not normally register on our day-to-day functional radar screens. He describes this in terms of a process of exploration, presentation, and interpretation, or the "imaginative disclosure" of otherwise unregistered meanings.[42]

All this may seem a long way from Kuyper's view of art's "mystical task" of reminding us of the beauty of the pre-fallen world and anticipating the shape of the world to come. However, even if they do not define art in terms of beauty, most neo-Calvinist philosophers of art would agree that art is normative in the way it depicts human life and the world. It does so by celebrating what is good and whole and by exposing and lamenting what is evil and broken. Most importantly, it shows art as an indispensable feature of societal life and human existence and a unique cultural calling alongside other cultural practices that does not need any exterior justification. Since Christians often ignore and dismiss the arts *or* romanticize and idolize them, this is an important insight.

WHAT SHOULD WE DO?

Before we discuss Kuyper's relevance and potential contribution to our own time, it is important to point out some weaknesses. I will focus on three in particular. These concern his account of Calvinism's influence on art, his appeal to common grace for defending classical art, and his emphasis on beauty as the core of the aesthetic.

Kuyper's attempt to attribute the success of Dutch painting in the Golden Age to Calvin's doctrine of election lacks proper evidence. Although it may well be true that the doctrine of election is compatible with the new attention given by art to the common man, there is no

---

[42]For Zuidervaart's notion of art and artistic truth as "imaginative disclosure," see Lambert Zuidervaart, *Artistic Truth: Aesthetics, Discourse, and Imaginative Disclosure* (Cambridge: Cambridge University Press, 2004).

historical evidence that they are causally related. The more likely explanation is that this interest in ordinary people and their day-to-day lives was a result of the need to meet the demands of a new buyer's market. In other words, it was an accidental by-product of Calvin's ban on visual images and statues in the church that artists were forced to broaden their range of subject matter beyond religious and biblical topics.[43] Having lost their ecclesiastical commissions, they needed to find new work and clients. The new repertoire appeased the taste of the rising middle class, which, as it happened, was also largely Calvinist. So while it is true that Calvin's doctrine of election elevated the previously neglected "common man," it cannot be said to have exercised a direct influence on painting.

Another weakness in Kuyper's lecture is the tension between two Calvinist principles: the principle of "common grace," which stresses that God bestows good gifts on believers and unbelievers alike, and the principle of "antithesis," the idea that there is a fundamental and irreconcilable difference in the way believers and nonbelievers engage with the world. In his lecture on art, Kuyper emphasizes the principle of common grace. In his lectures on politics and on science, however, he had foregrounded the doctrine of the antithesis. In those contexts, he would stress that there are two kinds of science and politics—one practiced by believers under the guidance of the Holy Spirit, and the other by unbelievers. It was the doctrine of the antithesis that inspired Kuyper to create a Christian university and political party. Yet, while there are "two kinds of science," one Christian and one apostate, there are not "two kinds of art." Instead, Kuyper believes that, by virtue of common grace, the unbelieving Greeks had accomplished the highest forms of art and that their principles are still valid for today. As a consequence, Kuyper is often very critical of the art of his own time that does not conform to those principles, whether produced by believers or unbelievers.

---

[43]Philip Benedict, "Calvinism as Culture? Preliminary Remarks on Calvinism and the Visual Arts," in *Seeing Beyond the Word: Visual Arts and the Calvinist Tradition*, ed. Paul Corby Finney (Grand Rapids, MI: Eerdmans, 1999), 19-45.

The tension between Calvin's doctrine of common grace and that of the antithesis in Kuyper is never really resolved and can be seen reflected in some of the differences between thinkers after him. In his book *Modern Art and the Death of a Culture*, Rookmaaker, for instance, emphasizes the antithesis in his analysis of modern art by outlining the schism between art shaped by a Christian worldview and that by modern secular thought. By contrast, Seerveld, in his book *Rainbows for the Fallen World*, shows how modern art, even though no longer shaped by Christian principles, had nevertheless opened up new avenues for art that enabled it to grow. This is reflected in the title of one of his chapters, "Modern Art and the Birth of a Christian Culture."[44]

A final weakness is Kuyper's emphasis on beauty as the key characterization of art and his further claim that beauty is the expression of divine perfection: "The world of sounds, the world of forms, the world of tints, and the world of poetic ideas, can have no other source than God."[45] In this characterization Kuyper follows a long tradition of Christian thinking about beauty and the arts that merges biblical insights with Platonic and neo-Platonic thought and, in modern times, Romantic notions. One problem with this approach is that it uncritically privileges beauty over other manifestations of God's presence in creation, such as acts of kindness or justice. It also fails to recognize that beauty itself is part of the fallen creation. Most problematic is that this kind of "beauty theology" uncritically applies premodern thinking about beauty to our modern notion of art. It is important to remember, however, that when premodern thinkers speculated about beauty, they rarely had in mind the kind of objects we now class as art. Instead, they contemplated such things as natural or divine light, the order of the cosmos, or, as in the case of Plato, the beauty of the human form in the context of homoerotic love. To transfer these metaphysical speculations on beauty to contemporary conceptions of art is by no means

---

[44]Seerveld, *Rainbows for the Fallen World*, 156-201.
[45]Kuyper, *Lectures on Calvinism*, 156-57.

straightforward and often problematic. It is therefore not surprising that Christian thinkers after Kuyper have taken different positions on this issue. Whereas Dooyeweerd and Rookmaaker follow Kuyper in defining art in terms of beauty and harmonic order, Seerveld, Wolterstorff, and Zuidervaart depart from him on this crucial point.

Given these weaknesses, perhaps it is possible to say that Kuyper's main contribution in this lecture does not lie in any specific view of art—after all, this was not his area of expertise—but in the way he draws attention to some fundamental Calvinist principles and their potential applications to the sphere of art and the aesthetic. This enables us to explore what might be considered the unique and irreducible characterization of art in distinction from other human activities that also construct meaning such as science or myth or religion. We can affirm that art, while created as originally good, is, alongside everything else, tainted and broken by sin and in ongoing need of redemption. We can be inspired by Kuyper's Calvinist notion of common grace when drawing on non-Christin thinkers and artists who provide valuable insights for our inquiry. Some of them have made important contributions to a better understanding of art as a cultural practice or of the role of the body and the various senses in our primordial aesthetic encounters with the world. In doing so they implicitly affirm Calvin's positive theology of creation and the original goodness of all things bodily and physical. This, in turn, enables a fruitful dialogue between Kuyper and other thinkers on the role of art as—on my "definition"—the articulation of embodied, affective, lived human experience.

Finally, does all this mean that Kuyper does not see any place for art in church? I don't think that would be the right conclusion. For one, Kuyper argued for the importance of congregational singing to enhance worship in the church. Although, like Calvin, he is cautious about visual images as "crutches" for (or, worse, replacements of) the Word, there is nothing specific in his lecture that forbids any use of art in worship contexts. Perhaps a fresh Kuyperian understanding of the arts could even inspire a new form of Protestant liturgical art that activates the senses as well as the mind. Perhaps such art can not only, as Rembrandt once did, humanize the major figures of the Bible—prophets, priests, and kings—but also tap into the experience of the "common" man and woman and imaginatively capture something of their lived experience as believers, moments of unshaken faith but also those of doubt, even despair. Ultimately, such art should be able to connect the worship of the King taking place on Sunday with the kingdom work done throughout the week, seeking justice and the common good. But this will take some time to develop.

FOR FURTHER READING

Begbie, Jeremy. *Voicing Creation's Praise: Towards a Theology of the Arts*. Edinburgh: T&T Clark, 1991.

Brand, Hilary, and Adrienne Chaplin. *Art and Soul: Signposts for Christians in the Arts*. Downers Grove, IL: InterVarsity Press, 2007.

Dyrness, William. *Visual Faith: Art, Theology, and Worship in Dialogue*. Grand Rapids, MI: Baker Academic, 2001.

Finney, Paul Corby, ed. *Seeing Beyond the Word: Visual Arts and the Calvinist Tradition*. Grand Rapids, MI: Eerdmans, 1999.

Graham, Gordon, ed. *The Kuyper Center Review*. Vol. 3, *Calvinism and Culture*. Grand Rapids, MI: Eerdmans, 2013.

Rookmaaker, Hans. *The Complete Works of Hans Rookmaaker*. Edited by Marleen Hengelaar-Rookmaaker. 6 vols. Carlisle, UK: Piquant, 2001–2002.

Seerveld, Calvin. *A Christian Critique of Art and Literature*. Toronto: Tuppence Press, 1995.

———. *Rainbows for the Fallen World*. Toronto: Tuppence Press, 1980.

———. *Redemptive Art in Society*. Sioux Center, IA: Dordt College Press, 2014.

Taylor, David W. *The Theater of God's Glory: Calvin, Creation, and the Liturgical Arts*. Grand Rapids, MI: Eerdmans, 2017.

Wolterstorff, Nicholas. *Art in Action: Toward A Christian Aesthetic*. Grand Rapids, MI: Eerdmans, 1980.

———. *Art Rethought: The Social Practices of Art*. Oxford: Oxford University Press, 2015.

Zuidervaart, Lambert. *Art, Education, and Cultural Renewal: Essays in Reformational Philosophy*. Montreal: McGill-Queen's University Press, 2017.

———. *Artistic Truth: Aesthetics, Discourse, and Imaginative Disclosure*. Cambridge: Cambridge University Press, 2004.

6

KUYPER AND THE FUTURE

BRUCE ASHFORD

RUSSIAN WINTERS DO NOT AFFORD many options for how to spend one's evenings. When the temperature regularly drops to 20 or 30 below zero, there is little to do other than hole up in the house with a mug of hot tea and a good book. So, when I found myself living in Russia during the late 1990s, I had plenty of time on my hands and read plenty of books. And this is how I first learned about Abraham Kuyper.

I was raised Baptist and had received a fine education at a Baptist seminary. As a child, I was, of course, accidentally Baptist. I was Baptist because my mother and father were Baptist. But now, by the time I was a twenty-something adjunctive professor at several universities in the city of Kazan, I was a convictional Baptist. I admire the Baptist tradition for many things, but more than any of those are its high view of Scripture and its commitment to evangelism and missions.

Yet the one thing the Baptist tradition does not have is a unified approach to public theology. Contemporary American Baptists are fed by two historical streams of Baptist life—Anabaptism and English Reformation Baptism. I knew that I could not fully embrace the Anabaptist approach to politics and public life because, by conviction, I thought that Christians should participate actively in politics and public life. I felt more of an affinity with the English Reformation

Baptists, but they are not known for having constructed a comprehensive philosophy of society.

Thus, when I found myself living in Kazan, I was actively seeking alternative sources for a Christian philosophy of society. This time in Kazan provided the perfect context for reflecting on and articulating such a philosophy for three reasons. First, I was intellectually and existentially ready for what Kuyper had to offer. As an adolescent, two questions had nagged at me constantly. The first had to do with the coherence of the Christian faith, and that question was answered quite well during my seminary days. The second question, however, concerned the nature of Christ's lordship and the relation of biblical revelation to the whole architecture of society and culture, and this question was not addressed in much depth during my seminary days.

This intellectual and existential void leads to the second reason I was especially well poised to receive Kuyper's public theology while living in Kazan. Russian society was "secular" in the sense that social order had long ago been severed from sacred order. The Communist revolution had spared no expense in displacing Christianity from its default position and persecuting persons and communities who resisted. Generations after the revolution, as I lived in Kazan, I sensed that most Russians had learned to manage life without reference to God. Historic Christian teaching seemed implausible, even unimaginable. Because I rubbed elbows daily with university professors and students, I experienced their deep skepticism about my Christian faith. Many of them expressed their disbelief in God, in a transcendent and objective moral law, and in any meaning or purpose for their lives. Russia's cultural institutions—especially its families, educational institutions, and political parties—reflected this deep sense of loss. Kuyper's public theology had been developed in relation to a secular revolution—the French Revolution—and thus appeared especially helpful in speaking to the Russian situation.

Third, Kuyper's public theology made sense to me. As I delved into *Lectures on Calvinism*, I found his imaginative construal of God's design for a nation's social architecture deeply and profoundly biblical. Kuyper observed certain patterns in Scripture and in history that reveal a creation order and a lawful ordering of society. Using a spatial analogy to articulate this ordering, Kuyper rightly recognized that God's normative social architecture includes a variety of different spheres of culture, each with its own unique reason for being, each with limits to its jurisdiction. As such, the spheres are revealed as a sort of ontological system of checks and balances. Moreover, God is sovereign over the spheres and calls his people to work out their salvation within those spheres. God's saving works and word are relevant, at one level or another, to our activities in those spheres. Kuyper's construal made sense of the biblical teaching and of the world as I experienced it, and it gave me a mandate to bring my Christian faith to bear on my cultural activities.

Upon returning to the United States just after the dawn of the twenty-first century, I realized immediately how relevant Kuyper's public theology was for America's rapidly secularizing society and its cultural institutions. As I see it, the framework of thought set forth in *Lectures on Calvinism* has a bright future. This was Kuyper's hope also, as evidenced by his final lecture at Princeton, "Calvinism and the Future."[1] In it, he reviews what he had argued up to that point, reiterating that Calvinism is a life-system relevant to the totality of human life rather than merely a "dogmatical" or "ecclesiastical" system.[2] Based on its holistic relevance, therefore, Kuyper now wishes to show the relevance of the neo-Calvinist worldview for the modern world, the era in which he lived that is a forebear to our own. By summarizing this concluding lecture, we can discern the broad contours of Kuyper's relevance for our modern secular age.

---

[1] Abraham Kuyper, *Lectures on Calvinism* (1931; repr., Grand Rapids, MI: Eerdmans, 1999), 171-99.
[2] Kuyper, *Lectures on Calvinism*, 171.

WHAT DID KUYPER SAY?

The malaise of modernity.[3] To show why the Calvinist worldview is needed for the healing of Western society, Kuyper begins by diagnosing the West's ills. Despite its ever-increasing scientific, medical, and technological advancements, Kuyper argues, the West nonetheless is experiencing serious moral and spiritual degeneration. Ours is a "state of malaise,"[4] he says, one in which "the hypertrophy of our external life results in a serious atrophy of the spiritual."[5] Western society had so vigorously exercised its muscles in the realm of the material that the more important muscles of spiritual life had shriveled from disuse.

This moral and spiritual degeneration carried with it a general spirit of discontent that made itself heard, Kuyper argues, in several ways. It revealed itself "on all sides" with complaints of "empoverishment, degeneracy, and petrifaction."[6] It further made itself known through the pessimistic philosophy of Arthur Schopenhauer and the sacrilegious mockeries of Friedrich Nietzsche. Most notably, it was revealed in the anarchism of countless thousands of Westerners who "would rather demolish and annihilate everything, than continue to bear the burden of present conditions."[7]

Can the modern West engage in a process of self-correction? Can it naturally evolve out of the present moral and spiritual degeneracy and into a higher phase? Kuyper points out that in the past, societies could correct themselves because they were open to correction on the basis of a Christian worldview. But modern societies, infected by the modern spirit, are not open to correction. "The modern philosophy, which

---

[3]Charles Taylor, *The Malaise of Modernity* (Toronto: House of Anansi Press, 1991). Various Kuyperians have shown real affinity for Taylor's analysis, which mirrors some aspects of Kuyper's thought. See James K. A. Smith, *How (Not) to Be Secular: Reading Charles Taylor* (Grand Rapids, MI: Eerdmans, 2014); and Robert Joustra and Alissa Wilkinson, *How to Survive the Apocalypse: Zombies, Cylons, Faith, and Politics at the End of the World* (Grand Rapids, MI: Eerdmans, 2016).
[4]Kuyper, *Lectures on Calvinism*, 173.
[5]Kuyper, *Lectures on Calvinism*, 172.
[6]Kuyper, *Lectures on Calvinism*, 173.
[7]Kuyper, *Lectures on Calvinism*, 173.

gains the day, considers itself in ever-increasing measure as having *outgrown* Christianity."[8]

The helplessness of modern Christianity. After diagnosing the West's malaise, Kuyper lays the blame at the feet of Christian churches that had "fallen asleep" and become "forgetful of their duties in reference to humanity at large, and the whole sphere of human life."[9] With Christian churches thus shrinking from their God-given task of serving the common good, deistic and atheistic philosophers took it on themselves to rebuild society from the ground up, this time replacing biblical teaching about human fallenness with the assumption that human nature is uncorrupted.[10] As has been noted elsewhere in this volume, Kuyper blames the French Revolution, which was undergirded by a godless comprehensive life-system to rival Christianity.

To make matters worse, Kuyper argued, modern Christians had responded wrongly to the modern spirit, revising the faith in a misguided attempt to protect it. Led by theologians such as Friedrich Schleiermacher and Albrecht Ritschl, these Christians wanted to reshape historic Christianity, hoping to make it more appealing to modern people by removing supernatural elements and replacing them with more patently mystical or altruistic morals. Although they wanted to honor Christ, they effectively dishonored him by reducing Christianity to a humanitarian ideology.

This new conception of Christianity rejected the Bible's authority and thus soon rejected many of its central teachings. Kuyper writes that this modern theology is

> a theology which virtually destroys the authority of the Holy Scriptures as a sacred book; which sees in sin nothing but a lack of development; recognizes Christ for no more than a religious genius of central significance; views redemption as a mere reversal of our subjective mode of thinking; and indulges in a mysticism dualistically opposed to the world

---

[8]Kuyper, *Lectures on Calvinism*, 175 (emphasis original).
[9]Kuyper, *Lectures on Calvinism*, 175.
[10]Kuyper, *Lectures on Calvinism*, 176.

of the intellect,—such a theology is like a dam giving way before the first assault of the inrushing tide. It is a theology without hold upon the masses, a quasi-religion utterly powerless to restore our sadly tottering moral life to even a temporary footing.[11]

Indeed, Christians must reject this humanitarian revisioning of Christianity, with its reduction of the faith to a mystical and practical affair, and instead embrace the Calvinist world- and life-view.

Although there is nothing wrong with mystical and practical manifestations of the Christian faith, Kuyper argues, it is a grievous error to *reduce* the faith to such manifestations. When confined to such limits, Christianity ceases to be Christianity altogether. Although Christ fed the hungry and healed the sick, the primary element of his ministry was the proclamation of himself as God and Savior, of the forgiveness of sins through his blood, of his second coming to set the world to rights.[12] The church grew strong on the back of its many martyrs, and those "martyrs shed their blood not for mysticism and not for philanthropic projects, but for the sake of convictions such as concerned the acceptance of [doctrinal] truth and the rejection of error."[13] No one would die for Schleiermacher's Jesus, because Schleiermacher's Jesus had not died for them.

The need for Calvinist Christianity. Although Roman Catholics could be of some help, Kuyper argues, what is really and truly needed is a return to Calvinism, both in its doctrinal forms and in its worldview manifestations. Indeed, one cannot have a Calvinist worldview without fidelity to Scripture and its attendant Calvinist doctrine, but neither can one hold to Calvinist doctrine consistently without also espousing a Calvinist world- and life-view. Kuyper writes:

> Therefore, let us not stop half-way. As truly as every plant has a root, so truly does a principle hide under every manifestation of life. These

---

[11]Kuyper, *Lectures on Calvinism*, 182-83.
[12]Kuyper, *Lectures on Calvinism*, 187-88.
[13]Kuyper, *Lectures on Calvinism*, 189.

principles are interconnected, and have their common root in a fundamental principle; and from the latter is developed logically and system-
atically the whole complex of ruling ideas and conceptions that go to
make up our life and world-view. With such a coherent world and
life-view, firmly resting on its principle and self-consistent in its
splendid structure, Modernism now confronts Christianity; and
against this deadly danger, ye, Christians, cannot successfully defend
your sanctuary, but by placing, in opposition to all this, a life- and
world-view of your own, founded as firmly on the base of your own
principle, wrought out with the same clearness and glittering in an
equally logical consistency.[14]

It is here, in Kuyper's exhortation to revive the Calvinist worldview in
full, that his chapter applies theology to society most overtly. Calling his
American Calvinist counterparts to action, he makes four proposals.

First, Kuyper argues, "Calvinism should no longer be ignored where
it still exists, but rather be strengthened where its historical influences
are still manifest."[15] It would be ungrateful, to say the least, to ignore
one's own heritage, especially when that heritage holds the key to the
revival of Western churches and societies. Thus, instead of ignoring
their heritage, Calvinists should revive it and put it to work in church
and society.

Second, he urges his audience to engage in a historical study of the
principles of Calvinism.[16] Only with a retrieval of Calvin's writings, and
of his progeny's theological and philosophical writings, can the Calvinist project be renewed in full.

Third, and closely connected to historical study, Kuyper argues that
the church should develop Calvinist principles "in accordance with the
needs of our modern consciousness and their application to every department of life."[17] In other words, a historically and biblically

---

[14]Kuyper, *Lectures on Calvinism*, 189-90.
[15]Kuyper, *Lectures on Calvinism*, 192.
[16]Kuyper, *Lectures on Calvinism*, 193.
[17]Kuyper, *Lectures on Calvinism*, 194.

anchored Calvinism must write itself anew in response to modernity's unique challenges.

Finally, he urges Calvinists to "cease being ashamed of" their Calvinist principles and heritage.[18] Indeed, if Reformed churches—whether in the United States, Canada, or the Netherlands—would successfully combat the corrosive effects of the modern worldview, they must proudly and happily embrace the confessional convictions that would allow them to do so.

As Peter Heslam notes, Kuyper's four exhortations serve as a kind of "autobiographical program" for Kuyper in that they represent the causes for which he had labored for most of his life.[19] Indeed, Kuyper had drawn on Calvinist doctrine in his sermons from the pulpit, systematic theology lectures at the Free University, and devotional articles written for the religious weekly he founded. He reasoned from Calvinist principles when constructing the philosophy of society—sphere sovereignty—undergirding the Stone Lectures. He was inspired by Calvinist convictions when he founded a university, a daily Christian newspaper, and a religious weekly. His Calvinist life-system shaped the Anti-Revolutionary political party he founded and guided his leadership first as a parliament member and later as a prime minister of the Netherlands.

The prospect of success. In his concluding remarks, Kuyper explores whether adherence to the Calvinist world- and life-view and Calvinistic labors on behalf of society would be successful. Curiously, he begins by asking the question, "Whence are the differences?"[20] That is, what accounts for diversity in creation, among individuals and between cultures? For Kuyper, this question unlocks the divergent visions of Calvinism and modernity. Modernity, Kuyper avers, answers the question by appealing to Darwin's notion of "selection,"

---

[18]Kuyper, *Lectures on Calvinism*, 194.
[19]Peter Heslam, *Creating a Christian Worldview: Abraham Kuyper's Lectures on Calvinism* (Grand Rapids, MI: Eerdmans, 1998), 243.
[20]Kuyper, *Lectures on Calvinism*, 195.

whereas Calvinism answers with an appeal to divine "election." Thus, for Calvinists, everything owes its reason for being to God and his sovereign will.[21]

Kuyper's appeal to God's sovereign election reveals his mood about the future. The success of a Calvinist program, Kuyper states, is not ultimately in our hands but in the hands of God. Calvinists should *act* in accordance with the Calvinist worldview and in conformity with Reformed confessions. But in their acting, they must remember that success is determined by God alone. "The quickening of life comes not from men: it is the prerogative of God."[22]

Kuyper concludes by drawing an analogy with the Aeolian Harp, a stringed instrument that made music when wind passed through it. In this analogy, people acted by placing the harp, for example, on the porch in the hopes that a breeze might bring it to life. But until the wind blew, the harp remained silent. Similarly, Kuyper argues:

> Let Calvinism be nothing but such an Aeolian Harp,—absolutely powerless, as it is, without the quickening Spirit of God—still we feel it our God-given duty to keep our harp, its strings turned aright, ready in the window of God's Holy Zion, awaiting the breath of the Spirit.[23]

Thus, Kuyper's lectures, bristling as they were with calls to action, conclude not with assurance of victory but with candid preparation for the battle ahead. Despite his activism, Kuyper does not appear triumphalist—or even optimistic—when considering the church's ability to counteract the prevailing toxicity of modernity.[24] God's wind might blow even now, but such a phenomenon is beyond our control.

---

[21]Kuyper, *Lectures on Calvinism*, 197.
[22]Kuyper, *Lectures on Calvinism*, 199.
[23]Kuyper, *Lectures on Calvinism*, 199.
[24]For a brief summary of Kuyper's pessimism with regard to history, drawing not only on *Lectures* but also on *Common Grace* and other writings, see Heslam, *Creating a Christian Worldview*, 243-49.

WHAT DID KUYPERIANS DO?

In an essay published as a one-hundredth anniversary commemoration of the Stone Lectures, James Skillen wrote, "While in many ways [Kuyper] was a product of his time, he was much more than that. His life and writings had such influence and exhibited such creativity that one hundred years later, we are still mining his work with value."[25] Nowhere is Kuyper's legacy more fruitful than in the broad and programmatic agenda laid out in his lecture on "Calvinism and the Future."

The following areas represent the most significant strengths of Kuyper's work as they have been received and have energized the Kuyperian movement. First is his argument that the ideologies spawned by modernity would cause great harm to Western society and culture, leading it to abort its vital heritage of Christian truth rather than cherish it. The second is his recognition that these ideologies were not merely philosophical but essentially idolatrous and therefore deeply religious. Finally is his insight into the inherent weakness of modern theology and his argument that the Calvinist worldview was sturdy enough not only to stem the tide of modern unbelief but also to help renew modern society and reform its cultural institutions.

The ongoing malaise of modernity. Building off a legacy bestowed by his mentor, Guillaume Groen van Prinsterer, Kuyper was ever aware of the poisonous legacy of modernity.[26] Although Groen focused almost exclusively on the unbelieving ideology of the French Revolution, Kuyper broadened the scope, looking not only at the French Revolution but also at German pantheism and English Darwinism. Together, these unbelieving ideologies would continue to throw the West into convulsions unless, by God's grace, Western societies recognized their rotten

---

[25]James Skillen, "Why Kuyper Now?," in *Religion, Pluralism, and Public Life: Abraham Kuyper's Legacy for the Twenty-First Century*, ed. Luis E. Lugo (Grand Rapids, MI: Eerdmans, 2000), 365.

[26]As Harry Van Dyke notes in the introduction to Groen's magnum opus, *Unbelief and Revolution*, Kuyper was profoundly influenced not only by Groen's personality, and not only was Kuyper's thinking influenced by the content of *Unbelief and Revolution*, but "Kuyper would shape his entire public career fighting 'the Revolution' as defined by his mentor." Groen van Prinsterer, *Unbelief and Revolution*, trans. Harry Van Dyke (Bellingham, WA: Lexham Press, 2018), xxii.

fruits and attacked them at the very roots. Kuyper's *Lectures* were prophetic in this respect, preceding as they did the rise of major revolutionary movements such as the National Socialism of Germany (Nazism) and the Communist Socialism of the USSR as well as the more minor social and political convulsions to which the West has become prone since the rise of unbelieving ideologies.

These unbelieving ideologies have been worked out in detail by a number of intellectual histories but in especially helpful ways by sociologist Philip Rieff and philosopher Charles Taylor. Rieff and Taylor both recognize the dangerous consequences of severing society and culture from their roots in Judeo-Christian religion and morality. Each in his own way argued that if the West would flourish in the future, it must regain its belief in God and the moral law.

Rieff argues that the West is in the midst of a historically unprecedented movement to sever social order from sacred order.[27] Historically, all civilizations have understood the need for sacred order to shape social order.[28] Sacred order, Rieff argues, shaped cultural institutions and products, which in turn shaped society. But in the West, he argues, our cultural elite have conspired to cut social order free from sacred order, leaving social order to float on its own. With religion thus neutered, Rieff argues, cultural institutions and products become "deathworks," purveyors of social decay rather than the mediators of life they were intended to be. In Rieff's view, social decay will continue unless or until Western societies manage to recover the necessity and beauty of the Judeo-Christian "thou shalt" and "thou shalt not."[29]

Similarly, philosopher Charles Taylor argues that the contemporary era in Western civilization is one in which Christianity has been

---

[27]Philip Rieff, *My Life Among the Deathworks: Illustrations of the Aesthetics of Authority*, vol. 1 of *Sacred Order/Social Order*, ed. Kenneth S. Piver (Charlottesville: University of Virginia Press, 2006).

[28]Rieff, *Deathworks*, 13.

[29]Philip Rieff, *The Crisis of the Officer Class: The Decline of the Tragic Sensibility*, ed. Alan Woolfolk, vol. 2 of *Sacred Order/Social Order*, ed. Kenneth S. Piver (Charlottesville: University of Virginia Press, 2007), 6-7, 166-70.

displaced from the default position. Living within an "immanent frame" of reference, Westerners consider historic, biblical Christianity implausible and unimaginable.[30] With Christianity thus decentered and considered implausible, an explosion of ideological options rush in to fill the void. Among the crippling effects of Christianity's replacement by countless competing options is that Westerners find themselves confused and disoriented, in a state of perpetual intellectual and spiritual unease. Moreover, Western society has reduced morality to self-authorization.[31] This brings about an ironic situation in which Westerners are increasingly concerned about universal freedom, equality, and justice while at the same time decreasingly able to justify them. This causes problems not only in terms of public policy-making but also public discourse, as citizens cannot articulate why anyone disagreeing with them should acquiesce to their self-authorized moral code.[32] In such a situation, all we can do is shout each other down. This we do with increasing verve and decreasing civility.

Thus, Kuyper's prophetic and radical critique of modernism is confirmed not only by twentieth-century revolutions but also contemporary social and cultural decay. In response to this reality, it is incumbent on Kuyperian Christians to continue to identify and speak against the ways in which unbelieving ideology convulses our societies and corrupts our cultural institutions. This is what Alvin Plantinga, Nicholas Wolterstorff, and the Reformed epistemologists sought to do for the discipline of philosophy and the sphere of education. It is what Hans Rookmaaker, Calvin Seerveld, and others aimed to achieve in the sphere of art. It is what James Skillen and the Center for Public Justice aim to do in the political sphere. By "calling the bluff" of unbelieving ideologies, revealing their inability to account for reality or to cause human flourishing, we help make the case for a constructive alternative—neo-Calvinist Christianity.

---

[30]Charles Taylor, *A Secular Age* (Cambridge, MA: The Belknap Press of Harvard University Press, 2007), 83.
[31]Taylor, *Secular Age*, 580-89.
[32]Taylor, *Malaise of Modernity*, 18.

The inherently religious nature of unbelieving modernity. Kuyper was also right to recognize the inherently religious nature of unbelieving modernity. For Kuyper, all of humanity is religious. We are worshipers at heart, worshiping either God or idols, and our worship, being heartfelt, naturally radiates outward into our social, cultural, and political lives. Dutch economist and politician Bob Goudzwaard elaborated on this aspect of Kuyper's thought, arguing that three basic principles help us make sense of the relationship between religion and society. First, each person serves a god of some sort. Second, each person is transformed into the image of his chosen god. Third, each society is transformed into the image of its dominant gods.[33]

The Kuyperian view is further vindicated not only by biblical teaching but also by the veritable explosion of idolatrous ideologies in the modern age. Consider, for example, the work of Kuyperian political scientist David Koyzis, revealing the idolatrous nature of classical liberalism, conservatism, nationalism, democratism, and socialism.[34] Each of these ideologies elevates some aspect of the created world to the level of absolute, unquestioned power. The biblical term for such absolutizing is idolatry, and the effects are as damaging today as they were in Scripture. By absolutizing individual autonomy (classical liberalism), cultural heritage (conservatism), the titular people group (nationalism), the voice of the people (democratism), or material equality (socialism), ideologues enable one aspect of creation—the absolutized aspect—to become a sort of cudgel, beating down other aspects of God's good creation.[35]

The inherent weakness of modern theology. Kuyper was right to reject modern theology for its heterodoxies and heresies. Both at its

---

[33]Bob Goudzwaard, *Aid for the Overdeveloped West* (Toronto: Wedge, 1975), 14-15. James K. A. Smith makes this connection between worship, society, and culture in *Desiring the Kingdom: Worship, Worldview, and Cultural Formation*, Cultural Liturgies 1 (Grand Rapids, MI: Baker Academic, 2009).

[34]David Koyzis, *Political Visions & Illusions: A Survey & Critique of Contemporary Ideologies*, 2nd ed. (Downers Grove, IL: IVP Academic, 2019).

[35]Koyzis, *Political Visions & Illusions*, 27-62.

historical headwaters with Schleiermacher and its "downstream" contemporary iterations today, liberal theology is far too weak to undergird the church. In "Modernism: A Fata Morgana in the Christian Domain," Kuyper argued that modern theology represented a toxic compromise with the spirit of the age, based on a superficial understanding of reality and a distorted understanding of the Christian faith.[36] In retrospect, Kuyper's critique has proven prescient and prophetic. Although in Kuyper's time, liberal denominations were experiencing expansive growth, within mere decades they began a steep decline across Europe and the United States.

The cause for this decline is not difficult to discern. By the end of the twentieth century, many of the West's seminaries and divinity schools were busy deconstructing Christian Scripture and dissolving the biblical Christ in the acid baths of historical criticism. As a result, the graduates of these institutions took their newly acquired liberalism into America's pulpits, causing churches and denominations that had grown large and strong on a diet of biblical theology to become increasingly moribund.[37]

In response, we must resist this "quasi-religion" that is "utterly powerless to restore our sadly tottering moral life to even a temporary footing."[38] If our churches and denominations want to really and truly follow the Lord Christ, we must do so by looking for guidance from the same Scriptures that Jesus treated as authoritative (Mt 5:18). We must not hold a low view of Scripture in glaring contradiction to the high view Christ held.

The inherent strength of the Calvinist worldview. Whereas "modern" Christianity is a quasi-religion incapable of stemming the tide of

---

[36]Abraham Kuyper, "Modernism: A Fata Morgana in the Christian Domain," in *Abraham Kuyper: A Centennial Reader*, ed. James D. Bratt (Grand Rapids, MI: Eerdmans, 1998), 87-124.

[37]For example, see Kevin Flatt, *After Evangelicalism: The Sixties and the United Church of Canada* (Montreal: McGill-Queen's University Press, 2013). Flatt demonstrates the steep numerical and spiritual losses incurred by the United Church of Canada's abrupt and decisive rejection of its evangelical past. Also, see Thom S. Rainer, "A Resurgence Not Yet Realized: Evangelistic Effectiveness in the Southern Baptist Convention Since 1979," *Southern Baptist Journal of Theology* 9, no. 1 (Spring 2005): 54-69.

[38]Kuyper, *Lectures on Calvinism,* 182-83.

unbelief, neo-Calvinist Christianity is true religion, capable not only of stemming the tide of unbelief but renewing society and redirecting cultural institutions toward their true end in God. Christianity is not merely a path to salvation, nor a system of dogmatics, but a worldview that issues forth in an overarching philosophy of society. The challenge for neo-Calvinists in the twenty-first century, as Craig Bartholomew so aptly writes, is to follow Kuyper's example by "[developing] an integrally biblical Christian worldview and [living] creatively and thus plausibly from this perspective in our particular contexts."[39]

Unlike Kuyper's "modern" Christianity, the neo-Calvinist worldview arises from Scripture and thus possesses the power and vitality to stand as a bulwark against unbelieving ideology. Neo-Calvinism recognizes that grace restores nature and, therefore, that God's saving works and word are relevant to every sphere of culture.[40] And, as Kuyper's *Lectures* demonstrated, this worldview works itself out in a philosophy of society that secures the uniqueness and integrity of each sphere of culture by placing it under God's sovereign rule, as mediated by his Word. This philosophy of society is Kuyper's most distinctive contribution and the one from which twenty-first-century Christians stand to benefit most.

This philosophy of society can serve as a bulwark against contemporary iterations of Revolutionary ideology. Building on Koyzis's excavation of the idolatrous underpinnings of modern political ideologies, there is much work to be done examining the "revolutionary" unbelief that serves as a connective tissue of sorts between ideologies such as liberalism, socialism, and progressivism. As French political scientist Pierre Manent and American political philosopher Daniel Mahoney have argued, this revolutionary ideology—which they describe as "humanitarian religion" or "the religion of humanity"—is squarely at odds with Christianity and therefore must be resisted.

---

[39]Craig Bartholomew, *Contours of the Kuyperian Tradition: A Systematic Introduction* (Downers Grove, IL: InterVarsity Press, 2017), 9.
[40]Bruce Riley Ashford, "What Hath Nature to Do with Grace? A Theological Vision for Higher Education," *Southeastern Theological Review* 7, no. 1 (Summer 2016): 3-22.

This "humanitarian religion" envisions humanity as intrinsically good, peaceful, and unified.[41] Yet our original goodness, such a view argues, has been corrupted by the rise and development of nation-states. Nation-states foster warmongering, religious divisions, economic disparity, and other evils. Thus, humanitarians argue that we must bring peace and unity to the world by minimizing or obliterating the nation-state, weakening or undoing its borders, and fostering among global humanity the sense of camaraderie we would have felt if we had not been corrupted by civilization. This vision of humanity, which is found in prototypical form in Immanuel Kant's *Perpetual Peace*, finds proponents today among elite actors in the European Union, the United States, and the United Nations. Despite its popularity, however, this vision of humanity aligns neither with Scripture nor reality. It offers an essentially atheistic view of life, a false anthropology, and a heretical and utopian eschatology.[42]

Moreover, the neo-Calvinist worldview provides an account of pluralism that secures the rights of religious communities and keeps church and state in check. As Kuyper argues in *Lectures*, "sovereignty" is the key issue for a Christian philosophy of society. As the sovereign, God has delegated his authority to humans; he has separated life into separate spheres, given each sphere its own distinct reason for being and its own jurisdiction, and called us to bring our cultural doings into conformity with his will for each sphere. Thus, with creation's normative order consisting of a plurality of authorities, we must repel the ever-present human desire to totalize.

---

[41]Daniel J. Mahoney, *The Idol of Our Age: How the Religion of Humanity Subverts Christianity* (New York: Encounter Books, 2018); Pierre Manent, "La tentation de l'humanitaire," *Géopolitique*, no. 68 (2000): 8.

[42]As James Skillen notes, although Kuyper's writings do not bequeath a developed theory of international relations, Kuyper did envision two types of globalization, the first type being a sort of unjust global control and the second, a more organic integration of life characterized by justice and fostered by common grace under the lordship of Christ. In Skillen's reading, "for Kuyper any kind of worldwide development would have to be evaluated in terms of whether justice was being done to the diverse spheres of social life, to diverse nations, and to the rest of creation." Skillen, "Why Kuyper Now?," 372.

Indeed, the neo-Calvinist worldview is custom-built to resist the totalitarian temptations in free societies. Drawing on the lessons learned from the rise of communism and National Socialism, we must resist the softer forms of tyranny to which Western societies are ever susceptible. The humanitarian religion dominating the Western landscape possesses within it a false anthropology that makes it unreasonably optimistic about human nature and thus about the future. If humanity could only weaken the grip of religion and minimize or eliminate the nation-state, as the argument goes, we could usher in an era of universal flourishing and harmony. Of course, in order to usher in this era, the mechanism for change is politics. And since injustice and inequality can be found in every sphere of culture, everything must be politicized. Thus, this new era can be ushered in effectively only by weakening the mediating institutions—religious and familial—most likely to oppose it and by strengthening the state.[43] In response to such totalitarian temptations, neo-Calvinists must argue compellingly for the sort of societal pluralism espoused by Kuyper.

One last application bears mentioning. A Kuyperian philosophy of society may be a potentially fecund resource for Islamic societies wishing to curate forms of democracy that do not undercut basic Islamic principles.[44] In the field of international studies, there is a sharp disagreement

---

[43] This is the insight highlighted by a number of emerging social and political philosophers, but most clearly by Polish political philosopher Ryszard Legutko. Legutko, having been born under communist totalitarianism but, more recently, having served as a member of the European Union's Parliament, argues that twentieth-century Soviet society and twenty-first-century Western society are all too similar in their openness to totalitarian temptations. He writes, "If the old communists lived long enough to see the world of today, they would be devastated by the contrast between how little they themselves had managed to achieve in their antireligious war and how successful the liberal democrats have been. All the objectives the communists set for themselves, and which they pursued with savage brutality, were achieved by the liberal democrats who, almost without any effort and simply by allowing people to drift along with the flow of modernity, succeeded in converting churches into museums, restaurants, and public buildings, secularizing entire societies, making secularism the militant ideology, pushing religion to the sidelines, pressing the clergy into docility, and inspiring powerful mass culture with a strong antireligious bias in which a priest must be either a liberal challenging the church or a disgusting villain." Ryszard Legutko, *The Demon in Democracy: Totalitarian Temptations in Free Societies* (New York: Encounter Books, 2016), 167.

[44] A fascinating recent development is political scientist Shadi Hamid's embrace of Kuyper's public theology as a supplement and complement to his own Islamic view of the proper relationship of religion, politics, and public life. See, for example, Robert Nicholson's interview with Hamid.

between two streams of thought. On one side of the debate are thinkers who argue that nations cannot adopt democracy fruitfully unless or until they become culturally fit for it. On the other side are thinkers who argue that democracy is precisely the factor that makes nations culturally fit. Regardless of which stance one takes, the question arises as to what type of democracy could be curated to resonate with that nation's religion and culture. Many Islamic societies wish to reject theocracy yet also are rightly hesitant to embrace notions of "state sovereignty" or "popular sovereignty," concepts rooted in Western liberalism and individualist anthropology that are antithetical to Islamic teaching. Thus, as John L. Hiemstra has argued, Kuyper's sphere sovereignty could provide for Islamic societies a blueprint for how to affirm divine sovereignty while at the same time rejecting theocracy and promoting basic freedoms.[45]

WHAT SHOULD WE DO?

Sir Isaac Newton once remarked, "If I have seen further it is by standing on the shoulders of giants."[46] Indeed, one of God's great gifts to his people is the existence of "giants" who have gone before us and on whose shoulders we can stand. These giants are not saints—or rather, they are flawed saints just like the rest of us. We need not commend everything in their heart to stand firmly on their shoulders.

Abraham Kuyper is just such a giant for twenty-first-century Christians seeking to see more clearly in our own day. Moreover, his neo-Calvinist worldview and philosophy of society are fruitful resources not only in traditional Dutch Reformed circles but also for other ecclesiastical traditions and in other national contexts. In my own American and Southern Baptist context, I and other scholars have found Kuyper's

---

Robert Nicholson, "Is the Struggle with Islam Reshaping the Modern World? An Interview with Shadi Hamid," *Providence*, September 25, 2018, https://providencemag.com/2018/09 /struggle-islam-reshaping-modern-world-interview-shadi-hamid/.

[45]John L. Hiemstra, "A Calvinist Case for Tolerant Public Pluralism: The Religious Sources of Abraham Kuyper's Public Philosophy," *Religious Studies and Theology* 34, no. 1 (2015): 53-83.

[46]Herbert Westren Turnbull, ed., *The Correspondence of Isaac Newton: 1661–1675*, vol. 1 (Cambridge: Cambridge University Press for the Royal Society, 1959), 416.

framework for public theology amenable to, and instructive for, our own tradition. Similarly, Kuyper's work has been embraced by churches and Christian leaders in communist China. One of the most prominent Kuyperian pastors, Wang Yi, was recently arrested and sentenced to nine years in prison for criticizing the government on a broad array of issues, including abortion, the Tiananmen Square massacre, and Xi Jinping's authoritarian policies and actions.[47] Moreover, Kuyper's public theology has been adopted by scholars, leaders, and institutions in contexts as diverse as South Africa, England, Korea, Brazil, and Canada.

Yet much work remains to be done in applying a neo-Calvinist worldview in creative and plausible ways for our contemporary context. Kuyper's imaginative philosophy of society can and should be brought to bear as a prophetic voice and a bulwark against the unbelieving ideologies, such as humanitarian religion, that proliferate in the contemporary West. It should be employed to secure the freedom of religious communities, and to keep church and state in check by resisting totalizing temptations.

Further still, the neo-Calvinist recognition of creation's goodness and its normative order should be brought to bear on contested issues concerning the physical, material world, such as pollution, transgenderism, and transhumanism. It should be employed to counter the Pelagian anthropology and historic determinism Western thought leaders have borrowed from Marx and carried over into critical gender, race, and sex theory. It should also be leveraged to counter a resurgent ethno-nationalism that seeks to privilege members of the titular ethnic group over other communities, often suppressing their religious identity and fostering other forms of unjust treatment. In this last instance, we stand to be more consistently Kuyperian than Kuyper himself, whose ethnocentrism undermined his valuable contributions, especially the concept of sphere sovereignty.

---

[47]Paul Mozur and Ian Johnson, "China Sentences Wang Yi, Christian Pastor, to 9 Years in Prison," *New York Times*, January 2, 2020, www.nytimes.com/2019/12/30/world/asia/china-wang-yi -christian-sentence.html.

More than a century now after the publication of his *Lectures*, Kuyper's so-called *neo*-Calvinism is not nearly as new as it was in 1898. Yet Kuyper saw the malaise of our contemporary era before any of us were born. Such a prophetic voice should turn our ear. Now more than ever, we need Kuyper's overarching vision for the implementation of a neo-Calvinist worldview. What Kuyper offers in his declarations of creation's inherent goodness and order, the radical lordship of Christ over all things, and the intrinsically religious nature of every worldview or totalizing principle is a robust Christianity well suited to meet the challenges of our late modern age.

Kuyper's Calvinist harp is poised to play. And while only God can bring the quickening wind of the Spirit, only we can keep that harp "turned aright," ready to receive God's power when he graces to give it. May we be the people who attend to this harp daily. And may we be those who never tire of pleading with the Lord to send and resend the breeze of the Spirit that this harp might be continually brought to life.

FOR FURTHER READING

Ashford, Bruce Riley. *Letters to an American Christian*. Nashville: B&H Publishing, 2018.

Bailey, Justin. *Reimagining Apologetics*. Downers Grove, IL: IVP Academic, forthcoming.

Ballor, Jordan J., and Robert Joustra, eds. *The Church's Social Responsibility: Reflections on Evangelicalism and Social Justice*. Grand Rapids, MI: Acton Institute, 2015.

Bennett, Kyle D. *Practices of Love: Spiritual Disciplines for the Life of the World*. Grand Rapids, MI: Brazos Press, 2017.

De Jong, Marinus. "The Church Is the Means, the World Is the End: Klaas Schilder's Thought on the Relationship Between Church and World." PhD diss., Theologische Universiteit Kampen, 2019.

Goudzwaard, Bob, and Craig G. Bartholomew. *Beyond the Modern Age: An Archaeology of Contemporary Culture*. Downers Grove, IL: IVP Academic, 2017.

Joustra, Robert, and Alissa Wilkinson. *How to Survive the Apocalypse: Zombies, Cylons, Faith, and Politics at the End of the World*. Grand Rapids, MI: Eerdmans, 2016.

Kaemingk, Matthew. *Christian Hospitality and Muslim Immigration in an Age of Fear*. Grand Rapids, MI: Eerdmans, 2018.

Monsma, Steve. *Healing for a Broken World: Christian Perspectives on Public Policy*. Wheaton, IL: Crossway, 2008.

Mouw, Richard J. *Uncommon Decency: Christian Civility in an Uncivil World*. Downers Grove, IL: InterVarsity Press, 1992.

Pinson, J. Matthew, Matthew Steven Bracey, Matthew McAffee, and Michael A. Oliver. *Sexuality, Gender, and the Church*. Nashville: Welch College Press, 2016.

Schuurman, Derek. *Shaping a Digital World: Faith, Culture and Computer Technology*. Downers Grove, IL: IVP Academic, 2013.

7

KUYPER AND RACE

VINCENT BACOTE

AS WE HAVE SEEN throughout this collection of essays, Abraham Kuyper was a man of many talents and powerful intellect. He was truly a great figure. It is impossible to look at his career and deny his great intellect, gifts for organization, prolific publishing record, and vision for a Christianity with twin pieties of private and public virtue. There is much to his legacy worth reflection, celebration, and further cultivation. Yet, as should be expected when one believes in the truth of post-fall human depravity, it is a certain truth that even great people have feet of clay. Kuyper was not without flaws. Even in this brief collection, we have seen references to significant flaws in his person and writing, especially in his language about race.[1] An examination of the Stone Lectures should rightly praise Kuyper's important theological and cultural insights, but it should also take seriously these grievous flaws.

As we consider these flaws, important questions arise: How do we understand statements that betray a blatant racism against Africans? Some have argued that the logical conclusion of such sentiments,

---

[1]In his Stone Lectures, it is Kuyper's comments on race that are most striking and problematic, thus our inclusion here. However, our inclusion of commentary on only race in this volume is not intended to suggest that this is Kuyper's only theological flaw worth considering.

particularly Kuyper's racist language and the role of his theology in apartheid South Africa, is that Kuyper's theology is irredeemable, wholly interwoven with colonialism and racism. Others have argued that Kuyper was simply a "man of his time," expressing the common sentiments of his day. The latter approach downplays the culpability of Kuyper for his language, chalking up his word choices to ignorance or placing blame on the society in which Kuyper lived rather than the man himself. Neither of these approaches, however, will suffice. Instead, this chapter will argue that we can neither downplay nor totalize the flaws of Kuyper. He is neither mere hero nor mere villain. Rather, he is a man with clay feet who must be critically engaged. Kuyper's legacy unavoidably includes these problematic, deeply troubling comments on race. What, then, does it look like to take his *full* legacy seriously, passing on the good gifts that Kuyper offers while lamenting his sin?

Before proceeding further, it is important to properly set the table in order to proceed with integrity. To do this requires remembering the setting in which Kuyper makes his remarks as presented in the first part of this volume; in a very real way he is—as we all are—a person of his time. While this does not excuse his language, it is important to remember these lectures were given in a time, place, and occasion, as this helps us refrain from immediately evaluating what we read as if Kuyper should have known all that we now know. With this in mind, we need to look at not only what it said but also how it fits in Kuyper's larger aspiration in the Stone Lectures: his aim to present a "life-system" of Calvinism as response to the challenges of modernity. In addition, it is important to evaluate Kuyper in a way that helps us to make the most of what he offers even when critiques are offered, including voices of strident and more moderate responses. Last, as we proceed, we also need to be willing to shine the searchlight of truth on ourselves just as we do with Kuyper.

WHAT DID KUYPER SAY?

I begin this section with a trip down memory lane I will never forget. As a divinity school student with an interest in theology that engaged culture and politics, I looked forward to reading Kuyper's Stone Lectures. In these lectures, I found an immensely helpful theological basis for Christian participation in public life. Indeed, Kuyper gave words and concepts to what had only been intuitions for me; encountering his work on theology of culture felt like I was breathing in, as I have written before, "much needed oxygen."[2] *At first*, Kuyperian thought seemed like a very ideal theological home. Yet, as we will see below, I discovered this was a residence with serious complications and dysfunctions, particularly related to race. It would almost be an understatement to say it caused a major crisis for me. I will never forget where I was and what went on in my mind when confronted with these words.[3] How could someone who was, on the one hand, so devoted to articulating the wonder of God's pluriform creation affirm accounts of *racial* diversity that led to claims of inferiority and threat? In the final section of this essay, I will share how I think we can face the truth about Kuyper's failings in this area and take a path that is neither angry rejection of Kuyper nor benign acceptance that avoids the distressing reality. But first, we must see what he wrote.

As we take a closer look at Kuyper's own statements on race in the Stone Lectures, a brief comment is needed. Each of the quotes that we'll survey must be understood in the context of Kuyper's argument—an argument that has been helpfully unpacked throughout this volume.

---

[2]"Reading Kuyper's text on theology of culture was like breathing some much needed oxygen." Vincent Bacote, *The Spirit in Public Theology: Appropriating the Legacy of Abraham Kuyper* (Grand Rapids, MI Baker: Academic, 2005), 7.

[3]Richard Mouw has reflected on this challenge, working to confront the racist elements in Kuyper's thoughts, in his short introduction to Kuyper. See Richard Mouw, "Race: Adding Another 'Neo,'" in *Abraham Kuyper: A Short and Personal Introduction* (Grand Rapids, MI Eerdmans, 2011), 80-85. This challenge has also been explored by other Kuyper and neo-Calvinist scholars. In 2016, the annual Kuyper Conference—then hosted at Princeton Seminary, now at Calvin University—explored the theme of Kuyper and race, addressing aspects of Kuyper's treatment of race. Selected papers from this conference were published in the *Journal of Reformed Theology* 11, no. 1-2 (January 2017).

Contextualizing these statements within his broader argument, though, does little to soften the landing of these words. Though some quotes are long, the length is important for understanding the setting where Kuyper expresses his views. As we'll see firsthand, these quotes are deeply problematic, without excuse, and indicative of postlapsarian sinfulness. But, in order to shine the light of truth on them, we must read them for what they are. After all, our work as those seeking to learn from and apply Kuyper's insights in a new century is not to be "uncritical fan[s]" but to take what Kuyper has offered us and hold it in the light of the gospel, creatively applying what is good and true and offering a needed corrective and rebuke to what is not. We must, as I have argued elsewhere, "decide what to bring from Kuyper's era and what to leave in the past."[4]

Kuyper on race in his first Stone Lecture, "Calvinism a Life-System."
In this first lecture, Kuyper writes:

> In China it can be asserted with equal right that Confucianism has produced a form of its own for life in a given circle, and with the Mongolian race that form of life rests upon a theory of its own. But what has China done for humanity in general, and for the steady development of our race? Even so far as the waters of its life were clear, they formed nothing but an isolated lake. Almost the same remark applies to the high development which was once the boast of India and to the state of things in Mexico and Peru in the days of Montezuma and the Incas. In all these regions the people attained a high degree of development, but stopped there, and, remaining isolated, in no way proved a benefit to humanity at large. This applies more strongly still to the life of the colored races on the coast and in the interior of Africa—a far lower form of existence, reminding us not even of a lake but rather of pools and marshes.[5]

Kuyper makes this observation while presenting a theory of the development of civilizations as part of his argument that Calvinism as a

---

[4]Bacote, *Spirit in Public Theology*, 155. As I wrote here, this is certainly applicable to race but extends to more of Kuyper's thought.
[5]Abraham Kuyper, *Lectures on Calvinism* (1931; repr., Grand Rapids, MI: Eerdmans, 1999), 32.

worldview offers positive development of society. This statement about the inferiority of African societies is made as one observation among several others.

Kuyper's claims about the inferiority of other ethnic groups continues in this lecture in his understanding of the development of civilization. "From the high-lands of Asia," he writes:

> Our human race came down in groups, and these in turn have been divided into races and nations; and in entire conformity to the prophetic blessing of Noah the children of Shem and of Japheth have been the sole bearers of the development of the race. No impulse for any higher life has ever gone forth from the third group.[6]

Here Kuyper observes, in a seemingly matter-of-fact manner, that civilization has developed in accordance with the Genesis 9 blessings of Shem and Japheth and the supposed "curse of Ham" (it is actually Canaan who is cursed).[7] This statement occurs as Kuyper is beginning to make his argument that civilization moves forward as a result of intermarriage ("commingling of blood" is Kuyper's language for this).[8] Such an argument similarly betrays Kuyper's sense of racial superiority and inferiority: just as "botanists harvest large profits" through the "crossing of different breeds," so "the commingling of blood" is a means by which humanity continues to develop.[9]

---

[6]Kuyper, *Lectures on Calvinism*, 35.

[7]As George Harinck notes in "Wipe Out Lines of Division," the concept of the "curse of Ham" was already "declared obsolete in the academic circles of [Kuyper's] days." George Harinck, "Wipe Out Lines of Division (Not Distinctions)," *Journal of Reformed Theology* 11, no. 1-2 (January 2017): 83.

[8]An irony is that when Kuyper writes "The South African Crisis" he states a different view of intermarriage: "The Boers are not sentimental but men of practical genius. They understood that the Hottentots and the Bantus were an inferior race and that to put them on an equal footing with whites, in their families, in society, and in politics, would be simple folly. They have understood, further, the danger of mixed liaisons, and to save their sons from this scourge they have inculcated the idea that carnal intercourse with Kaffir women is incest. On the other hand, they have treated their slaves as good children. They have habituated them to work and have softened their manners. In South Africa you will find no one more skillful in dealing with the natives than a Boer patriarch." See Abraham Kuyper, "The South African Crisis," in *Abraham Kuyper: A Centennial Reader*, ed. James D. Bratt (Grand Rapids, MI: Eerdmans, 1998), 339.

[9]Kuyper, *Lectures on Calvinism*, 35-36.

Kuyper on race in his third Stone Lecture, "Calvinism and Politics."
Statements like these are not simply found in the first of Kuyper's Stone
Lectures. These problematic, racist statements that betray a sense of
racial superiority continue throughout his Stone Lectures. In his third
lecture he writes:

> The historic development of a people shows, as a matter of course, in
> what other ways authority is bestowed. . . . In a word it may assume a
> variety of forms, because there is an endless difference in the devel-
> opment of nations. A form of government like your own could not exist
> one day in China. Even now, people in Russia are unfit for any form of
> constitutional government. And among the Kaffirs and Hottentots of
> Africa, even a government, such as exists in Russia, would be wholly
> inconceivable. All this is determined and appointed by God, through the
> hidden counsel of His providence.[10]

This statement occurs as Kuyper makes the case for republican form of
government (in line with Calvin). As the quote reveals, this form of
government is granted by God in settings where the people have suffi-
ciently developed as a society. Africans (at least those in South Africa)
and others, in Kuyper's view, have not, and this is in accordance with
the hand of divine providence.

*Kuyper on race in his sixth Stone Lecture, "Calvinism and the
Future."* We have identified a number of statements throughout the
Stone Lectures in this section and will conclude with a statement from
Kuyper's final lecture, which not only highlights his sense of racial su-
periority and inferiority but also uses language now considered derog-
atory for various people groups. In this lecture, Kuyper writes:

> The problem concerns the fundamental question: *Whence are the differ-
> ences?* Why is not all alike? Whence is it that one thing exists in one state,
> another in another? There is no life without differentiation, and no dif-
> ferentiation without inequality. The perception of difference the very
> source of our human consciousness, the causative principles of all that

---

[10]Kuyper, *Lectures on Calvinism*, 84.

exists and grows and develops, in short the mainspring of all life and thought. . . . To put it concretely, if you were a plant you would rather be a rose than mushroom; if insect, butterfly rather than spider; if bird, eagle rather than owl; if a higher vertebrate, lion rather than hyena; and again, being man, richer than poor, talented rather than dull-minded, of the Aryan race rather than Hottentot or Kaffir. Between all these there is differentiation, wide differentiation.[11]

Kuyper makes these statements as he contrasts election and selection (evolution by natural selection). He goes on to conclude there is a sense that across history the doctrine of election has restored "peace and reconciliation to the hearts of the believing sufferer,"[12] presumably because it better explains why there are differences of various kinds in the world, a better explanation than the hand of blind natural force.

As we conclude this brief survey of Kuyper's statements on race in the Stone Lectures, I want to bring us back to what I said at the beginning of this section, the literary equivalent of breaking the fourth wall in cinema. I vividly remember reading Kuyper's words about race. I will never forget where I was or how unsettled I was upon reading these words. Although Kuyper again makes these statements about the inferiority of Africans in a matter-of-fact manner as part of his larger discussion about how to regard types of differences, the words were jarring for me and others.

WHAT DID KUYPERIANS DO?

There has been some writing specific to Kuyper and race on the Stone Lectures, although it is important to note that the majority of engagement with Kuyper and race is in relationship to questions of South Africa and apartheid.[13] While the category of race/ethnicity was not

---

[11]Kuyper, *Lectures on Calvinism*, 195-96.

[12]Kuyper, *Lectures on Calvinism*, 197.

[13]Among the books and articles addressing Kuyper on South Africa and apartheid, see Allan Boesak, *Black and Reformed: Apartheid, Liberation, and the Calvinist Tradition* (New York: Orbis Press, 1984); H. Russel Botman, "Is Blood Thicker Than Justice? The Legacy of Abraham Kuyper for South Africa," in *Religion, Pluralism, and Public Life: Abraham Kuyper's Legacy for the*

present in Kuyper's language about sphere sovereignty, the dysfunctional development and adaptation of this prominent idea in Kuyper was part of the basis for apartheid, and many (mistakenly in my view) regard him as the father of apartheid. While it is true that Kuyper's ideas were used as part of the theological basis for apartheid, this does not mean that Kuyper himself made the argument for rigid racial separateness in society. We have to ask whether the use of Kuyper's ideas as part of the construction of apartheid is a clear development of what he taught or a convenient distortion and selective use of his language and concepts in service of constructing a racist society. In my judgment, at most we can say with Craig Bartholomew that Kuyper was partially responsible.[14] Beyond this, we need to assess what appears in the Stone Lectures. But even so, the question remains: What of Kuyper's words above? How should we respond to such racist statements and to the man who wrote them?

As scholars have interacted with Kuyper, they have done so in a number of ways: critique and rejection, critique situated in history, and critique tied to theological themes. While each approach is clear to reject Kuyper's racist statements, their approach to Kuyper and Kuyperian thought as a whole differs.

Critique and rejection. In an address later published as an essay, Peter Paris's engagement with Kuyper's language about human development offers this critique:

> In my judgment, Kuyper was a prototypical nineteenth-century exemplar
> of theological scholarship bent on preserving and promoting the myth

---

Twenty-First Century, ed. Luis E. Lugo (Grand Rapids, MI: Eerdmans, 2000), 342-61; P. J. Strauss, "Abraham Kuyper and Pro-apartheid Theologians in South Africa: Was the Former Misused by the Latter?," in *Kuyper Reconsidered: Aspects of His Life and Work*, ed. Cornelis van der Kooi and Jan de Bruijn (Amsterdam: VU Uitgeverij, 1999), 218-27; J. C. Adonis, "The Role of Abraham Kuyper in South Africa: A Critical Historical Evaluation," in Van der Kooi and De Bruijn, *Kuyper Reconsidered*, 259-72; George Harinck, "Abraham Kuyper, South Africa, and Apartheid," speech at the opening ceremony of the Abraham Kuyper Institute for Public Theology at Princeton Theological Seminary, *The Princeton Seminary Bulletin* 23, no. 2 (Spring 2002): 184-87; Craig Bartholomew, *Contours of the Kuyperian Tradition: A Systematic Introduction* (Downers Grove, IL: IVP Academic, 2017), 152-57.
[14]Bartholomew, *Contours of the Kuyperian Tradition*, 152.

of European cultural and racial superiority. Most importantly, he contended with shameless arrogance that African peoples had made virtually no contributions whatsoever to human civilization. Similar promotions of the same myth by countless numbers of Europeans greatly advanced their dictatorial program over all spheres of human endeavor in Africa and throughout their respective empires. . . . If he be listed among the best of nineteenth-century Calvinist theologians, Kuyper's perspective must be relegated to the trash bin of history.[15]

Ending with his arresting image of the "trash bin of history," Paris argues that, in the end, to take Kuyper's racist statements seriously, and reject such statements, we must reject Kuyper's insights in their entirety. His entire body of work is awash in the "myth of European cultural and racial superiority" and, like many of Kuyper's time, is irredeemably awash with racism.

Critique situated in history. James Bratt similarly argues about Kuyper on race (in reference to both the Stone Lectures and Kuyper's support of the Boers in South Africa):

In the United States and his native land, Kuyper applauded "commingling of blood" as the fount of social progress and cultural vitality. But in South Africa he praised the Boers' absolute ban on "race" mixture (regarded as "incest") as their highest mark of morality and their only hope for the future.

The only explanation for such a reversal was Kuyper's full-blown subscription to contemporary European race theory, to which he added a dollop of biblical imagery. The theory postulated first a stark hierarchy of fixed qualities, with the "Aryan race" on top and the "Negro" at the very bottom. It also interpreted history as a unified evolutionary development. Kuyper had repeated this at Princeton . . . Kuyper's biblical addendum was the "prophetic blessing of Noah." . . . It was as if, one observer has said, Kuyper rejected social Darwinism for a social version

---

[15]Peter J. Paris, "The African and African-American Understanding of Our Common Humanity: A Critique of Abraham Kuyper's Anthropology," in Lugo, *Religion, Pluralism, and Public Life*, 271-72.

of Mendelian genetics, crossing "a materialistic theory of selection . . . with an idealistic theory of election."[16]

In their critiques, both Paris and Bratt reveal that Kuyper was subject to a prevailing view on race that regarded those of African descent as inferior. To look seriously at Kuyper requires acknowledging this influence and its presence in his statements on race. However, they part ways on what the reality of such views in his body of work must mean for our use of his work. While Paris calls for rejection, Bratt makes a bracing critique without the same summary judgment.

Critique tied to theological themes. While these two approaches encompass the dominant methods of engaging Kuyper and his statements on race, recently, a third approach has emerged. Daniel Camacho has also written an interesting article on Kuyper and race that merits our attention. Camacho considers the relationship between the doctrine of common grace and Kuyper's views on race. Here are couple of his statements and queries at length:

> Kuyper's theological anthropology, his vision of how God has shaped humanity, assumes that common grace is concentrated primarily around a golden—or white—stream of humanity. While common grace covers the world, in Kuyper's eyes, it is distributed along certain lines of social development and civilization building. All of this does not preclude a common grace in other peoples, but theirs is a lower form of existence. Darker, indigenous peoples are characterized by a spiritual and cultural stagnation and immaturity. Yet, the lower peoples can still benefit and grow from the advancements that Calvinism, Europe, and now America have contributed to the flourishing of the human race. All of this is part of Kuyper's theological vision. All of this, in spite of our best wishes, is part of the Kuyperian legacy. . . .

---

[16]James D. Bratt, *Abraham Kuyper: Modern Calvinist, Christian Democrat* (Grand Rapids, MI: Eerdmans, 2013), 293-94. In this quote Bratt refers to an article that makes similar observations about Kuyper on race, concluding he had unsuccessfully addressed tensions in his thought because of his desire to support the Boers and his ideas about God's action in the world and historical developments. See Dirk Th. Kuiper, "Groen and Kuyper on the Racial Issue," in Van der Kooi and De Bruijn, *Kuyper Reconsidered*, 69-81.

While Kuyper confessed his vision as a creed, its deployment, its impact, has been felt on a broader aesthetic and institutional level. That is because race is not simply a proposition; it does not operate merely on the level of a "worldview." Racial biases have seeped deeply into our imaginations and desires. Segregated schools and churches have further inculcated race as a *habit* through practice.[17]

Camacho asks whether common grace, the doctrine that emphasizes God's generosity to creation and opens the way toward Christian engagement in society, is linked with Kuyper's statements of racial hierarchy. While one might debate the tight connection made by Camacho (as I do), it is not hard to see a potential connection when common grace, a doctrine connected to development, is set beside Kuyper's seemingly matter-of-fact observations about the levels of development in different groups and the (at least) implied or (at most) asserted value judgments about those of African descent. We are further invited to consider the extent to which common grace factors into segregation (seemingly more than apartheid is in mind here).

Each of these approaches demonstrates serious engagement with Kuyper's racist statements and a wholesale rejection of them. However, they differ in their *rationale* for such statements. (Were Kuyper's statements reflective of the general milieu in nineteenth-century thought? Or were these statements directly arising from core theological concepts in his work?) But for all that these engagements with Kuyper offer us, they do not yet give us a way to *critically* engage Kuyper on this subject. At this point, we might ask whether there are critiques that conclude with a more constructive approach. In relationship to what is written in the Stone Lectures, the answer is "not really." Craig Bartholomew and H. Russell Botman have written constructive critiques related to Kuyper's legacy in South Africa, as noted above, but not directly related to the Stone Lectures. But I believe such an approach is called for when reading

---

[17]Daniel José Camacho, "Common Grace and Race," The Twelve Blog by Reformed Journal, March 26, 2014, https://blog.reformedjournal.com/2014/03/26/common-grace-and-race-2/ (emphasis original).

Kuyper. A need for critical, constructive engagement that does not downplay his faults but gives us a way forward sets the stage for, once again, returning to the story of my "Kuyper crisis experience."

WHAT SHOULD WE DO?

When confronted with Kuyper's language on race, I was thrown into a vortex of confusion. Let the reader understand: in Kuyper I had finally found someone with a theology of public engagement for which I had long searched. The internal vexation was distressing. What do you do when someone plays your music and then you discover tunes that are worse than discordant? What do you do when you hoped this person would be the centerpiece of your dissertation research and you imagine facing interrogation from those who would wonder, "Why would you give attention to the work of such a racist?" (Full disclosure: I have sometimes been asked this question.) My resolution of the vexation emerged as part of the birth of a critical thinking mindset.[18] As noted at the beginning of this chapter, this means telling the truth of the good and the horrific. This is necessary if we are to move forward with integrity.

We have to first make the observation that Abraham Kuyper was a man of his time (and perhaps on this he is just true to the modern era) on race, not to make excuses but to be honest about his time and place. One of the best ways to move forward is to put Kuyper in conversation with himself, specifically heeding these words from Richard Mouw:

> The topic of race is one on which we need to do more than just a little aggiornamento. Much of Kuyper's thinking on this subject requires straightforward repudiation. This is especially important to be clear about, since there are some whose knowledge of Kuyper is limited to his reputation as one of the influences on Afrikaner *apartheid* thinking that long characterized white Dutch Reformed culture in South Africa.[19]

---

[18]For one direct example, see Vincent Bacote, "Critical Thinking Is Obeying the Commandment of Loving Your Neighbor as Yourself," interview by Bart Noort, *Theological University Kampen Magazine*, December 2014.

[19]Mouw, *Kuyper: A Short and Personal Introduction*, 81.

A good place to start is with approaching Kuyper in the way he approached Calvinism. In Kuyper's final lecture he states:

> What the descendants of the old Dutch Calvinists as well as of the Pilgrim fathers have to do, is not to copy the past, as if Calvinism were a petrifaction, but to go back to the living root of the Calvinist plant, to clean and to water it, and so to cause it to bud and to blossom once more, now fully in accordance with our actual life in these modern times, and with the demands of the times to come.[20]

Later in the same lecture, he continues:

> To repristination I am as averse as any man; but in order to place for the defence of Christianity, principle over against principle, the world-view over against world-view, there lies at hand, for him who is a Protestant in bone and marrow, only *the Calvinistic principle* as the sole trustworthy foundation on which to build.[21]

Sometimes figures are presented to us in a manner that suggests we best honor them by passing on their thoughts with a commitment to preservation. While Kuyper had a personality that might suggest he thought his views should be treated in this manner, it is far better for us to take his views and treat them in the manner he sought to treat Calvinism. When we take this approach, we resist the temptation of letting our various emotional responses lead us to quickly put Kuyper in the dustbin as Paris suggested. For certain, we should prune Kuyper's troubling views on race from his legacy and consider how to make his legacy blossom anew from within as well as considering ways to update and develop this living tradition.

We can further look within Kuyper's work for trajectories that counter negative beliefs and practices on race. In a quote more related to differences in gender, we observe Kuyper's argument for equality:

> If Calvinism places our entire human life immediately before God, then it follows that all men or women, rich or poor, weak or strong, dull or

---

[20]Kuyper, *Lectures on Calvinism*, 171.
[21]Kuyper, *Lectures on Calvinism*, 191 (emphasis original).

talented, as creatures of God, and as lost sinners, have no claim whatsoever to lord over one another, and that we stand as equals before God,
and consequently equal as man to man.[22]

Within the text this view of equality gets qualified by Kuyper in the
subsequent sentences (and others with similar ideas throughout the
lectures), where he argues that whatever hierarchies there are among
humans come from God's hand of providential generosity. Although
Kuyper says that those in higher positions are to serve others, it is sadly
the case that often history has revealed a far different story.

An improved legacy will not deny God's hand of providence in history
or the acknowledgment of differences of various kinds between persons,
but it will seek to avoid theological accommodations for various social,
cultural, and political dysfunctions that thwart the flourishing of fellow
divine image bearers. In this regard, Camacho states:

> What would it mean to begin to unhook common grace from the legacy
> of white supremacy? To start, it would mean listening to and dialoging
> with marginalized voices. Additionally, it would mean recognizing the
> cultural contextualizations of Christian discipleship. . . .
>
> I think that the Kuyperian tradition still presents to us opportunities
> for moving forward when it comes to issues of race and culture. If indeed
> this whole world were to be *graced*, then perhaps I can—in spite of sin—
> see the goodness in the color of my skin, in the texture of my hair, in the
> poetry of Kendrick Lamar, and in the dance of my people (though
> Kuyper was iffy about dancing). All of this matters to God; all of this is
> theologically significant.[23]

Even if one does not agree that common grace is connected to White
supremacy, there have certainly been many challenges with race within
Reformed Christianity and beyond (besides apartheid). Camacho dis-
plays not only a critique but an invitation to make the most of common
grace by actively affirming the goodness of all members of the human

---

[22]Kuyper, *Lectures on Calvinism*, 27.
[23]Camacho, "Common Grace and Race."

race and welcoming the fruits from their stewardship of the culture. This is one way to make more of Kuyper's legacy by pursuing neglected trajectories for bringing God glory. A further dimension of Kuyper's thought that opens the way to improving and developing his legacy comes from this observation about the church in the Stone Lectures:

> If the churches are formed by the union of confessors, and are united only in the way of confederation, then the differences of climate and of nation, of historical past, and of disposition of mind come in to exercise a widely variegating influence, and multiformity in ecclesiastical matters must be the result. A result, therefore, of very far-reaching importance, because it annihilates the absolute character of every visible church, and places them all side by side, as differing in degrees of purity, but always remaining in some way or other a manifestation of one holy and catholic Church of Christ in Heaven.[24]

In this statement and others, Kuyper acknowledges a kind of perspectivalism. While here he speaks of multiformity in terms of the ecclesiological manifestation and theological reflection, the principle itself holds for our understanding of all reality. Kuyper is aware that truth is complex and that contributions can come from many places besides his own tradition.

He recognizes that different cultures will have different yet legitimate perspectives. Although it was his view that the highest forms of culture and development were in Europe and America, within this principle is the recognition that other voices from other cultures may have legitimate perspectives. An implication of this for us today is that we should lend an ear to these other voices, for it is quite possible that they will have noticed facets of truth to which we are blind yet which we need in order to have a better understanding of reality and practice of life. This means that we should take a communal approach to matters such as theology, indeed all domains of knowledge. Moreover, it means that we learn to consider others, whom we may explicitly or implicitly regard

---

[24]Kuyper, *Lectures on Calvinism*, 63-64.

as beneath us culturally, as valued members of the human community and body of Christ who have a significant contribution to our life as a Christian community on earth.

While Kuyper's opinions on race in particular suggest he could hardly imagine the day when those of African descent would be notable contributors to society, this principle at its best expresses a recognition of the need for contributions from the breadth of society if we are to have as complete an understanding of truth as humanly possible. This kind of *neo*-Kuyperian perspectivalism can be of great benefit to the church and the world.

Where do we go from here? When we put Kuyper in conversation with himself, with clear eyes we look at both the brilliance of Kuyper along with his frailty. Then, rather than walking away from the tradition because of glaring imperfections, we look at the positives already present within neo-Calvinism and dare to imagine a better version of this faith and worldview. This is what I chose to do when thinking, "What shall I do with Kuyper?" I saw that he was troubling and helpful at the same time. I decided that I could be honest about ways that his work offers valuable contributions as well as troubling and sometimes horrific dimensions. In my view, Christian integrity requires me to be honest about what is helpful and useful while also admitting my dismay at Kuyper's failings. I then move from this assessment to stewardship of his legacy, bringing forward what is good. This is an approach that looks at the present and considers how to contextualize the tradition and, while aware of Kuyper's frailties, also is quick to ask, "What might we be missing on race or other important issues?" This is a neo-Calvinism that has critical appreciation of Kuyper and humbly seeks to honor God and serve him in the created order. All readers of the Stone Lectures can be a part of this task and opportunity.

FOR FURTHER READING

Adonis, J. C. "The Role of Abraham Kuyper in South Africa: A Critical Historical Evaluation." In *Kuyper Reconsidered: Aspects of His Life and Work*. Edited by Cornelis van der Kooi and Jan de Bruijn. Amsterdam: VU Uitgeverij, 1999.

Boesak, Allan. *Black and Reformed: Apartheid, Liberation, and the Calvinist Tradition*. New York: Orbis Press, 1984.

Botman, H. Russel. "Is Blood Thicker Than Justice? The Legacy of Abraham Kuyper for South Africa." In *Religion, Pluralism, and Public Life: Abraham Kuyper's Legacy for the Twenty-First Century*. Edited by Luis E. Lugo. Grand Rapids, MI: Eerdmans, 2000.

Eglinton, James. "*Varia Americana* and Race." *Journal of Reformed Theology* 11, no. 1-2 (January 2017): 65-80.

Harinck, George. "Wipe Out Lines of Division (Not Distinctions)." *Journal of Reformed Theology* 11, no. 1-2 (January 2017): 81-98.

Journal of Reformed Theology: Special Issue on Neo-Calvinism and Race 11, no. 1-2 (2017).

Joustra, Jessica. "An Embodied *Imago Dei*." *Journal of Reformed Theology* 11, no. 1-2 (January 2017): 9-23.

Kuiper, Dirk Th. "Groen and Kuyper on the Racial Issue." In *Kuyper Reconsidered: Aspects of His Life and Work*. Edited by Cornelis van der Kooi and Jan de Bruijn. Amsterdam: VU Uitgeverij, 1999.

Liou, Jeff. "Taking Up #blacklivesmatter." *Journal of Reformed Theology* 11, no. 1-2 (January 2017): 99-120.

Liou, Jeff, and David Robinson. "Our Racist Inheritance: A Conversation Kuyperians Need to Have." *Comment Magazine*. May 14, 2015. www.cardus.ca/comment /article/our-racist-inheritance-a-conversation-kuyperians-need-to-have/.

Mouw, Richard. "Race: Adding Another 'Neo.'" In *Abraham Kuyper: A Short and Personal Introduction*. Grand Rapids, MI: Eerdmans, 2011.

Strauss, P. J. "Abraham Kuyper and Pro-apartheid Theologians in South Africa: Was the Former Misused by the Latter?" In *Kuyper Reconsidered: Aspects of His Life and Work*. Edited by Cornelis van der Kooi and Jan de Bruijn. Amsterdam: VU Uitgeverij, 1999.

8

LOST IN TRANSLATION

THE FIRST TEXT OF THE STONE LECTURES

GEORGE HARINCK

INTRODUCTION

In his inaugural speech on *Souvereiniteit in eigen kring* (sphere sovereignty) at the opening of the Vrije Universiteit on October 20, 1880, in de Nieuwe Kerk in Amsterdam, Abraham Kuyper sketched the national, scholarly, and Reformed aspirations of this new university. The Vrije Universiteit was a Dutch-language university, functioning under national law. But in his closing remarks Kuyper also pointed to the international relevance of the Vrije Universiteit. Expressions of support had been received from Germany, Italy, Scotland, Switzerland, and the United States.[1] This reminded Kuyper of the international character of the Synod of Dort of 1618–1619, and he made just that comparison, saying that scholarship and the Reformed confession knew no national borders.[2]

I thank the editors and the members of the research group of the Neo-Calvinism Research Institute at Theological University Kampen and the members of the Herman Bavinck Center for Reformed and Evangelical Theology at Vrije Universiteit Amsterdam for their comments on a previous version of this text.
[1] See *De Heraut*, October 24, 1880.
[2] Abraham Kuyper, *Souvereiniteit in eigen kring: Rede ter inwijding van de Vrije Universiteit, den 20sten October 1880 gehouden, in het koor der Nieuwe Kerk te Amsterdam* (Amsterdam: J. H. Kruyt, 1880), 41. There is no English translation of the full text of this publication in print that includes this remark by Kuyper.

The Dutch language unfortunately hampered the international outreach and relevance of the Vrije Universiteit. Until 1900, only a dozen students from the Boer republics in South Africa, and sons from Dutch American families, enrolled there. They all spoke or understood Dutch. The scholarship and Reformed character of the university were attractive, but its Dutch language was not. Nowadays this is seen as a historical limitation, but in the first decade of the Vrije Universiteit this was not considered to be a handicap. The focus of the university was national. Before 1890 only one publication by Kuyper or one of the other professors is known to have been translated, into German.

Interestingly, Kuyper's most famous text, his *Stone Lectures on Calvinism*, were delivered in 1898 in English. Nearly every text Kuyper produced was published first in Dutch, then translated in full or in part in another language. But this text was *originally* presented in English. The history of the text of these lectures is the topic of this chapter. The present historiography presents the creation of the Stone Lectures as a haphazard process in which Kuyper played a negative role and which led to a deficient English edition of the lectures. I think this presentation is not correct. In order to put the record straight, I present an alternative history in this chapter that shows how Kuyper, having learned from difficulties in previous translation projects and without putting pressure on his American colleagues, succeeded in obtaining a translation that met his high standards.

THE ART OF TRANSLATING

Kuyper's publications were aimed at a national audience, but in the fall of 1889, when he started to write an encyclopedia of theology— his first academic work since his publications on church historical topics in the 1860s (in Dutch and in Latin)—Kuyper seemed to have remembered his remarks in *Souvereiniteit in eigen kring* and decided to cross the modern language barrier. From the start, he planned to publish his encyclopedia simultaneously in the Netherlands and in the United States. He admired the United States for its religious freedom and democratic character. He learned about the country through the press but also through firsthand information from Dutch immigrants, including his son Frederik, who had crossed the Atlantic in 1886. These immigrants imported Kuyper's publications where they still read Dutch.[3] Their interest whetted Kuyper's appetite for American engagement.

Kuyper spoke English quite well, but he had no experience writing in English. So, for an American edition of his encyclopedia he needed to find a translator and a publisher. On the request of Kuyper, his Amsterdam publisher J. A. Wormser approached the theologian Geerhardus Vos, a young Dutchman living in the United States, about Kuyper's plan. Vos had been offered a professorship at the Vrije Universiteit in 1886 but turned it down, taking up a professorship at the Theological School of the Christian Reformed Church in Grand Rapids instead.[4] He mastered both Dutch and English and was fascinated by neo-Calvinist theology and worldview. Since Vos himself was not well-acquainted with the American publishing world, he wrote to B. B. Warfield, a professor at Princeton Theological Seminary, for advice on whether it would be preferable to publish the book in English:

> The Holland language is very little read outside of the small country in which it is spoken, while to an English book not only the new, but also a large part of the old world lies open, English being read everywhere. The question was therefore put to me, whether I could make a rough guess at the size of the edition. Secondly, I am asked for information as to a reliable firm, which might be inclined to publish the book here. Finally,

---

[3] About the Dutch American reading culture, see George Harinck, "D. J. Doornink and the Early Years of the Dutch-American Book Selling Trade (1860 to 1880)," in *Across Borders: Dutch Migration to North America and Australia*, ed. Jacob E. Nyenhuis, Suzanne M. Sinke, and Robert P. Swierenga (Holland: Van Raalte Press, 2010), 113-34.

[4] George Harinck, "Geerhardus Vos as Introducer of Kuyper in America," in *The Dutch-American Experience: Essays in Honor of Robert P. Swierenga*, ed. Hans Krabbendam and Larry J. Wagenaar (Amsterdam: VU Uitgeverij, 2000), 242-62.

there is a question, as to whether, if the book was to be published in English, I would undertake to furnish the translation.[5]

Warfield knew Kuyper's name and work and had referred to him in the April 1889 issue of *The Presbyterian Review* as "to be classed with [Charles] Hodge and [Eduard] Böhl, as nearly the only ones in the nineteenth century who have written truly standard works on Reformed theology."[6] In his letter, Vos expressed his doubt that there would be a market in the United States for the book Kuyper had in mind, but he also stressed the importance of the intended publication:

> So far as I know it would be the first modern attempt to write on the Encyclopedia of Theology from a reformed-Calvinistic point of view. I have no doubt, but the writer is eminently qualified to do the work thoroughly. He has done more than anybody else for the revival of the old orthodoxism and the old orthodox theology in Holland and unites in a wonderful manner the practical gifts of the leader of a religious movement, with a well-trained systematic mind.[7]

With Warfield's advice, in February 1890 Vos wrote to Kuyper that he would do the translation. Vos guessed that the translation would take him two years, but that was no problem for Kuyper, who had calculated that it would take four years to write the Dutch version of the encyclopedia.[8] The encyclopedia was a work in progress, which meant that Vos did not receive proof sheets of the book immediately. In the meantime, Vos translated a rather long text by Kuyper titled "Calvinism and Confessional Revision."[9] But the timing was still a complication. He wrote Warfield in 1891: "My regular work is so manyfold, that I can only snatch

---

[5]G. Vos to B. B. Warfield, 22 October 1889, Benjamin B. Warfield Papers, Special Collections, Princeton Theological Seminary Libraries, Princeton, NJ.

[6]"Reviews of Recent Theological Literature," *The Presbyterian Review* 10 (April 1889): 336.

[7]Vos to Warfield, 22 October 1889, Warfield Papers. For unknown reasons, this quotation has not been included in this letter as published in James T. Dennison Jr., ed., *The Letters of Geerhardus Vos* (Phillipsburg, NJ: P&R Publishing, 2005), 129-30.

[8]Vos to A. Kuyper, 1 February 1890. Dennison, *Letters of Geerhardus Vos*, 134.

[9]Abraham Kuyper, "Calvinism and Confessional Revision," trans. Geerhardus Vos, *The Presbyterian and Reformed Review* 2, no. 7 (July 1891): 369-99.

a few spare moments." Another difficulty for Vos was Kuyper's style: "I had my doubts about several things, and on the whole found it hard to anglicize the style."[10]

On the request of Warfield, Vos also translated an article on theological developments in the Netherlands by Herman Bavinck, professor at the Theological School in Kampen. This article, titled "Recent Dogmatic Thought in the Netherlands," published in 1892, was the first introduction of Kuyper's activity to an American academic readership. And its introduction was a positive one: Kuyper "does not produce a new theology, but reproduces the old in an independent and sometimes in a free manner," Bavinck wrote. "The various Reformed doctrines to him are not loosely connected *loci communes*, but, being most intimately related, they form one world of ideas, one strictly coherent system."[11] A similarly positive judgment of Kuyper's work came from a review of his article on confessional revision, published in 1891. The review noted that Kuyper's article was "the mature judgment of a champion of the Reformed Churches, . . . looking at the matter in the dry light of reason."[12] Following this, two rectoral addresses by Kuyper in 1892 and 1893 were translated by the Presbyterian minister John H. De Vries of Yonkers, a native from Amsterdam.[13] The introduction of Kuyper to an American audience continued to broaden through the influence of American Congregationalist minister and writer William Elliot Griffis, who had no Dutch background but was a member of a Pilgrim Fathers Memorial Committee. In 1891, Griffis visited the Netherlands and wrote an article in an American magazine on an evening he

---

[10]Vos to Warfield, 12 February 1891, Warfield Papers.

[11]H. Bavinck, "Recent Dogmatic Thought in the Netherlands," *The Presbyterian and Reformed Review* 3, no. 10 (1892): 226.

[12]Unsigned review of "Calvinism and Confessional Revision," by Abraham Kuyper, *The Christian Intelligencer*, July 29, 1891.

[13]Abraham Kuyper, "Calvinism and Art," trans. John H. De Vries, *Christian Thought: Lectures and Papers on Philosophy, Christian Evidence, Biblical Elucidation* 9 (February 1892): 259-82, (June 1892): 447-59; Abraham Kuyper, "Pantheism's Destruction of Boundaries," trans. John H. De Vries, *The Methodist Review* 75, no. 4 (July/August 1893): 520-37, no. 5 (September/October 1893): 762-78.

spent at Kuyper's home in Amsterdam.[14] Reformed Dutch Americans knew Kuyper since the 1880s, but now his name became known in a broader circle. Kuyper welcomed these endeavors, and on November 29, 1891, he listed some of the translations in his weekly *De Heraut*, concluding, "As far as the defense of Calvinism is concerned, the news from America is not unfavorable."[15]

Unfortunately, when the Dutch proofs of Kuyper's encyclopedia arrived in 1893, Vos could not find the time to do the translation.[16] Thus, the *Encyclopædie der heilige godgeleerdheid* was published in Dutch in Amsterdam in 1894, while the English translation remained in *statu nascendi*. Griffis did not know of this translation project when he, on February 8, 1893, recommended De Vries to Kuyper as "a very competent translator."[17] A month later De Vries, who had started translating Kuyper's *E voto Dordraceno*, asked Kuyper to appoint him as his authoritative translator.[18] On Griffis's recommendation, Kuyper suggested De Vries to translate the encyclopedia.[19] De Vries wrote to Kuyper that he was willing to do it, and then Kuyper asked Vos if De Vries would be a good successor on the project. Vos doubted that he would. He had read De Vries's translation of "Calvinism and Art" and found it sometimes very poor, and often too literal. "I would feel sorry if a work of such importance would be introduced [here] in imperfect form."[20]

Despite his experience, De Vries did not seem to be the right translator. From 1893 to 1895, Kuyper therefore worked with two other translators, the Dutch Americans Abel H. Huizinga and J. Poppen, but they both got only halfway through the work.

[14]William E. Griffis, "An Evening with Dr. Kuyper," *The Christian Intelligencer*, August 31, 1892.

[15]"De berichten uit Amerika, in zooverre het de verdediging van het Calvinisme geldt, luiden niet ongunstig."

[16]That summer, Vos had moved to Princeton Theological Seminary, where he became Warfield's colleague.

[17]W. E. Griffis to J. H. De Vries, 8 February 1893, Abraham Kuyper Papers, Historical Documentation Center for Dutch Protestantism, Vrije Universiteit Amsterdam.

[18]J. H. De Vries to A. Kuyper, 7 March 1893, Kuyper Papers.

[19]See J. H. De Vries to Kuyper, 3 April 1893, Kuyper Papers.

[20]Vos to Kuyper, 11 May 1893, in Dennison, *Letters of Geerhardus Vos*, 173.

In 1896, Kuyper again approached De Vries to translate the work, and he accepted the job. He started translating anew. "I am at work on volume II at the rate of 16 pages a week. I have 55 pages done," he wrote to Kuyper.[21] De Vries finished the translation of the second volume of the *Encyclopædie* in the summer of 1897. De Vries (supported by Warfield) argued that an introduction to volume one would need to be added—not the historical chapters in the current volume, for they would not interest the Americans, according to De Vries—and published as one book. Kuyper gave in grudgingly. In September 1897, Scribner's Sons in New York agreed to publish the book, titled *Encyclopedia of Sacred Theology: Its Principles.*

So much of Kuyper's struggles with translating make clear that he was hurt by the fact he could not write well in English. Given this, Kuyper had to depend on his translators, who either did not finish the job, had difficulty translating him, or translated him poorly. Further complicating his plans, the work of translation was also time consuming. Kuyper learned that translating his work for the American market was a complicated enterprise.

THE LECTURES

In 1896, Kuyper was invited by Princeton Theological Seminary, on the initiative of Geerhardus Vos, to deliver the Stone Lectures of 1897–1898, six in all. Kuyper would not come until the following academic year. In an interview Kuyper gave to a Dutch newspaper in January 1897, he said he had already chosen Calvinism as the topic for his lectures.[22] But once again, his experience navigating the Dutch and English languages, and Dutch and American audiences, was less straightforward than he might have hoped.

When Vos found out in the fall of 1897 that Kuyper had not yet started writing his lectures, he started to get nervous. Kuyper would have to

---

[21]J. H. De Vries to Kuyper, 16 March 1896, Kuyper Papers.
[22]"Dr. Kuyper naar Amerika," *Algemeen Handelsblad*, January 16, 1897.

deliver six lectures in October next year, and Vos knew that translations were time consuming and generated unforeseen complications. He therefore impressed on Kuyper the urgency of this translation, asking who it was he had commissioned to do the work and suggesting he might want to postpone the lectures. "The time between now and 1898-99 may be also rather short for the translation," Vos wrote. "When would it be possible for you to furnish the Dutch text?"[23]

Over the next few months, Kuyper wrote his lectures in Dutch and, according to one historical witness, did not translate them himself but asked American friends to do this.[24] However, there is no direct evidence of Kuyper requesting this. In the spring of 1898, he hired the twenty-year-old Ethel Ashton, from Great Britain. She lived with the Kuyper family in Amsterdam for half a year and gave conversation lessons to Kuyper's three daughters and also to Kuyper. During mealtimes, only English was spoken, so Kuyper's English fluency was improved as well. Ashton's talents were both conversational and literary, having already published poems and stories.[25] She wrote about her time with the Kuyper family at the Prins Hendrikkade in Amsterdam in 1921, a quarter of a century after she had lived there.[26]

One day in April 1898, a dismal Kuyper joined his family at coffee time. He had received the translation of his first lecture from America

---

[23]Vos to Kuyper, 11 October 1897, Kuyper Papers: "Misschien is de tijd tusschen nu en 1898-1899 ook rijkelijk kort voor de vertaling." Dennison, *Letters of Geerhardus Vos*, 200, translated "rijkelijk kort" incorrectly as "short enough" instead of "very short."

[24]Johannes Stellingwerff, *Dr. Abraham Kuyper en de Vrije Universiteit* (Kampen: Kok, 1987), 232-33, writes that Kuyper translated the lectures himself, but I found no proof for this. According to Ethel Ashton, "Een herinnering aan den zomer van 1898," in *Herinneringen van de oude garde aan den persoon en levensarbeid van Dr. A. Kuyper*, ed. Henriëtta Sophia Susanna Kuyper and Johanna Hendrika Kuyper (Amsterdam, 1922), 173, the lectures were translated into English for Kuyper.

[25]In 1897 she published in *The Gentlewoman: An Illustrated Weekly Journal for Gentlewomen*. In the Netherlands she published a poem, "In Praise of Amsterdam," in *Onder Neerlands vlag: Album ter herdenking van het vijf en twintig jarig bestaan van den Nederlandschen militairen bond, 1874–1899* (Amsterdam: Van Holkema & Warendorf, 1899), 182-83. On Kuyper's death she published the poem "Dr. Abraham Kuyper," in *The American Daily Standard*, January 10, 1921, and in *Gedenkboek ter herinnering aan het overlijden van Dr. A. Kuyper en de sprake die daarbij uit de pers voortkwam* (Amsterdam: W. ten Have, 1921), 289-90; it was also published under the title "A Portrait" in Ashton, "Een herinnering," 178-79.

[26]Ashton, "Een herinnering," 173-80.

and was dissatisfied. The translation did not articulate what he meant nor how he wanted to say what he meant; it was too literal.[27] So, Kuyper changed his plan. He decided that he would improve the translation himself, with the help of a native speaker. On the suggestion of his daughter Henriette he asked Ashton to do this, and she gave him "linguistic guidance" for four months. "He wanted the lectures in English as pure and as exact as possible," Ashton wrote. "Even the finest nuance of his meaning should be understood."[28] By fine-tuning the translations himself together with Ashton, Kuyper overcame the disadvantage of translators distorting his text. The literal translations of the lectures were arriving from America this spring. As late as July he received the translation of the fourth lecture by Nicolaus M. Steffens from Dubuque, Iowa. In a letter accompanying his translation, Steffens communicated how difficult and time consuming the translation had been and his own meticulous efforts to capture Kuyper's words:

> So far as my translation is concerned, I found my work connected with it a bit difficult in some passages. How true is what Buffon says: *Le style c'est l'homme*. And allow me to say: you are so terribly original, such a pronounced individual. I have done what I could to present Dr. Kuyper as well as I could to our American public in English. This is how I performed my task. First I read the original several times; next I made a literal translation; then I attempted to remove the Dutch idioms from the translation; in the final product I have tried to remain true to the original, to be clear in communicating your thoughts, and finally to make the English as good as possible in diction and style. After that I turned the manuscript over to my friend, Dr. W.O. Ruston, a mature American preacher, who returned it to me with his comments, which I incorporated, and finally, to determine whether or not the translation would commend itself to an audience, I read my translation to a German American, pastor [H.] Ficke, an eminent man of letters, and

---

[27] Ashton, "Een herinnering," 175-76.
[28] Ashton, "Een herinnering," 177.

to Dr. [A.] McClelland, his colleague, both of whom gave a favorable judgment of my work.[29]

Despite the hard work of Steffens, I presume that Kuyper and Ashton reworked his translation as well to make the style similar, as they did with the other five lectures. Peter Heslam, the British author of a dissertation on the Stone Lectures, was struck by the fact that the style and expressions of "the actual text of the *Lectures,*" what I call the Kuyper-Ashton text in this chapter, were coherent.[30] In light of the joint elaboration of the various lecture texts by Kuyper and Ashton, this is no surprise.

In July 1898, the lectures were completed. Ten copies of the Kuyper-Ashton text were typeset and printed on sheets, on one side only, and bound by the Amsterdam bookbinder J. A. van Waarden in full cloth, with a red spine and red corners combined with beige leatherette on the boards.[31] Kuyper would leave for the United States on August 11. The day before, he had given Ashton one of the ten copies of the "big red book," as she described it, with a dedication: "To Miss Ashton, presented by the author, in thankful remembrance of her linguistic guidance."[32]

Shortly after, Griffis was also in Amsterdam as a foreign journalist for the inauguration of Queen Wilhelmina on September 6. He visited Kuyper's home in the weeks after Kuyper had left and got a copy of the book, holding the Kuyper-Ashton text on loan from one of Kuyper's daughters.[33]

---

[29]N. M. Steffens to Kuyper, 30 June 1898 [translation by the author], in George Harinck, "*We live presently under a waning moon*": *Nicolaus Martin Steffens as Leader of the Reformed Church in America in the West in Years of Transition (1878–1895)* (Holland: Van Raalte Press, 2013), 178. Peter S. Heslam, *Creating a Christian Worldview: Abraham Kuyper's Lectures on Calvinism* (Grand Rapids, MI: Eerdmans, 1998), 59, mistakenly dated this letter January 30, 1898.

[30]Heslam, *Creating a Christian Worldview*, 62.

[31]Seven copies of the same typeset are extant: four at Special Collections in the library of Princeton Theological Seminary, one at the Historical Documentation Center at Vrije Universiteit Amsterdam, one in the private collection of Tj. Kuipers, Ermelo, and one in the private collection of George Harinck. Three other copies are not located, but both Ashton and H. Bavinck received a copy from Kuyper. See H. Bavinck to Kuyper, 17 April 1899, Kuyper Papers; Bavinck's references to quotes and page numbers in this letter are proof that he received the same typeset.

[32]Ashton, "Een herinnering," 177.

[33]W. E. Griffis, diary, 16 September 1898: "Read Dr. Abraham Kuyper's (Princeton, Stone) Lectures on Calvinism (printed, not published, copy loaned by his daughter)." William Elliot Griffis Collection, Special Collections, Alexander Library, Rutgers University, New Brunswick, NJ.

WARFIELD'S NOTE

Thus far, we are presented with a coherent picture of the creation of the text of Kuyper's Stone Lectures. But as we press into the story of this text, problems arise. In the literature on the making of the Stone Lectures, a note Warfield inserted in his copy of the book with the Kuyper-Ashton text has been the cornerstone of another and quite different historical reconstruction of the making of this text. In order to research its meaning and its relation to the Kuyper-Ashton text, let us first quote Warfield's note in full:

> *Note*: the "Stone Lectures" in Princeton Theological Seminary were delivered in the autumn of 1898 by Dr. A. Kuyper, of the Free University of Amsterdam. About ten days before the lectures were to begin Dr. Kuyper sent his Dutch ms. and asked that it might be translated for his use. In the short time remaining it seemed necessary to engage more than one hand at the task and the following gentlemen kindly undertook to render the several lectures into English, viz: the Rev. J.H. de Vries, pastor of the Second Presbyterian Church, Princeton, who translated lectures I and V.; the Rev. A.H. Huizinga, P.D. of Fishkirk, N.Y., who translated lecture II; the Revd. Professor Henry E. Dosker D.D. of Holland, Michigan, who translated lecture III; the Revd. Professor N.M. Steffens of Dubuque, Iowa, who translated lecture IV; and the Rev. Dr. G. Vos, of Princeton, who translated lecture VI.–
>
> The translated text was then set on type at Princeton and the printed sheets provided to Dr. Kuyper for use in the rostrum. Only a dozen copies were taken off the types—of which the following is one. Before the lectures were issued to the public in English, (New York: Fleming H. Revell Co. [1899]), the text was much altered by Dr. Kuyper himself with a view to bettering the English, but with the effect of waning it sadly. The authoritative text must ever be the Dutch text, which appeared in Amsterdam in one season: of the two English texts, that issued by the Revells has Dr. Kuyper's own imprimatur, but even the hasty text contained in this volume is better.–
>
> These sheets are worthy of preservation for themselves therefore: and they are worthy of it also as a *souvenir* of an interesting occasion, and as

a means of communicating the labor of love of the gentlemen who per-
mitted themselves to be hurried through the task of translating these
lectures for the use of the lecturer in the rostrum.

    B.B. Warfield.[34]

This note contradicts many aspects of the history as presented in the
previous section, which documented that the English text of the lectures had been established very carefully by Kuyper and Ashton. In light
of this previous account, Heslam's appreciation for the consistency of
the English text is understandable, but he had also read Warfield's note
and therefore wrote:

> It is a tribute to the skill of the translators that, despite the hybrid origins
> of the English texts and the speed with which it was made ready, its ex-
> pression and style are accurate and consistent throughout. There are no
> stylistic differences between the lectures themselves that can be attributed
> to their several translators.[35]

Given the difficulties American translators had encountered with
Kuyper's text in previous years and our discussion about the quality of
the translation, it is hard to believe that there were no stylistic differences in translations produced by five different people.

How, then, do we understand this note in Warfield's book and the
contradictions that ensue? We talk about a Kuyper-Ashton text, made
from April till July 1898 and printed in Amsterdam in August, and
Warfield talks about the same text but made in America and printed in
Princeton in October 1898. To get to the heart of these contradictions,
we must take a closer look at Warfield's note. In it, he wrote that around
October 1—that is, ten days before Kuyper had to give his first lecture

---

[34]This note was published for the first time in 1987 in Johannes Stellingwerff, ed., *Geboekt in eigen huis: Bevattende een opsomming van de werken van Abraham Kuyper zoals vermeld in de catalogus van de bibliotheek van de Vrije Universiteit, een essay van J. Stellingwerff benevens twee herdrukte redes van Abraham Kuyper* (Amsterdam: VU Uitgeverij, 1987), 33, and again in 1998 in Heslam, *Creating a Christian Worldview*, 62. Heslam published parts of Warfield's note, and his text slightly differs from Stellingwerff's. I have compared their transcribed texts with the original and established the literal and full text, with paragraphs and parentheses, as presented here.
[35]Heslam, *Creating a Christian Worldview*, 62.

in Princeton—he received a handwritten text in Dutch, the manuscript, of Kuyper's lectures, and he asked them to be translated for his use. This raises at least three significant questions. First, why would Kuyper have written to Warfield? He had not met him yet, and he was not his Princeton contact. Vos had been the Princeton agent who maintained contacts with Kuyper, and he had translated his Dutch texts and had advised him on translations and translators.

This brings us to the second question: Why did Kuyper not send the book with the Kuyper-Ashton text instead of a handwritten text, a manuscript? Kuyper had taken copies of the Kuyper-Ashton text with him from the Netherlands. In August, he had left a copy at Scribner's and Sons publishers at Fifth Avenue, New York, hoping they would be willing to publish the lectures; they did not, and on October 17 they returned "the volume" to Kuyper.[36]

Why, in the third place, would Kuyper have sent Warfield the text at all? About ten days or two weeks before October 10, the date Kuyper would give his first lecture, Kuyper was hiking in Keene Valley and traveling, via Elizabethtown, Boston, and Hartford, to New York. He arrived at Fifth Avenue Hotel, Madison Square, on October 1. On October 3 and 4, he visited Princeton as planned and met Warfield for the first time: "On Monday and Tuesday I went to have a look in Princeton, and I liked it there," he wrote in a letter to his wife. "De Vries and his wife and Vos and his wife were most cordial, and Dr. Warfield was very courteous."[37] On that occasion, when he met two of the five translators Warfield mentioned, he might as well have handed over the text of the lectures instead of sending it from Keene Valley or another place.

---

[36]Charles Scribner's Sons to Kuyper, 17 October 1898, Kuyper Papers; Frances L. Patton to Kuyper, 26 November 1898, Kuyper Papers: "I wrote Mr. Scribner in regard to the publication of your lectures and expressed my interest in them and the hope I had in seeing them in print. Mr. Scribner wrote me a very pleasant letter in reply: but it was discouraging so far as the prospect of him undertaking the publication of the lectures was concerned. He evidently feared that there would be some pecuniary risk in the matter—the demand for Calvinistic literature not being very great just now in this country. I am sorry for this: but I have done my best."

[37]Kuyper to J. H. Kuyper-Schaay, 8 October 1898, in *Kuyper in America: "This Is Where I Was Meant to Be,"* ed. George Harinck (Sioux Center, IA: Dordt College Press, 2012), 32-33.

One explanation for sending the manuscript may be that Kuyper was worried his lectures would not be translated in time. Therefore, he sent his manuscript from Keene Valley the moment he had finished his editing. Kuyper, however, knew from experience with earlier translators how time consuming translating was, so it was uncertain they would get the job done in two weeks' time at all.

These three questions make us wonder: What did Kuyper do with the Kuyper-Ashton text after his arrival in the United States? On September 17, Kuyper wrote to his wife from his hotel in Keene Heights in the Adirondack Mountains. He was restless because in all his weeks in the United States he still had not received mail from home. Then he continued, referencing the *Lectures*: "This week I have taken to hand one lecture a [day] to shorten it, so now they have all been reduced to 34 pages each. I have had to work hard on them. Sometimes from 9 to 4 o'clock. But now I have finished, that at least gives me peace."[38] Kuyper's use of the word *pages* in this letter suggests he worked in a book, the English Kuyper-Ashton text. Further, his reference to the reduction of each lecture to thirty-four pages corresponds with the number of pages in this book. The sixth lecture was thirty-four pages, but the other lectures were all longer, with a maximum of forty-three pages.[39] Kuyper's letter to his wife also gives the impression the text of the lectures was ready for presenting; there is no hint that the next phase had to be a hasty translation of a Dutch manuscript.

By September 17, Kuyper was at peace as far as the lectures were concerned. If he had finished a Dutch text that had to be translated into English before October 10, the date of his first Stone Lecture, why would he have waited almost two weeks before sending the manuscript to Warfield, who wrote in his note he received the text around October 1? And as to the mail and time, another difficulty surfaces. Translating is a

---

[38]Kuyper to Kuyper-Schaay, 17 September 1898, in Harinck, *Kuyper in America*, 22.
[39]The lectures in the book holding the Kuyper-Ashton text have an unequal length: Lecture 1, 37 pages; Lecture 2, 43 pages; Lecture 3, 38 pages; Lecture 4, 38 pages; Lecture 5, 35 pages; Lecture 6, 34 pages.

time-consuming job. J. H. De Vries translated sixteen pages of the *Encyclopædie* in a week, and one Stone Lecture was twice as long. Henri De Vries, another Dutch American Kuyper translator and a brother of J. H. De Vries, was a fast worker. He could do three Kuyper pages a day.[40] How then could Dosker, Huizinga, Steffens, Vos, and J. H. De Vries (who had to do two lectures) have translated the lectures within ten days? Even if these five men, ministers and academics who had just started a new season of preaching and teaching, had been willing to put all their daily work aside—which is highly implausible—and translated as fast as H. De Vries, it would have taken them several days to complete the work. De Vries and Vos were in Princeton and theoretically could have started their work the day the manuscript was in Warfield's mailbox, but Dosker lived in Michigan, Steffens in Iowa, and Huizinga in New York.[41] At least two days would be lost by mailing back and forth, and one more day for type setting and printing—although it is possible the publishing house dealt independently with the lectures, since on October 10 only the first lecture had to be ready. In either case, this time span for the translation work does not seem realistic. Alongside this evidence, we should also remind of the case of Steffens, who had written to Kuyper in July of the meticulous work he had done translating the fourth lecture in the spring. Would Steffens begin translating a Dutch text on exactly the same topic anew in the fall, implying that his work in the spring had been in vain?

Warfield's account of the way these lectures were translated, within ten days and by five different authors, does not fit with Kuyper's experience with the complexities of translating, nor with Heslam's praise of the stylistic coherence of the text. The stylistic coherence that Heslam notes would be possible only after the texts had been seriously edited—and in Warfield's account, there was no time for that.

---

[40]H. De Vries to Kuyper, 1 October 1896, Kuyper Papers.

[41]In the time span of the crucial ten days, Huizinga wrote a letter to Kuyper, inviting him to his home in Fishkill, New York. He wrote about health issues and the Stone Lectures: that he could not attend these and how they would be received in the United States. Huizinga does not mention the work that at that time should have occupied him day and night, the translation of the second lecture. Abel H. Huizinga to Kuyper, 8 October 1898, Kuyper Papers.

In short, Warfield's version of the history of the text is highly implausible. Might it be that he was mistaken when he wrote his note, maybe decades after 1898? His account would fit better with all the other archival and textual information we have if it referenced an earlier date Kuyper sent him his texts, for example December 1897 or January 1898. In that case, perhaps Warfield as an intermediary had indeed sent Kuyper's lectures to these translators[42]—although Kuyper knew all the men personally from earlier translation projects and the short period of ten days is the linking piece in Warfield's story. But then again, setting aside Ashton's colliding account, it is exactly this time slot that turns his note into a problematic source. For if Warfield was right that Kuyper sent him a manuscript around October 1, what then about the account of Ashton, the translation letter of Steffens, the binding by Van Waarden, the references to a "book," and Kuyper's letters to his wife?

SOLUTIONS

Even if we correct the dates in Warfield's text, problems remain in Warfield's account. In an October 19 reference to Kuyper's Stone Lectures, recounting his disappointment that he could not attend Kuyper's fourth lecture, Warfield wrote him that his "only solace is that, having a proof-copy of the lecture, I can read it in my study."[43] But to what does Warfield's reference of a "proof-copy of the lecture" refer? Was he referring to the book with the Kuyper-Ashton text? And why did Warfield call this book a "proof copy"? Perhaps this was because the sheets were printed on one side only. Griffis did not take the bound Kuyper-Ashton-text as a proper book either; he referred to it as a "printed, not published copy."[44] Or was Warfield referring to loose printed sheets indeed, as he

---

[42]Steffens's wording in his letter to Kuyper of June 30, 1898, suggests that someone other than Kuyper asked him to translate and that there were more translators: "Enclosed please find the translation of your fourth lecture, which was entrusted to me" ("Ingesloten vindt gij s.v.p. de vertaling van uwe vierde lezing, die mij toevertrouwd [was]"). Steffens to Kuyper, 30 June 1898, in Harinck, "We live presently under a waning moon," 175, 177.

[43]Warfield to Kuyper, 19 October 1898, Kuyper Papers.

[44]Griffis, diary, 16 September 1898, Griffis Collection: "Read Dr. Abraham Kuyper's (Princeton, Stone) Lectures on Calvinism (printed, not published, copy loaned by his daughter)."

seems to do in the note in his copy of the Kuyper-Ashton text, and did his note end up in the wrong book?[45] Since these presumed sheets are not extant, we cannot check this possibility.[46]

Other Kuyper scholars, Johan Stellingwerff and Peter Heslam, have also dealt with this problem of conflicting data. In their reports, they referenced only a few sources and did not see the letters I found or the different copies of the book holding the Kuyper-Ashton text. Even so, they realized the tension between Ashton's account and Warfield's note. Stellingwerff's solution—and, Heslam's, following in his footsteps—resolved these tensions by taking Warfield's note as the point of reference and making Ashton's story fit with it. What I call the Kuyper-Ashton text is in their books referred to as the translation made in October 1898.

Stellingwerff's account resolves the tension between the two narratives by suggesting two reasons why Kuyper rewrote his lectures. His first reason is that a statement by Griffis, during his visit to the Netherlands, caused Kuyper to rework the lectures. In *The Christian Intelligencer* of September 21, 1898, Griffis published an article titled "The Inauguration of Queen Wilhelmina." He had attended this ceremony on September 6 as a foreign journalist, and on this trip he had also visited Kuyper's home. On August 4, Griffis had dinner with Kuyper, his wife, and Ethel Ashton, among others.[47] In his article "The Inauguration of Queen Wilhelmina," dated "Amsterdam, September 7th, 1898," he wondered if Calvinism would once more be dominant in the new era

---

[45]Warfield wrote in his note "sheets," whereas the Kuyper-Ashton text is a bound book; later on in his note he referred again to the book as "these sheets."

[46]Warfield's clause "having a proof-copy of the [fourth] lecture" is the only source that still makes me hesitant about my interpretation of this translation history.

[47]Griffis, diary, 4 August 1898, Griffis Collection: "Dinner with Dr. A. Kuyper, wife, 2 daughters, miss of Hilversum, son and English lady [Ashton], correspondent of The Gentlemen of England." See also Stellingwerff, *Kuyper en de Vrije Universiteit*, 233; and William Elliot Griffis, *The American in Holland: Sentimental Rambles in the Eleven Provinces of the Netherlands* (Boston: Houghton Mifflin, 1899), 372: "I dine at the house of a Dutch scholar on Prinz Hendrik Kade. I find a delightful party. Wife ('vrouwtje'), two daughters, older son and his betrothed, and a rector's daughter from England make an hour golden-winged. Then, in the garden, after-dinner tea is served."

under Wilhelmina, who is "strongly on the side of historic Christianity."[48] He especially pointed his American readers to Kuyper's enthusiasm for this development and alluded to his upcoming Stone Lectures at Princeton, "where he will protect, defend and illuminate" Calvinism.[49] But when he wrote this, on September 7, Griffis had not yet read the Stone Lectures. When leaving the Netherlands, on September 15, one of the first things he did aboard the ship was read the book with the Kuyper-Ashton text ("printed, not published") he had borrowed from one of Kuyper's daughters.[50]

According to Stellingwerff, Kuyper may have become nervous because of a clause in Griffis's article: "If he can wield his pen in English as in his mother tongue," Griffis wrote, "then I prophesy for this book (that must grow out of the Stone Lectures) a warm welcome among thinking men."[51] Stellingwerff unjustly suggests that Griffis had read Kuyper's Stone Lectures,[52] and he invented the assumption that this clause made Kuyper decide to send the Dutch manuscript of his lectures to Warfield and ask him to have them translated into proper English. But we don't know if Kuyper read the article, even if Stellingwerff's suggestion fits well in the timeline. Griffis's article was published on September 21, and according to Warfield's note, Kuyper sent the manuscript to Princeton one week later. And Griffis had advised Kuyper several times before on translations and recommended J. H. De Vries to him.

However, in the week before Griffis's article was published, Kuyper had given the finishing touch to the meticulously edited Kuyper-Ashton text of the Stone Lectures in Keene Valley, and he was satisfied. Would one loose remark about a future publication have made him doubt all

---

[48]William Elliot Griffis, "The Inauguration of Queen Wilhelmina," *The Christian Intelligencer*, September 21, 1898.
[49]Griffis, "The Inauguration."
[50]Griffis, diary, 16 September 1898, Griffis Collection.
[51]Griffis, "The Inauguration." This last clause was quoted in Stellingwerff, *Kuyper en de Vrije Universiteit*, 238.
[52]Stellingwerff, *Kuyper en de Vrije Universiteit*, 237: "Intussen verscheen de eerste beoordeling van de Stone-lectures in de *Christian Intelligencer* van 21 september" (Meanwhile the first review of the Stone Lectures was published . . .).

of his and Ashton's meticulous labor? While it is possible Griffis's remark made Kuyper that nervous, it is not very plausible.

Second, Stellingwerff (and later, Heslam) argues that Kuyper found new information for his lectures in the library of the passenger liner RMS *Lucania*, on which he sailed from Liverpool to New York in August, and in the New York Public Library.[53] In September, Kuyper then used these libraries to revise the Dutch manuscript of the lectures (Kuyper "inserted the information he had found in his lectures"[54]), which it is assumed he had taken with him—alongside the book with the Kuyper-Ashton text. Stellingwerff and Heslam base this solution on notes Kuyper made on publications by George Bancroft, Henry Cabot Lodge, and Franklin B. Hough. These notes are in Kuyper's archive.[55] Stellingwerff asked, "Was it Griffis's remark [in *The Christian Intelligencer*] that made him [Kuyper] to send the Dutch texts to [P]rof. Warfield in Princeton with the request to have these translated for him, ten days before delivering the first lecture?"[56] Heslam wrote:

> Having now made several changes to the text of his lectures, he sent the emended [*sic*] manuscripts to Warfield at Princeton with the request that they should be speedily translated into English. Because of the changes he had made, and despite the laborious efforts of Ethel Ashton, he now required that the entire text of his lectures should be translated once more.[57]

This second solution has two weaknesses. One is the date these notes were taken by Kuyper. His notes on Bancroft's 1891 edition of his *History of the United States* were written on the letterheaded paper of the *Lucania*, so during or after his crossing of the Atlantic in August.

---

[53]Stellingwerff, *Kuyper en de Vrije Universiteit*, 235. Stellingwerff does not make clear how he knows Kuyper visited the public library. Heslam copied this information from Stellingwerff.

[54]Stellingwerff, *Kuyper en de Vrije Universiteit*, 235: Kuyper "verwerkte het gevonden materiaal nog in zijn lectures."

[55]Inv.nr. 318, nr. 48, 52, Kuyper Papers.

[56]Stellingwerff, *Kuyper en de Vrije Universiteit*, 238: "Was het deze opmerking die hem bewoog om tien dagen voor de eerste lecture zou worden gehouden, de nederlandse teksten naar prof. Warfield te Princeton zenden met het verzoek ze voor hem te doen vertalen?"

[57]Heslam, *Creating a Christian Worldview*, 61. Thus, Warfield wrote in his note, "He now required that the entire text of his lectures should be translated."

In the Kuyper-Ashton text (Stellingwerff's and Heslam's October trans-
lation), Bancroft is quoted only once, in the third lecture, on politics.
This quotation is not in Kuyper's *Lucania* notes but is an older one
Kuyper had used already in 1874,[58] and it had been taken from Ban-
croft's 1853 edition of his *History of the United States*.[59] In the 1899
English edition of the Stone Lectures, composed in Amsterdam after
Kuyper's return from the United States, he referred to both editions of
Bancroft's book.

The notes on the book of Cabot Lodge are on blank paper. They may
also have been written down during or after Kuyper's sea voyage, but
there is no evidence for it one way or the other. In the Kuyper-Ashton
text (or the October translation), Cabot Lodge is absent. The 1899
English edition of the third Stone Lecture, on politics, has in a footnote
one quotation from Cabot Lodge's book on Hamilton, and that one is
in Kuyper's notes. So, notes on two of the three authors Stellingwerff
and Heslam mentioned do not appear in the Kuyper-Ashton text (or the
October translation).

This edition does contain seven citations from Hough's *American
Constitutions*.[60] Stellingwerff stated these notes were taken from a copy
of Hough's book in the New York Public Library;[61] Heslam added "in
the center of Manhattan."[62] I leave aside that a public library, now at the
two-block section of Fifth Avenue between Fortieth and Forty-Second
Streets, did not exist in New York in 1898, and focus on the date. The
notes on Hough's book are on blank paper. It is possible that these notes
were not taken in New York, but in Amsterdam, before Kuyper left for

---

[58]Abraham Kuyper, *Het calvinisme, oorsprong en waarborg onzer constitutioneele vrijheden* (Amsterdam: B. van der Land, 1874), 69.

[59]George Bancroft, *History of the United States from the Discovery of the American Continent to the
Declaration of Independence*, 15th ed. (Boston: Little, Brown, 1853).

[60]Franklin B. Hough, *American Constitutions: Comprising the Constitution of Each State in the
Union, and of the United States, with the Declaration of Independence and Articles of Confederation*
[. . .], 2 vols. (Albany: Weed, Parsons & Co., 1871–1872). Kuyper mistakenly wrote Hugh instead
of Hough. He cites Hough—with the same misspelling—again in Abraham Kuyper, *Antirevolutionaire staatkunde*, vol. 1 (Kampen: Kok, 1916), 457.

[61]Stellingwerff, *Kuyper en de Vrije Universiteit*, 235.

[62]Heslam, *Creating a Christian Worldview*, 61.

the United States.[63] An argument in favor of Amsterdam is that the handwriting indicates that someone other than Kuyper has taken the notes from Hough's book.[64] From the notes, it is clear that the transcriber was a Dutchman: in the transcript the word *page* is abbreviated as "bl." or "pag.";[65] an American would have written "p." for *page*. The only ground for the assumption the notes were taken in New York may be that Hough's book was not available in one of the university libraries in the Netherlands in 1898. But so far as we can tell—other sheets with quotations may have been lost—the citations of these three authors in the Stone Lectures cannot bridge the gap between Ashton's memories and Warfield's note.

The other weakness of this solution is that the American authors mentioned in Kuyper's notes are referenced only in the third lecture in the Kuyper-Ashton text (Stellingwerff's and Heslam's October translation). If, because of the new information, Kuyper had to rework this one lecture so radically that he had to write a new lecture in Dutch, this does not necessarily necessitate changes to the five other lectures as well. Additionally, why would he rewrite the whole third lecture in Dutch for some additional quotations, when every citation he used was in native English? The only quotes of the three books Stellingwerff mentioned were Hough's. The seven citations from his work appear in an uninterrupted row in one paragraph in lecture three. If they had been added by Kuyper in August or September, a simple insert would have sufficed. There was no need for a new translation.

Finally, it is noteworthy that seven out of "ten" (Ashton[66]) or "a dozen" (Warfield) copies of the book with the Kuyper-Ashton text are around, including Warfield's. If these were in fact the afterward-bound sheets of the October text, as Warfield stated in his note and Stellingwerff and

---

[63]Transcript of pages I, 5-9, and II, 544-51, 564-67, and 573-76 of Hough, *American Constitutions*, inv.nr. 318, Dossier betreffende de reis naar Amerika, nr. 58 and 59, Kuyper Papers; quote from Cabot Lodge, *Alexander Hamilton* (Boston, 1892), 256, inv.nr. 318, nr. 52, Kuyper Papers.
[64]Stellingwerff, *Kuyper en de Vrije Universiteit*, 235.
[65]As in the Dutch *bladzijde* ("bl.") or *pagina* ("pag.").
[66]Ashton, "Een herinnering," 177.

Heslam argued, this would mean that two different sets of ten copies of the Stone Lectures would have been produced in 1898: the "big red book" Ashton received from Kuyper on August 10 and the same "printed, not published, copy loaned by his daughter" to Griffis in September 1898,[67] and another set whose features we don't know because no copy survived. All in all, Stellingwerff's and Heslam's reconstruction of the history of the text of the Stone Lectures on the basis of Warfield's note raises more questions and no solutions.

PRINT

As we have seen, the reconstruction of the history of the text of Kuyper's Stone Lectures based on Warfield's note is contradicted by other sources and leads to the kind of problems we have expanded on. The reconstruction that takes its starting point from Ashton's account, on the other hand, is consonant with evidence from several other sources, or at least the evidence does not contradict the account.

There is one more argument that favors the set we know to be called the Kuyper-Ashton text instead of the October translation, and that is a technical argument regarding the printing history of the book. We know that the red-white books had been bound in Amsterdam by bookbinder Van Waarden. Warfield's copy of the Stone Lectures, however, did not have this signature binding. According to librarian Ken Henke from the Special Collections Department in Princeton Theological Library, the binding of Warfield's copy was, instead, similar to other bindings of books from his library.[68] Since Warfield's copy is dissimilar from the other known copies of the Stone Lectures—there is no title or author mentioned on front or spine—Warfield's copy had

---

[67]W. E. Griffis to Kuyper, 21 October 1898, Kuyper Papers: "I send you greetings and kindest wishes from my home and study room. I had a most delightful time in Holland and everything was fully up to my expectations and some greatly exceeded them. Your daughter was so kind to lend me her private copy of your lectures on Calvinism, which I greatly enjoyed reading on the voyage. I shall return them carefully as soon as I am able to get the lectures in their ordinary course of publication."

[68]The call number of Warfield's copy in the library of Princeton Theological Seminary is SCF 2363 and is "For use in library only."

probably been rebound (like the copy at the Vrije Universiteit), and the two-page note was then included in the new binding. As a solution to this difference, Kuyper's bibliographer, Tjitse Kuipers, suggested there may be two sets because of two different bindings that have survived: one is a full red binding (bound in Princeton, he says, with title, subtitle, and author's name on the front cover) and one is a red and white binding (bound in Amsterdam, with title, subtitle, and author's name on the front cover and title on the spine).[69] But Kuyper left Princeton on October 22, the day after he had delivered his final lecture, so there does not seem to have been much time to make bound copies for him.

Specialists in printing and printing history have tried to solve the problem of the conflicting sources by answering the question where the book with the Kuyper-Ashton text or the October translation were printed. Their research on the paper type and the type setting resulted in the conclusion that the book with the Kuyper-Ashton text had been set and printed in the Netherlands. They gave two technical reasons for this conclusion. The first is the typographical measurement: the setting width is exactly 24 cicero (cic.), which was the typographical size in the Netherlands around 1900, based on the Didot point system, in which a point is 0.376065 mm (DIN 16507). A cic. is 12 points. According to the American Bureau of Standards, the Anglo-Saxon world at that time used the pica point, which was 0.35146 mm (or 0.013837 in.). The American pica point is smaller than the Didot point of the Netherlands. If this text had been typeset in the United States, it is almost certain this had been done with American materials, and the setting width would be a little smaller because of the smaller pica point. Additionally, the font style is a typical lean letter as produced by the Dutch publishing company Joh. Enschedé from Haarlem. So, the Kuyper-Ashton text was set and printed in the Netherlands—that is, before Kuyper left Amsterdam on August 11, 1898.

---

[69]Tjitze Kuipers, *Abraham Kuyper: An Annotated Bibliography, 1857–2010* (Leiden: Brill, 2011), 291.

The second reason for the production of the book with the Kuyper-Ashton text in the Netherlands is its similarity with two other books by Kuyper that had been published around 1898 by publishing house Höveker & Wormser in Amsterdam: *De crisis in Zuid-Afrika*, published in 1900, and the Dutch edition of the Stone Lectures, *Het calvinisme: Zes Stone lezingen, in October 1898 te Princeton (N.J.) gehouden* in 1899. The setting width of these three books is exactly the same, and the paper type of *Het calvinisme* is very similar to the paper of the book holding the Kuyper-Ashton text.[70] The results of this technical analysis do not support Warfield's account and are in line with Ashton's version and with the other archival data.

The overall conclusion must be that the information in Warfield's note does not correspond with the other sources on the history of the text of Kuyper's Stone Lectures. These other sources are of a various nature, but they support each other. Because of Warfield's standing as an academic, his key role in Kuyper's visit to Princeton, and the precise character of the information he offers in his note, it is understandable that previous researchers have fully relied on this source. They did not compare his information with other sources and therefore had no reasons to doubt Warfield's note. But when all sources are taken into account, there is only one source that is incompatible with all the others, and that is precisely what Warfield's note historiography relied on. This fact leaves us bewildered, not understanding how he could misinterpret the historical situation of 1898, but the evidence forces us not to rely on his note in explaining the history of the text of Kuyper's Stone Lectures.

CLOSING REMARKS

By the end of December 1898 Kuyper had returned to the Netherlands. Ethel Ashton had returned to England, and in the new year Kuyper made the Dutch and the English text ready for printing on his own. It

---

[70]I thank G. Post van der Molen and Henk Porck (Royal Library, The Hague, the Netherlands) for their research.

is understandable that Kuyper reworked his English text, having extended his English vocabulary and improved his sense of the English language while traveling in the United States, but for him, who was used to writing *aus einem Gusz*, this work of correcting and amending a text was unusual. The book was published in Dutch with Höveker & Wormser in Amsterdam and Pretoria. The English edition was a combined effort of T&T Clark and Simpkin, Marshall, Hamilton, Kent & Co. in London and Revell (who provided a different binding for the American edition) in New York.[71] Kuyper had not succeeded in publishing his encyclopedia in Dutch and English at the same time, but with the Stone Lectures he succeeded: in June 1899 they were published in both languages at the same time in the Netherlands, South Africa, Great Britain, and the United States. After this major translation project, Kuyper did not have any difficulties in reaching the American market. He published no more books in America, but during his lifetime many of his articles were published in translation.

As we have seen in the first part of this chapter, the translation of the Stone Lectures was not an incident but part of a deliberate and broader effort to internationalize. Ernst Troeltsch recognized this feature of neo-Calvinism, and the key role these lectures played in this effort, and wrote:

> The international character of Calvinism . . . is . . . displayed in the active translation activity, by which everything of importance which appears is translated into English for the benefit of the English-speaking peoples. Kuyper's book itself is a monument of this international spirit.[72]

This second part of the chapter was on the difficulties this translational drive brought along and the specific historical misunderstandings that have developed regarding the translation of the Stone Lectures. The overall aim was to put the record straight and show that the presentation

---

[71]H. Revell to Kuyper, 9 December 1898, Kuyper Papers.
[72]Ernst Troeltsch, *The Social Teaching of the Christian Churches, Volume II* (London: Allen & Unwin / New York: Macmillan, 1931), 618.

and publication of the lectures in English was not an incident, not an enterprise that almost exceeded Kuyper's powers, but one that was well organized and intrinsically related to the nature of neo-Calvinism as an international movement. The Stone Lectures have not become the most famous and most dispersed book of this tradition by accident. Apart from the topic (a general introduction to neo-Calvinism) and apart from the timing (though Kuyper was the foremost Dutch politician at the time), he preferred lecturing in Princeton over attending the investiture of Queen Wilhelmina. Kuyper's careful preparation of the English text underlines that the lectures were meant to be the international introduction to neo-Calvinism from its inception.

CONCLUSION

JESSICA R. JOUSTRA

WHEN I FIRST ENCOUNTERED Kuyper's *Lectures on Calvinism,* there was a sense of grandiosity to them. *These* were the lectures that outlined the kind of robust, Calvinistic worldview that gives a comprehensive vision for life that provides the way for Christians to extend their faithful following of Jesus Christ into every area of society and culture. The lore of Kuyper's personality, bold claims, and important ideas surrounded his lectures, as my own friends and mentors received them with great acclaim. We've heard, throughout these chapters, of the importance of Kuyper's lectures, which provided "much needed oxygen" for the pursuit of faithful cultural and political engagement (alongside, as we've seen, deeply troubling claims of Kuyper's).[1] Richard Mouw has similarly reflected, in his own introduction to Abraham Kuyper, that in Kuyper's Stone Lectures he "discovered what [he] had been looking for: a vision of active involvement in public life that would allow me to steer my way between a privatized evangelicalism on the one hand and the liberal Protestant or Catholic approaches to public discipleship on the other hand."[2]

Such a vision, as Jonathan Chaplin and Richard Mouw describe in their chapters, provided the fodder for multiple institutions, including

---

[1]See Vincent Bacote, "Kuyper and Race," in *Calvinism for a Secular Age* (Downers Grove, IL: IVP Academic, 2021), 148. Each chapter has, in its own way, touched on both the aspects of the Stone Lectures that are life-giving and transformative and the aspects that are deeply problematic, damaging, and without excuse. This is clearly explored in Bacote's chapter, which is specifically devoted to how we engage Kuyperian thought, given his statements on race, but can be seen throughout the rest of the volume as well.

[2]Richard Mouw, *Abraham Kuyper: A Short and Personal Introduction* (Grand Rapids, MI: Eerdmans, 2011), ix.

educational and political organizations that have loomed large in my own communities: the Christian Labor Association (CLAC), Cardus, the Center for Public Justice (CPJ), the Institute for Christian Studies (ICS), and Calvin University—my own alma mater.

RECEIVING KUYPER'S LECTURES: THEN

You can imagine my surprise, then, when I discovered that these lectures —important and foundational as they were—were initially attended by only three or four dozen individuals.[3] Such humble beginnings do not, of course, negate the importance of Kuyper's lectures, but they do begin to paint a picture of the reception of Kuyper's words, both immediately and as their influence trickled through generations of Christians.

As James Bratt recalls in the preface, how one defines Calvinism is important for the story of the reception and influence of Kuyper's words. The original, small Princeton crowd that gathered to hear Kuyper was undoubtedly friendly to Calvinism. Important thinkers like B. B. Warfield left Kuyper's lectures impressed with, and edified by, the "passion, faith, and energy" of Kuyper.[4] On the one hand, the two spoke the same language: an affirmation of Calvinism's doctrine and ecclesial polity. But, as Bratt points out, Kuyper meant *more* by Calvinism than those at Princeton. Calvinism, Kuyper contended, "did not stop at a church order, but expanded into a *life-system*, and did not exhaust its energy in a dogmatical construction, but created a *life-* and *world-view*."[5] In short, as we've seen throughout this short volume, Kuyper's Calvinism was a worldview.

Although those in the crowd at Princeton were not the ones, in the end, to take up the call to champion a worldviewing Calvinism that Kuyper issued in these Stone Lectures, Kuyper's vision was not lost on American soil. For those who know these lectures of Kuyper's, we

---

[3]James D. Bratt, *Abraham Kuyper: Modern Calvinist, Christian Democrat* (Grand Rapids, MI: Eerdmans, 2013), 262.

[4]Bratt, *Abraham Kuyper: Modern Calvinist*, 264.

[5]Abraham Kuyper, *Lectures on Calvinism* (1931; repr., Grand Rapids, MI: Eerdmans, 1999), 171 (emphasis original).

quickly—and rightly—associate them with Princeton Theological Seminary, where he delivered them. But it is often forgotten that Kuyper's 1898 journey to America did not *end* in Princeton.[6] Kuyper continued on, stopping next in Michigan, where many Dutch Americans had settled (and remain to this day). During this leg of his journey, some of the familiar text of these Stone Lectures was revisited. Among other lectures and meetings, Kuyper once again delivered one of these Stone Lectures, his final lecture on Calvinism and the future. In this Dutch American crowd, and throughout the rest of his visits to Dutch American settlements, Kuyper met those "who would take up [his] charge."[7] These Dutch Americans, scattered throughout the United States in Michigan, Iowa, Illinois, and beyond, would take up Kuyper's call to proclaim and apply the Calvinistic worldview. They formed school systems, political think tanks, farming federations, labor unions, and more, all rooted in the distinctives of a Calvinistic worldview.

Kuyper's own reflections on a Calvinistic worldview in these lectures, as we've seen, take on several different tones. Some are deeply optimistic for the future and the possibilities of Calvinism. Calvinism, after all, is the worldview that "effectually secured" a "love for science,"[8] "restored to science *its domain*,"[9] and "emancipated" music, allowing for "its so splendid modern development."[10] Each of Kuyper's grand, optimistic claims about the Calvinistic worldview underscores his assertion that Calvinism "fit[s] itself to every stage of human development . . . every department of life!"[11] Alongside these claims, ringing with optimism and promise, he strikes a different tone, one that is ominous about

---

[6]For a thorough outline of Kuyper's 1898 journey, see Bratt, *Abraham Kuyper: Modern Calvinist*, 261-79.

[7]Bratt, *Abraham Kuyper: Modern Calvinist*, 264. Warfield "never comprehended the epistemological revolution Kuyper had suggested," writes Bratt. "Nor did the next several generations of American evangelicals and Fundamentalists who followed in Warfield's train."

[8]Kuyper, *Lectures on Calvinism*, 113.

[9]Kuyper, *Lectures on Calvinism*, 117 (emphasis original).

[10]Kuyper, *Lectures on Calvinism*, 168.

[11]Kuyper, *Lectures on Calvinism*, 171.

impending threats to Christianity. In the face of such danger, Calvinism is needed because it is the "only decisive, lawful, and consistent defense for Protestant nations against encroaching, and overwhelming Modernism;"[12] Modernism "now confronts Christianity; and against this deadly danger, ye, Christians, cannot successfully defend your sanctuary, but by placing in opposition to all this, *a life- and world-view of your own. . . . And this is equivalent to a return to Calvinism.*"[13] Indeed, argues Kuyper, the "*Calvinistic principle*" is the "sole trustworthy foundation on which to build."[14]

Both the Princeton crowd (who did not end up being a primary conduit of Kuyper's Calvinism in America) and the Holland, Michigan, crowd (who heard only Kuyper's address "Calvinism and the Future") heard the breadth of Kuyper's tones, ominous and optimistic. Surely, given Kuyper's optimism, he understands Calvinism as a Christian tradition that remains faithful to scriptural witness, to have an inherent worth and value. It is the Christian tradition that "embod[ies] the Christian idea more purely and accurately"[15] than other Christian traditions and "vindicates for religion its full universal character, and its complete universal application."[16]

But Calvinism also has a *particular* import in the face of the challenges of his day, Kuyper argues. There is something about the threat of modernity that could draw people toward Calvinism—necessitates an adherence to a Calvinist worldview—*and* something about Calvinism that can help counter these problems. In the face of modernism's challenges that Bruce Ashford helpfully describes in his chapter on Kuyper and the future, one must return to the Calvinistic life and worldview, which confesses the sovereignty of God and proclaims the means by which God's sovereignty—and

---

[12]Kuyper, *Lectures on Calvinism*, 12.
[13]Kuyper, *Lectures on Calvinism*, 90 (emphasis original).
[14]Kuyper, *Lectures on Calvinism*, 191 (emphasis original).
[15]Kuyper, *Lectures on Calvinism*, 17.
[16]Kuyper, *Lectures on Calvinism*, 52.

call to discipleship—extends into every square inch of life: philosophy, psychology, art, law, literature, medicine, science, and more.

RECEIVING KUYPER'S LECTURES: NOW

But what does this mean for us today?

Near the one-hundredth anniversary of Kuyper's delivery of his Stone Lectures, Peter Heslam penned a book on these lectures, *Creating a Christian Worldview*. Heslam referred to Kuyper's Stone Lectures as a "manifesto of Kuyperian Calvinism"[17] and contended that Kuyper's lectures remain relevant to, and important for, Heslam's own, late twentieth-century, primarily American readership. For such a claim, Heslam gave four reasons: first, these lectures summarize key aspects of Kuyper's thought; second, these lectures occurred at "the high point" of Kuyper's career;[18] third, unlike other works of Kuyper's that have been translated, his Stone Lectures were *intended* for a foreign, English-speaking audience; and fourth, by the time of Heslam's writing, these lectures were the work of Kuyper's that had traveled furthest, so to speak, and were "central to the transmission of Kuyper's influence abroad."[19]

Now, nearly two decades later, near the centennial of Kuyper's death, Heslam's rationale for attending to these lectures remains important. While the century has changed, these lectures remain works that were intended for an English-speaking, North American audience. They are a clear, comprehensive introduction to a Reformed, Calvinistic worldview that are self-consciously written for an audience that neither shares Kuyper's native tongue nor knows his home country. As a central voice in the second generation of Kuyperian scholarship, Herman Dooyeweerd, argued, these lectures are "the best example" of Kuyper's "reformational principles."[20]

---

[17]Peter Heslam, *Creating a Christian Worldview: Abraham Kuyper's Lectures on Calvinism* (Grand Rapids, MI: Eerdmans, 1998), 11.

[18]Heslam, *Creating a Christian Worldview*, 10.

[19]Heslam, *Creating a Christian Worldview*, 11.

[20]Herman Dooyeweerd, "Kuyper's wetenschapsleer," *Philosophia reformata: orgaan van de vereeniging voor calvinistische wijsbergeerte* 4 (1939): 197, translated by Peter Heslam in *Creating a Christian Worldview*, 10.

What we have tried to do in this little volume is not unlike Kuyper's original intention. Throughout these pages, we have sought to introduce— or reintroduce, as the case may be—these same Stone Lectures and Kuyper's basic principles of a Christian worldview to a primarily English-speaking, predominantly North American readership. In each chapter, we've taken the time to reflect on what Kuyper himself said in these lectures, attempting to mine the deep, important worldview insights that Kuyper grants us within them. But given the time that has passed between Kuyper's original writing and our own day, we've also attended to those who took up Kuyper's charge. "What did Kuyperians do?" these chapters have asked. In other words, what did those who heard Kuyper's message and took it to heart do with these principles; what difference does a Calvinistic worldview make in the real lives of people and their institutions? And finally we've asked, What should *we* do?

Where Kuyper's time felt the crisis of modernity, our time—in some ways—hardly feels different. As Richard Mouw observed, "The modernist project clearly remains a major challenge to the Christian faith in the twenty-first century."[21] The "state of *malaise*"[22] and waning religiosity of the Western world that Kuyper identified in 1898 is ongoing. In the West, we continue to grapple with the reality, as Bruce Ashford identifies, of "living within an 'immanent frame' of reference" where Christianity —theism, even!—is no longer a default worldview position and an "explosion of ideological options rush in to fill the void."[23] Kuyper's critique of modernism, in our own day, rings prophetic. What struck Kuyper as ideological fracture is in our day a seismic event: we are

---

[21]See Richard Mouw, "Kuyper and Life-Systems," in *Calvinism for a Secular Age* (Downers Grove, IL: IVP Academic, 2021), 17.

[22]Kuyper, *Lectures on Calvinism*, 173 (emphasis original). By this Kuyper means that there is some kind of ongoing discontent in the modern world. The root cause? The waning of spirituality and thus the waning of morality. This can be seen, he argues, in the upper echelons of academia (Schopenhauer, Nietzsche, etc.) but also in the masses: those resorting to anarchy or even nihilism. These many people, Kuyper argues, "would rather demolish and annihilate everything, than continue to bear the burden of present conditions."

[23]Bruce Ashford, "Kuyper and the Future," in *Calvinism for a Secular Age* (Downers Grove, IL: IVP Academic, 2021), 128.

"coming apart,"[24] as one prominent sociologist puts it; even in Kuyper's idealized America the republic has "fractured."[25]

But while the challenges of modernism that Kuyper identified in 1898 still seem true today, all has not remained unchanged. Kuyper's time is not our time. As Deborah Haarsma reminds us, "Many things in the science and faith arena have changed since Abraham Kuyper lectured in 1898."[26] Such a claim would certainly hold true in other spheres of life as well. "Scientific findings," she writes, "have exploded. The portrayal of science as an atheistic endeavor has become widespread."[27] There is, in our day, a seemingly irresolvable tension between science and faith that Christians must navigate. In such challenges, Kuyper's insistence on the importance of the Calvinist worldview remains an instructive guide in its offering of a "rich, compelling alternative: a full-bodied Christian faith, centered on Christ and Scripture, that encompasses all of life, including science"[28] and, of course, every other sphere of life.

But it is important to remember, as Vince Bacote rightly draws our attention to, that Kuyper himself does not apply Calvinism in an uncritical way. With a keen eye to the dangers of repristination and the depravity of humanity, he argues that we ought not "copy the past, as if Calvinism were a petrification, but go back to the living root of the Calvinist plant, to clean and to water it, and so to cause it to bud and to blossom once more."[29] In these final sections, we've tried to model a kind of Calvinistic pruning, taking what is good, right, and true of these lectures and the way they've been lived out by generations past and applying it to the challenges and questions of our own day.[30]

---

[24]Charles Murray, *Coming Apart: The State of White America, 1960–2010* (New York: Crown Forum, 2012).

[25]Yuval Levin, *The Fractured Republic: Renewing America's Social Contract in the Age of Individualism* (New York: Basic Books, 2016).

[26]Deborah B. Haarsma, "Kuyper and Science," in *Calvinism for a Secular Age* (Downers Grove, IL: IVP Academic, 2021), 103.

[27]Haarsma, "Kuyper and Science," 103n27.

[28]Haarsma, "Kuyper and Science," 104n28.

[29]Kuyper, *Lectures on Calvinism*, 171.

[30]This, of course, also includes naming and rooting out the problematic, troubling, and sometimes deeply damaging aspects of Kuyper's work. As we've seen in this volume, Kuyper's treatment of

THEOLOGICAL PRINCIPLES FOR
KUYPERIAN WORLDVIEWING

In moments of optimism where we might look with excitement and promise at the way Calvinism can guide and develop our engagement in every sphere of life *and* in those ominous times of crisis where Calvinism can speak an important word of assurance and corrective, Kuyper contended that the Calvinistic worldview *matters*. As Richard Mouw explained, Calvinism spells out the "big picture" of the world, setting forth "a life-system that highlights the inescapable reality of our living every moment before the face of God."[31]

But what is it about Calvinism that allows it to speak in this way, to "every department"—and, we could add, every time and season—"of life"? For Kuyper, at least three connected theological principles are woven throughout these Stone Lectures: Calvinism's claims of the sovereignty of God; its worldview that reintegrates the spheres of life; and its insistence on the full catholicity of the church, proclaiming a gospel that touches all of life.

First and foremost, as we've seen time and time again throughout these chapters, Calvinism has an overarching commitment to the sovereignty of God. In his lecture on Calvinism and religion, Kuyper insists again and again that "the confession of the absolute Sovereignty of the Triune God" remains primary, for "of Him, through Him, and unto Him are all things."[32] The "dominating principle" of Calvinism is God's sovereignty over all.[33] The confession of God's sovereignty is where the Calvinist worldview begins.

---

race is one of these aspects. In this volume, we've sought to clearly name Kuyper's strengths and weaknesses (even failures!) in his Stone Lectures, shining a light on the fullness of his work so that we can do the work of Calvinistic pruning well.

[31]Mouw, "Kuyper and Life-Systems," 19.

[32]Kuyper, *Lectures on Calvinism*, 46, cf. 58.

[33]Kuyper, *Lectures on Calvinism*, 79, cf. 22. Kuyper maintains the primacy of God's sovereignty in Calvinism. *This* is the "dominating principle," not—as many in his day, and in our own, would affirm—soteriology. While a consistent affirmation of God's sovereignty leads to important soteriological claims, these claims are not the *starting* point of Calvinism. For a helpful discussion on Calvinism's insistence on God's sovereignty—and its relation to soteriology—see Richard Mouw,

The confession of God's sovereignty has widescale implications. When Kuyper speaks of God's sovereignty, he is affirming *"the Sovereignty of the Triune God over the whole Cosmos,* in all its spheres and kingdoms, visible and invisible."[34] God is sovereign over not just our hearts and worship but over every aspect of life.[35] This foundational, primary point of Kuyper's is at the heart of his claims in the Stone Lectures and, unsurprisingly, comes through with force in the rest of his work as well. Those who know one thing of Kuyper often know his famous line at the founding of the Free University: "There is not a square inch in the whole domain of our human existence over which Christ, who is sovereign over all, does not cry: 'Mine!'"[36] Here too we hear a bold assertion of God's sovereignty.

Any claims of human authority and sovereignty must be understood, then, in the light of God's sovereignty. God is God—and we are not. But this does not leave humanity without agency. Rather, our agency and authority is *delegated* authority. In the case of politics, for example, Kuyper argues that "all authority of governments on earth originates from the Sovereignty of God alone."[37] Because all authority stems from God alone, we are also accountable to him for how we use this authority. We ought to use the authority God has granted to us in his way, for his purposes. Thankfully, we've also been left with clear patterns and signposts for how we ought to steward this authority; God has given us his Word, the good gift of his law, and even Jesus Christ as a living pattern and example so that we know how to carry out this authority properly, as God would have it—on earth, as it is in heaven. God's sovereign authority then extends over all of our lives; all

---

Calvinism in the Las Vegas Airport: Making Connections in Today's World (Grand Rapids, MI: Zondervan, 2004), 27-28.

[34]Kuyper, *Lectures on Calvinism*, 79 (emphasis original).

[35]See, for example, Kuyper's discussion on Calvinism, politics, and God's sovereignty in Kuyper, *Lectures on Calvinism*, 85, 98.

[36]Abraham Kuyper, "Sphere Sovereignty," in *Abraham Kuyper: A Centennial Reader*, ed. James D. Bratt (Grand Rapids, MI: Eerdmans, 1998), 488.

[37]Kuyper, *Lectures on Calvinism*, 82. Importantly, this authority is *given* and it is also limited. God alone is sovereign. For more on this, see Kuyper, *Lectures on Calvinism*, 96-97.

cultural spheres and all of human activity are *coram Deo*, before the face of God.[38]

Second, a worldview that begins with the affirmation of God's sovereignty is a worldview that reintegrates the spheres of life. God exercises his sovereignty over all of creation in a way that *must* form the guiding principle of every aspect of life: dogmatics, church, and piety, yes—but God's sovereignty extends beyond these to all of life, including politics, art, economics, science, and family life.[39]

This, Kuyper insists, is the genius of the Reformed worldview. It takes God's sovereignty so seriously that it insists it must affect our practice of law and medicine; it must undergird the way we pursue familial life; it animates and guides our art and philosophy. A sovereign God, as Kuyper says, "exercises its influence upon life in all its ramifications."[40] If we truly believe God is sovereign, and are rightly reading that Scripture proclaims this fact, we must produce a worldview that encompasses all of life—and Calvinism does this. Calvinism provides a reintegration of spheres (under the sovereign reign and rule of God) that have been disintegrated by the modern moral order. In a time where worldviews have been "thinn[ed]-out . . . and slic[ed]-up," stressing individuality and autonomy, the Calvinist worldview brings all things together under God's rule.[41] As Bratt affirms, Kuyper attends to the "interconnectedness of things," grounded in the sovereignty of God's rule and reign.[42]

Finally, a Calvinist worldview, built on the foundation of God's sovereignty, is one that insists on the full catholicity of the church, proclaiming a gospel that touches all of life. In these lectures, we've seen very clearly the "every square inch" nature of Kuyper's theology. Christ

---

[38]Kuyper, *Lectures on Calvinism*, 90.

[39]Kuyper, *Lectures on Calvinism*, 78, 171.

[40]Kuyper, *Lectures on Calvinism*, 194.

[41]Richard Mouw, "Mine! Kuyper for a New Century," in *Comment Magazine*, June 1, 2007, www.cardus.ca/comment/article/mine-kuyper-for-a-new-century/.

[42]James Bratt, "Preface," in *Calvinism for a Secular Age* (Downers Grove, IL: IVP Academic, 2021), xvii.

is King over "every department of human life."[43] There is nothing material or spiritual, personal or public that the gospel does not transform.

Kuyper's contemporary, Herman Bavinck, provided important theological reflection on, and language for, this important concept that is so evident in Kuyper's thinking: catholicity. In Kuyper's lectures, the language of catholicity does not occur, but Bavinck gave a rectoral address on the topic in 1888. In this address, he reminds his audience that the church fathers understood catholicity in three basic ways: (1) the local church is catholic (small *c*) because it "attaches itself to the universal church"; (2) the catholic church unites believers in all times and places; and (3) the church and the gospel it proclaims "embraces the whole of human existence."[44]

This third aspect of catholicity is where, Bavinck argued, the church has faltered. The church has failed to be catholic and thus has also failed to take God's sovereignty seriously when it proclaims a gospel that does *not* touch every aspect of our world and life. Again, Bavinck argues, this is the importance of Calvinism. Calvinism insists that the phrase "I believe in God the Father, Almighty, Creator of heaven and earth"[45] means that God is sovereign over all the things he has created, and the gospel is a story of God's redemption and restoration of those things.[46] In such an insistence, the church and the gospel it proclaims is not antagonistic to the things of the world, nor simply equivalent with the ways of the world, nor even takes the things of the world and elevates them to a new level.[47] Instead, it comes in and, like yeast in bread dough, leavens the whole thing.[48] The gospel matters in business. It matters in law. It matters in the household. It matters in the church. There certainly is self-denial, cross-bearing, and longsuffering inherent in following

---

[43]Kuyper, *Lectures on Calvinism*, 23.

[44]Herman Bavinck, "The Catholicity of Christianity and the Church," trans. John Bolt, *Calvin Theological Journal* 27 (1992): 221.

[45]Bavinck cites this line from the Apostles' Creed in Bavinck, "Catholicity," 236, cf. 237-38.

[46]This insistence that the Reformed tradition champions is not a *new* development, Bavinck argues—it is a *restoration* of how it was originally understood (Bavinck, "Catholicity," 236).

[47]Bavinck, "Catholicity," 228-31.

[48]Bavinck, "Catholicity," 231, 236.

Jesus. But there is also the "renewal of human beings" and then "by means of the Gospel [renewal of] the whole of life, state, society, and world."[49] The gospel demands that we pick up our cross and follow Jesus, but it also promises that this same Jesus is in the business of redeeming, renewing, and restoring all areas of life.

For Calvin, Bavinck argues, God's sovereignty, and thus the catholicity of the church, demands that the Bible be the "norm for all of life."[50] Such an approach to the Bible and its teaching is, in a nutshell, the importance of Calvinism. Calvinism thus presents the most coherent, all-encompassing, and most importantly, scriptural world- and life-view. Thus, we hear Kuyper's optimism (Calvinism transforms our lives and our world in line with God's creational intent) and his ominous need for a counter to the threats of his day (Calvinism is *the* robust worldview that can meet the challenges of modernity). For, as Kuyper and Bavinck both say, Calvinism proclaims the lordship of Christ over all the spheres of his creation and anticipates with eagerness the return of our King, so that all may know how wide, deep, and high is God's love—and his sovereign rule.

A KUYPERIAN ADDENDUM:
WORLDVIEW AND PIETY

Kuyper ends his lectures, however, with neither world-engaging optimism nor ominous tones of the battle with modernism. Instead, in full keeping with his insistence on the sovereignty of our God, who is the one who calls and equips us for engagement in every sphere, he reminds his listeners—and us today—that it is only through the Spirit of God that hearts will be awakened to hear this good news. We then, as Kuyper argues, ought to anticipate being used by God to proclaim this message of his all-encompassing reign and to participate with him in his work of renewing and restoring every square inch, in every sphere. Calvinism

---

[49]Bavinck, "Catholicity," 237.
[50]Bavinck, "Catholicity," 238.

is but an "Aeolian Harp" that needs the "quickening Spirit of God" to make melodious music. Thus, we stand "ready in the window of God's Holy Zion, awaiting the breath of the Spirit."[51]

There are a few moments like this throughout the Stone Lectures where we see glimmers of Kuyper's piety. He writes that "our prayer remains the deepest expression of all religious life"[52] and that "a Christianity that neglects the mystic elements grows frigid and congeals."[53] But such sentiments are not the bulk of these lectures. In them he focuses on the worldviewing, world-engaging nature of Calvinism. And, as a little volume that has sought to introduce not *all* of Kuyper's thought, but a particular work of Kuyper's, his Stone Lectures, we've focused here, too, on this aspect of his thought. We've tried to be honest in our introduction to it, not sugarcoating Kuyper's glaring faults, nor glossing over them, but letting the fullness of this text shine through, for better or worse. Alongside the "worse," we've also recognized what is good, right, and true in these lectures.

I think it would be a disservice to Kuyper's thought, however, not to include a small addendum to what we've compiled in these chapters. Al Wolters, a neo-Calvinist philosopher, has noted that the generations which followed after Kuyper were quick to pick up on his worldviewing, world-engaging themes. "Generally speaking," he writes, "neocalvinists are more noted for their intellectual ability and culture-transforming zeal than for their personal godliness or their living relationship with Jesus Christ."[54]

Whatever the cause,[55] such an emphasis has, at times, failed to accentuate that Kuyper was not only an important guide for the pursuit

---

[51]Kuyper, *Lectures on Calvinism*, 199.
[52]Kuyper, *Lectures on Calvinism*, 46.
[53]Kuyper, *Lectures on Calvinism*, 188.
[54]Al Wolters, "What Is to Be Done . . . Toward a Neocalvinist Agenda?," in *Comment Magazine*, December 1, 2005, www.cardus.ca/comment/article/what-is-to-be-done-toward-a-neocalvinist -agenda/.
[55]Perhaps some of this has to do with the fact that these Stone Lectures were much of what was accessible for English-speaking Kuyperians for quite some time. Only in the past few decades has much more of Kuyper's work been available in English. As Bratt notes in his preface, there have been multiple Kuyper volumes translated into English in just the past decade, including the Lexham Press series *Abraham Kuyper Collected Works in Public Theology*, eds. Melvin Flikkema and Jordan J. Ballor, 12 vols. (Bellingham, WA: Lexham Press), accessed April 20, 2020, https://lexhampress.com/product/55067/abraham-kuyper-collected-works-in-public-theology.

of faithful cultural and political engagement but also a man of deep piety and strong devotional life who wrote many meditations on the spiritual life, including *Near unto God*.

Kuyper's nightly routine can, perhaps, begin to shed a little bit of light on this aspect of his life and work. Each night, Kuyper would face the cross on his bedroom wall and confess that—yet again—he had not done enough to share in the sufferings of Jesus throughout his day.[56] This is, perhaps, a different picture of Kuyper than we might conjure up by simply reading the Stone Lectures, but it is nonetheless an important part of his life and thought.

For Kuyper, piety and practice, worldviewing and spiritual meditations were not antagonistic, but necessarily fed into one another. Kuyper's insistence that we must understand God's call for "every square inch" of our work and public life was paired with his equally strong insistence that we must be "near unto God" in piety, prayer, and worship.

In the end, the world-engaging, worldviewing nature of Kuyperian thought that loudly affirms God's call on every aspect of our lives is deeply tied to personal piety and intimacy with God. Kuyper himself weaves the two together in a mediation on Mark 12:30 in *Near unto God*. He writes:

> Everyone has some sort of view of the world, some ethical or moral and religious porch from which to look out at all that we can see and know of God's creation. What is of utmost importance is that God Almighty does not stay in the kitchen or the study or the family room when we view the world from that porch. . . .
>
> But our mind's capacity is not limited to our personal concept of God. To *think* Christianly—and to do so deeply—requires a comprehensive understanding of history, of doctrine, of science, of what is known in many, many areas. History itself is a blessing.

In addition to these works, a new volume of Kuyper's meditations, *Honey from the Rock* (Bellingham, WA: Lexham Press, 2018) has been translated. This volume, alongside Kuyper's well-known meditations, *Near unto God*, begins to give us a wonderful picture of Kuyper's piety.

[56]Richard J. Mouw, *All That God Cares About: Common Grace and Divine Delight* (Grand Rapids, MI: Baker Academic, 2020), 7.

And yet, loving God with the mind is more than imbibing academic knowledge. We *do* far more than *read* on any given day. What we eat, how we choose to spend our leisure time, how we behave when working— these things are the work of the mind at a very personal level, and they too need to be considered in our understanding of loving God. Our time is Christ's time, after all. . . .

One doesn't put on Christianity. Pushing and yearning will get us nowhere. Coming near unto God is a matter of knowing deeply how much he loves us and then giving him our lives in thanksgiving.

Love for God that comes from the heart and the soul is very much a matter of his planting. He is the source of our own devotion to him. But the mind is slightly different. We can train ourselves to think about him deeply, to work at accomplishing his will, to structure our lives in such a way that praise is in our every step. That process itself will bring us ever closer to God.[57]

In this brief meditation, Kuyper conveys his conviction that the gospel is not *either* public *or* private. It touches every aspect of our life: our public life and our personal devotion.

The message that Kuyper gives us within these lectures is an exciting one. For me, and many others, it has helped to orient the way in which the good news of the gospel of Jesus Christ matters in science, politics, art, and economics—and even in the work of neighborhood associations and school boards, cooking dinner and childcare, playing basketball and plucking weeds, and a host of other seemingly mundane tasks. But as we engage this vision of public, cultural discipleship, let us not forget Kuyper's insistence on the importance of being near unto God. After all, we are but an "Aeolian Harp—absolutely powerless, as it is, without the quickening of the Spirit of God."[58]

In steadfast trust and hope that our God is indeed sovereign, may we offer our full selves to his service, in every sphere of life.

---

[57] Abraham Kuyper, "With All Thy Mind," in *Near unto God*, trans. James C. Schaap (Grand Rapids, MI: Eerdmans, 1997), 95 (emphasis original).

[58] Kuyper, *Lectures on Calvinism*, 199.

LIST OF
CONTRIBUTORS

Bruce Riley Ashford (PhD, Southeastern Baptist Theological Seminary) is a professor, speaker, columnist, speech writer, and political consultant. He is senior fellow at the Kirby Laing Centre for Public Theology. He is a columnist for *First Things Magazine* and is the author or coauthor of nine books, including *The Doctrine of Creation, The Gospel of Our King, Letters to an American Christian, One Nation Under God: A Christian Hope for American Politics,* and *Every Square Inch: An Introduction to Cultural Engagement for Christians.*

Vincent Bacote (PhD, Drew University) is professor of theology and director of the Center for Applied Christian Ethics at Wheaton College. His publications include *The Spirit in Public Theology: Appropriating the Legacy of Abraham Kuyper* and *Reckoning with Race and Performing the Good News: In Search of a Better Evangelical Theology.*

James D. Bratt (PhD, Yale University) is professor of history emeritus at Calvin University. He is the author of *Abraham Kuyper: Modern Calvinist, Christian Democrat,* and editor of *Abraham Kuyper: A Centennial Reader,* providing English translations of Kuyper's most important shorter works.

Adrienne Dengerink Chaplin (PhD, Free University of Amsterdam) is a visiting research fellow at King's College London and a research associate at the Margaret Beaufort Institute in Cambridge. She has taught at the Institute for Christian Studies in Toronto, and has served as the co-president of the Canadian Society for Aesthetics. She is the founding curator of the traveling exhibition *Art, Conflict & Remembering: The*

Murals of the Bogside Artists, and the coauthor of *Art and Soul: Signposts for Christians in the Arts* and *The Philosophy of Susanne Langer: Embodied Meaning in Logic, Art and Feeling.*

Jonathan Chaplin (PhD, University of London) is senior fellow of Cardus, associate fellow at the UK think tank Theos, and a member of the divinity faculty at the University of Cambridge. He is former director of the Kirby Laing Institute for Christian Ethics, Cambridge, and associate professor of political theory at the Institute for Christian Studies, Toronto. He is author or editor of many books, articles, and journal special issues. His most recent book is *Faith in Democracy: Framing a Politics of Deep Diversity.*

James Eglinton (PhD, University of Edinburgh) is Meldrum Senior Lecturer in Reformed Theology at the University of Edinburgh. His most recent book, *Bavinck: A Critical Biography*, won the Gospel Coalition 2020 History and Biography Book of the Year, and was a Biography and Memoir finalist at the ECPA Christian Book Awards 2021. He is also author of *Trinity and Organism*, translator of *Christian Worldview* and *Herman Bavinck on Preaching and Preachers*, and coeditor of *Neo-Calvinism and the French Revolution*. His writings have also been featured in *The Times, Christianity Today, The Herald, The Gospel Coalition*, and *Desiring God.*

Deborah B. Haarsma (PhD, Massachusetts Institute of Technology) is president of BioLogos and an experienced research astronomer. She writes often on science and faith, including contributions to *Four Views on Creation, Evolution, and Intelligent Design* and *Christ and the Created Order*. She is the coauthor of *Origins* with her husband and fellow physicist, Loren Haarsma.

George Harinck (PhD, Free University of Amsterdam) is professor of history at the Free University of Amsterdam, and professor and director of the Neo-Calvinism Research Institute at Theological University of Kampen. He studied history at Leiden University and has published widely on the (international) history of neo-Calvinism and Dutch Protestantism since 1800.

Jessica R. Joustra (PhD, Fuller Theological Seminary and the Free University of Amsterdam) is assistant professor of religion and theology at Redeemer University and an associate researcher at the Neo-Calvinism Research Institute at the Theological University of Kampen. She is an editor and translator of Herman Bavinck's *Reformed Ethics* and associate editor for the *Bavinck Review*.

Robert J. Joustra (PhD, University of Bath) is associate professor of politics and international studies and the founding director of the Centre for Christian Scholarship at Redeemer University. He is editor and author of several books, including *The Religious Problem with Religious Freedom: Why Foreign Policy Needs Political Theology* and *How to Survive the Apocalypse: Zombies, Cylons, Faith, and Politics at the End of the World*.

Richard J. Mouw (PhD, University of Chicago) is president emeritus at Fuller Theological Seminary, and senior research scholar at the Paul B. Henry Institute for the Study of Christianity and Politics at Calvin University. He is the author of several books and essays on Abraham Kuyper's thought, including *Abraham Kuyper: A Short and Personal Introduction*.

BIBLIOGRAPHY

Abraham Kuyper Papers. Historical Documentation Center for Dutch Protestantism. Vrije Universiteit Amsterdam.

Adonis, J. C. "The Role of Abraham Kuyper in South Africa: A Critical Historical Evaluation." In Van der Kooi and De Bruijn, *Kuyper Reconsidered*, 259-72.

Algemeen Handelsblad. "Dr. Kuyper naar Amerika." January 16, 1897.

Ashford, Bruce Riley. *Letters to an American Christian*. Nashville: B&H Publishing, 2018.

———. "What Hath Nature to Do with Grace? A Theological Vision for Higher Education." *Southeastern Theological Review* 7, no. 1 (Summer 2016): 3-22.

Ashton, Ethel. "Dr. Abraham Kuyper." *The American Daily Standard*, January 10, 1921.

———. "Een herinnering aan den zomer van 1898." In *Herinneringen van de oude garde aan den persoon en levensarbeid van Dr. A. Kuyper*. Edited by Henriëtta Sophia Susanna Kuyper and Johanna Hendrika Kuyper. Amsterdam: W. ten Have, 1922.

———. *Gedenkboek ter herinnering aan het overlijden van Dr. A. Kuyper en de sprake die daarbij uit de pers voortkwam*. Amsterdam: W. ten Have, 1921.

———. *Onder Neerlands vlag: Album ter herdenking van het vijf en twintig jarig bestaan van den Nederlandschen militairen bond, 1874–1899*. Amsterdam: Van Holkema & Warendorf, 1899.

Audi, Robert, and Nicholas Wolterstorff. *Religion in the Public Square: The Place of Religious Convictions in Public Debate*. Lanham, MD: Rowman & Littlefield, 1997.

Bacote, Vincent E. "Critical Thinking Is Obeying the Commandment of Loving Your Neighbor as Yourself." Interview by Bart Noort. *Theological University Kampen Magazine*, December 2014.

———. *The Spirit in Public Theology: Appropriating the Legacy of Abraham Kuyper*. Grand Rapids, MI: Baker Academic, 2005.

Bailey, Justin. *Reimagining Apologetics*. Downers Grove, IL: IVP Academic, forthcoming.

Ballor, Jordan J., and Robert Joustra, eds. *The Church's Social Responsibility: Reflections on Evangelicalism and Social Justice*. Grand Rapids, MI: Acton Institute, 2015.

Bancroft, George. *History of the United States from the Discovery of the American Continent to the Declaration of Independence*. 15th ed. Boston: Little, Brown, 1853.

Barbour, Ian G. *Religion and Science: Historical and Contemporary Issues*. Rev. ed. San Francisco: HarperSanFrancisco, 1997.

Barna Group. *Gen Z: The Culture, Beliefs, and Motivations Shaping the Next Generation*. Ventura, CA: Barna Group, 2018.

Barth, Karl. *Church Dogmatics* I.2. Edited by G. W. Bromiley and T. F. Torrance. Translated by G. T. Thomson and Harold Knight. Edinburgh: T&T Clark, 1980.

Bartholomew, Craig. *Contours of the Kuyperian Tradition: A Systematic Introduction*. Downers Grove, IL: IVP Academic, 2017.

Bartholomew, Craig, ed. *In the Fields of the Lord: A Calvin Seerveld Reader*. Carlisle, UK: Piquant, 2000.

Bavinck, Herman. *Bilderdijk als denker en dichter*. Kampen: Kok, 1906.

———. "The Catholicity of Christianity and the Church." Translated by John Bolt. *Calvin Theological Journal* 27 (1992): 221-51.

———. "Defining Religious Consciousness: The Five Magnetic Points." In *The J. H. Bavinck Reader*, edited by John Bolt, James D. Bratt, and Paul J. Visser, translated by James A. De Jong, 145-98. Grand Rapids, MI: Eerdmans, 2013.

———. "Herman Bavinck's 'Common Grace.'" Translated by Raymond C. Van Leeuwen. *Calvin Theological Journal* 24, no. 1 (1989): 35-65.

———. "Recent Dogmatic Thought in the Netherlands." *The Presbyterian and Reformed Review* 3, no. 10 (1892): 209-28.

Begbie, Jeremy. *Voicing Creation's Praise: Towards a Theology of the Arts*. Edinburgh: T&T Clark, 1991.

Benedict, Philip. "Calvinism as Culture? Preliminary Remarks on Calvinism and the Visual Arts." In *Seeing Beyond the Word: Visual Arts and the Calvinist Tradition*. Edited by Paul Corby Finney. Grand Rapids, MI: Eerdmans, 1999.

Benjamin B. Warfield Papers. Special Collections. Princeton Theological Seminary Libraries. Princeton, NJ.

Bennett, Kyle D. *Practices of Love: Spiritual Disciplines for the Life of the World*. Grand Rapids, MI: Brazos Press, 2017.

BioLogos. "BioLogos." Accessed October 19, 2019. https://biologos.org/.

Boesak, Allan. *Black and Reformed: Apartheid, Liberation, and the Calvinist Tradition*. New York: Orbis Press, 1984.

Bolt, John. *A Free Church, A Holy Nation: Abraham Kuyper's Public Theology*. Grand Rapids, MI: Eerdmans, 2001.

Bonhoeffer, Dietrich. *Letters and Papers from Prison*. Edited by Eberhard Bethge. New York: Touchstone, 1971.

Botman, H. Russel. "Is Blood Thicker Than Justice? The Legacy of Abraham Kuyper for Southern Africa." In *Religion, Pluralism, and Public Life: Abraham Kuyper's Legacy for the Twenty-First Century*, edited by Luis E. Lugo, 342-61. Grand Rapids, MI: Eerdmans, 2000.

Bowlin, John, ed. *The Kuyper Center Review*. Vol. 4, *Calvinism and Democracy*. Grand Rapids, MI: Eerdmans, 2014.

Brand, Hilary, and Adrienne Chaplin. *Art and Soul: Signposts for Christians in the Arts*. Downers Grove, IL: InterVarsity Press, 2007.

Bratt, James D., ed. *Abraham Kuyper: A Centennial Reader*. Grand Rapids, MI: Eerdmans, 1998.

———. *Abraham Kuyper: Modern Calvinist, Christian Democrat*. Grand Rapids, MI: Eerdmans, 2013.

———. "Calvinism in North America." In *John Calvin's Impact on Church and Society, 1509–2009*, edited by Martin Ernst Hirzel and Martin Sallmann, 49-66. Grand Rapids, MI: Eerdmans, 2009.

———. "De Erfenis van Kuyper in Noord Amerika" [Kuyper's Legacy in North America]. In *Abraham Kuyper: zijn volksdeel, zijn invloed*, edited by C. Augustijn, J. H. Prins, and H. E. S. Woldring, 203-28. Delft: Meinema, 1987.

———. *Dutch Calvinism in Modern America: A History of a Conservative Subculture*. Grand Rapids, MI: Eerdmans, 1984.

———. "The Reformed Churches and Acculturation." In *The Dutch in America: Immigration, Settlement, and Cultural Change*, edited by Robert P. Swierenga, 191-208. New Brunswick, NJ: Rutgers University Press, 1984.

Calvin, John. *Institutes of the Christian Religion*. Edited by John McNeill. Translated by Ford Lewis Battles. 2 vols. Philadelphia: Westminster Press, 1960.

Camacho, Daniel José. "Common Grace and Race." *The Twelve Blog by Reformed Journal*, March 26, 2014. https://blog.reformedjournal.com/2014/03/26/common -grace-and-race-2/.

Campbell, Heidi A., and Heather Looy, eds. *A Science and Religion Primer*. Grand Rapids, MI: Baker Academic, 2009.

Cardus. "Comment Magazine." Accessed April 6, 2020. www.cardus.ca/comment/.

———. "Work & Economics—Cardus." Accessed April 6, 2020. www.cardus.ca /research/work-economics/.

Carlson-Thies, Stanley, and James W. Skillen, eds. *Welfare in America: Christian Perspectives on a Policy in Crisis*. Grand Rapids, MI: Eerdmans, 1996.

Center for Public Justice. "The Center for Public Justice." Accessed April 6, 2020. www.cpjustice.org.

———. "Public Justice Review: A Publication of the Center for Public Justice." Accessed April 6, 2020. www.cpjustice.org/public/public_justice_review.

Chaplin, Jonathan. "Civil Society and the State: The Neo-Calvinist Perspective." In *Christianity and Civil Society: Catholic and Neo-Calvinist Perspectives*, edited by Jeanne Heffernan Schindler, 67-96. Lanham, MD: Lexington, 2008.

———. *Herman Dooyeweerd: Christian Philosopher of State and Civil Society*. Notre Dame, IN: University of Notre Dame Press, 2016.

———. *Multiculturalism: A Christian Retrieval*. London: Theos, 2011.

———. "Rejecting Neutrality, Respecting Diversity: From 'Liberal Pluralism' to 'Christian Pluralism.'" *Christian Scholar's Review* 35, no. 2 (Winter 2006): 143-75.

Christian Farmers Federation of Ontario. "Christian Farmers Federation of Ontario." Accessed April 6, 2020. www.christianfarmers.org/.

The Christian Intelligencer. Unsigned review of "Calvinism and Confessional Revision," by Abraham Kuyper. July 29, 1891.

Citizens for Public Justice. "Citizens for Public Justice." Accessed April 6, 2020. https://cpj.ca/.

CLAC. "CLAC: Better Together." Accessed April 6, 2020. www.clac.ca/.

Copan, Paul, Tremper Longman III, Christopher L. Reese, and Michael G. Strauss, eds. *The Dictionary of Christianity and Science: The Definitive Reference for the Intersection of Christian Faith and Contemporary Science*. Grand Rapids, MI: Zondervan, 2017.

De Brès, Guido. *The Belgic Confession*. 1561. English translation available in *Our Faith: Ecumenical Creeds, Reformed Confessions, and Other Resources*, 25-68. Grand Rapids, MI: Faith Alive Christian Resources, 2013.

De Jong, Marinus. *The Church Is the Means, the World Is the End: Klaas Schilder's Thought on the Relationship Between Church and World*. PhD diss., Theologische Universiteit Kampen, 2019.

De Vries, John. *Beyond the Atom: An Appraisal of Our Christian Faith in This Age of Atomic Science*. 2nd ed. Grand Rapids, MI: Eerdmans, 1950.

Dennison, James T., Jr., ed. *The Letters of Geerhardus Vos*. Phillipsburg, NJ: P&R Publishing, 2005.

Donaldson, Dave, and Stanley Carlson-Thies. *A Revolution of Compassion: Faith-Based Groups as Full Partners in Fighting America's Social Problems*. Grand Rapids, MI: Baker Books, 2003.

Ecklund, Elaine Howard. *Religion vs. Science: What Religious People Really Think*. Oxford: Oxford University Press, 2018.

———. *Science vs. Religion: What Scientists Really Think*. Oxford: Oxford University Press, 2012.

Ecklund, Elaine Howard, and Christopher Scheitle. "Religious Communities, Science, Scientists, and Perceptions: A Comprehensive Survey." Paper prepared for presentation at the Annual Meetings of the American Association for the

Advancement of Science. February 16, 2014. www.aaas.org/sites/default/files /content_files/RU_AAASPresentationNotes_2014_0219%20%281%29.pdf.

Eglinton, James. *Trinity and Organism: Towards a New Reading of Herman Bavinck's Organic Motif*. London: T&T Clark, 2012.

Ensminger, Sven. *Karl Barth's Theology as a Resource for a Christian Theology of Religions*. London: T&T Clark, 2016.

Finney, Paul Corby, ed. *Seeing Beyond the Word: Visual Arts and the Calvinist Tradition*. Grand Rapids, MI: Eerdmans, 1999.

Flatt, Kevin. *After Evangelicalism: The Sixties and the United Church of Canada*. Montreal: McGill-Queen's University Press, 2013.

Flipse, Abraham C. "Creation and Evolution: History of the Debate in the Netherlands." BioLogos, November 17, 2014. https://biologos.org/articles/creation-and -evolution-history-of-the-debate-in-the-netherlands.

Glenn, Charles L. *The Ambiguous Embrace: Government and Faith-Based Schools and Social Agencies*. Princeton, NJ: Princeton University Press, 2000.

Goudzwaard, Bob. *Aid for the Overdeveloped West*. Toronto: Wedge, 1975.

———. *Capitalism and Progress: A Diagnosis of Western Society*. Grand Rapids, MI: Eerdmans; Toronto: Wedge Publishing, 1979.

———. *Globalization and the Kingdom of God*. Grand Rapids, MI: Baker Books, 2001.

Goudzwaard, Bob, and Craig G. Bartholomew. *Beyond the Modern Age: An Archaeology of Contemporary Culture*. Downers Grove, IL: IVP Academic, 2017.

Goudzwaard, Bob, and Harry de Lange. *Beyond Poverty and Affluence: Towards a Canadian Economy of Care*. Toronto: University of Toronto, 1994.

Gould, Lewis L. "1912 Republican Convention: Return of the Rough Rider." *Smithsonian Magazine*, August 2008. www.smithsonianmag.com/history/1912 -republican-convention-855607/.

Graham, Gordon, ed. *The Kuyper Center Review*. Vol. 3, *Calvinism and Culture*. Grand Rapids, MI: Eerdmans, 2013.

Griffis, William Elliot. *The American in Holland: Sentimental Rambles in the Eleven Provinces of the Netherlands*. Boston: Houghton Mifflin, 1899.

———. "An Evening with Dr. Kuyper." *The Christian Intelligencer*, August 31, 1892.

———. "The Inauguration of Queen Wilhelmina." *The Christian Intelligencer*, September 21, 1898.

Grundlach, Bradley J. "Protestant Evangelicals." In *The Warfare Between Science and Religion: The Idea That Wouldn't Die*. Edited by Jeff Hardin, Ronald L. Numbers, and Ronald A. Binzley. Baltimore, MD: Johns Hopkins University Press, 2018.

Guinness, Os. *The Global Public Square: Religious Freedom and the Making of a World Safe for Diversity*. Downers Grove, IL: InterVarsity Press, 2013.

Haan, Roelf. *The Economics of Honour: Biblical Reflections on Money and Property.* Grand Rapids, MI: Eerdmans, 2009.

Haarsma, Deborah B., and Loren D. Haarsma. *Origins: Christian Perspectives on Creation, Evolution, and Intelligent Design.* Grand Rapids, MI: Faith Alive Christian Resources, 2011.

Hardin, Jeff, Ronald L. Numbers, and Ronald A. Binzley, eds. *The Warfare Between Science and Religion: The Idea That Wouldn't Die.* Baltimore, MD: Johns Hopkins University Press, 2018.

Harinck, George. "Abraham Kuyper, South Africa, and Apartheid." Speech at the opening ceremony of the Abraham Kuyper Institute for Public Theology at Princeton Theological Seminary. *The Princeton Seminary Bulletin* 23, no. 2 (Spring 2002): 184-87.

———. "D. J. Doornink and the Early Years of the Dutch-American Book Selling Trade (1860 to 1880)." In *Across Borders: Dutch Migration to North America and Australia*, edited by Jacob E. Nyenhuis, Suzanne M. Sinke, and Robert P. Swierenga, 113-34. Holland: Van Raalte Press, 2010.

———. "Geerhardus Vos as Introducer of Kuyper in America." In *The Dutch-American Experience: Essays in Honor of Robert. P. Swierenga*, edited by Hans Krabbendam and Larry J. Wagenaar, 242-62. Amsterdam: VU Uitgeverij, 2000.

———, ed. *Kuyper in America: "This Is Where I Was Meant to Be."* Sioux Center, IA: Dordt College Press, 2012.

———. "Neo-Calvinism and Democracy: An Overview from the Mid-Nineteenth Century till the Second World War." In *The Kuyper Center Review.* Vol. 4, *Calvinism and Democracy*, edited by John Bowlin, 1-20. Grand Rapids, MI: Eerdmans, 2014.

———. "A Triumphal Procession? The Reception of Kuyper in the USA (1900–1940)." In Van der Kooi and De Bruijn, *Kuyper Reconsidered*, 273-82.

———. *"We Live Presently Under a Waning Moon": Nicolaus Martin Steffens as Leader of the Reformed Church in America in the West in Years of Transition (1878–1895).* Holland: Van Raalte Press, 2013.

———. "Wipe Out Lines of Division (Not Distinctions)." *Journal of Reformed Theology* 11, no. 1-2 (January 2017): 81-98.

The Heidelberg Catechism. 1563. English translation available in *Our Faith: Ecumenical Creeds, Reformed Confessions, and Other Resources*, 25-68. Grand Rapids, MI: Faith Alive Christian Resources, 2013.

Heslam, Peter. *Creating a Christian Worldview: Abraham Kuyper's Lectures on Calvinism.* Grand Rapids, MI: Eerdmans, 1998.

Hiemstra, John L. "A Calvinist Case for Tolerant Public Pluralism: The Religious Sources of Abraham Kuyper's Public Philosophy." *Religious Studies and Theology* 34, no. 1 (2015): 53-83.

History Matters. "Bryan's 'Cross of Gold' Speech: Mesmerizing the Masses." Accessed May 1, 2020. http://historymatters.gmu.edu/d/5354/.

Hoezee, Scott. *Proclaim the Wonder: Engaging Science on Sunday.* Grand Rapids, MI: Baker Books, 2003.

Holifield, E. Brooks. *Theology in America: From the Age of the Puritans to the Civil War.* New Haven, CT: Yale University Press, 2003.

Holmes, Arthur F. *Contours of a World View.* Grand Rapids, MI: Eerdmans, 1983.

Hough, Franklin B. *American Constitutions: Comprising the Constitution of Each State in the Union, and of the United States, with the Declaration of Independence and Articles of Confederation* [. . .]. 2 vols. Albany: Weed, Parsons & Co., 1871–1872.

Inazu, John. *Confident Pluralism: Surviving and Thriving Through Deep Difference.* Chicago: University of Chicago Press, 2016.

Joustra, Robert, and Alissa Wilkinson. *How to Survive the Apocalypse: Zombies, Cylons, Faith, and Politics at the End of the World.* Grand Rapids, MI: Eerdmans, 2016.

Kaemingk, Matthew. *Christian Hospitality and Muslim Immigration in an Age of Fear.* Grand Rapids, MI: Eerdmans, 2018.

Kemeny, P. C., ed. *Church, State, and Public Justice: Five Views.* Downers Grove, IL: InterVarsity Press, 2007.

Koyzis, David T. *Political Visions & Illusions: A Survey & Critique of Contemporary Ideologies.* 2nd ed. Downers Grove, IL: IVP Academic, 2019.

———. *We Answer to Another: Authority, Office, and the Image of God.* Eugene, OR: Pickwick Publications, 2014.

Kuiper, Dirk Th. "Groen and Kuyper on the Racial Issue." In Van der Kooi and De Bruijn, *Kuyper Reconsidered,* 69-81.

Kuipers, Tjitze. *Abraham Kuyper: An Annotated Bibliography, 1857–2010.* Leiden: Brill, 2011.

Kuyper, Abraham. *Abraham Kuyper Collected Works in Public Theology.* Edited by Melvin Flikkema and Jordan J. Ballor. 12 vols. (unnumbered). Bellingham, WA: Lexham Press.

———. *Antirevolutionaire staatkunde.* 2 vols. Kampen: Kok, 1916–1917.

———. *Bilderdijk en zijn nationale beteekenis.* Amsterdam: Höveker & Wormer, 1906.

———. "Calvinism: Source and Stronghold of Our Constitutional Liberties." In Bratt, *Abraham Kuyper: A Centennial Reader,* 279-322.

———. "Calvinism and Art." Translated by John H. De Vries. In *Christian Thought: Lectures and Papers on Philosophy, Christian Evidence, Biblical Elucidation.* Vol. 9 (February 1892): 259-82; (June 1892): 447-59.

———. "Calvinism and Confessional Revision." Translated by Geerhardus Vos. *The Presbyterian and Reformed Review.* Vol. 2, no. 7 (July 1891): 369-99.

———. "Common Grace." In Bratt, *Abraham Kuyper: A Centennial Reader,* 165-204.

——. *Guidance for Christian Engagement in Government.* Translated and edited by Harry Van Dyke. Grand Rapids, MI: Christian's Library Press, 2013.

——. *Het calvinisme, oorsprong en waarborg onzer constitutioneele vrijheden.* Amsterdam: B. van der Land, 1874.

——. *Honey from the Rock: Daily Devotions from Young Kuyper.* Translated by James A. De Jong. Bellingham, WA: Lexham Press, 2018.

——. *Lectures on Calvinism.* 1931. Reprint, Grand Rapids, MI: Eerdmans, 1999.

——. "Manual Labor." In Bratt, *Abraham Kuyper: A Centennial Reader,* 231-54.

——. "Modernism: A Fata Morgana in the Christian Domain." In Bratt, *Abraham Kuyper: A Centennial Reader,* 87-124.

——. *On the Church.* Edited by John Halsey Wood Jr. and Andrew M. McGinnis. *Abraham Kuyper Collected Works in Public Theology,* edited by Melvin Flikkema and Jordan J. Ballor. Bellingham, WA: Lexham Press, 2016.

——. "Pantheism's Destruction of Boundaries." Translated by John H. De Vries. *The Methodist Review* 75, no. 4 (July/August 1893): 520-37; no. 5 (September /October 1893): 762-78.

——. *Pro Rege: Living Under Christ's Kingship: Volume 3.* Edited by John Kok with Nelson D. Kloosterman. Translated by Albert Gootjes. *Abraham Kuyper Collected Works in Public Theology,* edited by Melvin Flikkema and Jordan J. Ballor. Bellingham, WA: Lexham Press, 2019.

——. *The Problem of Poverty.* Edited by James W. Skillen. Grand Rapids, MI: Baker Books, 1991.

——. *Scholarship: Two Convocation Addresses on University Life.* Translated by Harry Van Dyke. Grand Rapids, MI: Christian's Library Press, 2014.

——. "The Social Question and the Christian Religion." In *Makers of Modern Christian Social Thought: Leo XIII and Abraham Kuyper on the Social Question,* edited by Jordan J. Ballor, 45-118. Grand Rapids, MI: Acton Institute, 2016.

——. "The South African Crisis." In Bratt, *Abraham Kuyper: A Centennial Reader,* 323-60.

——. *Souvereiniteit in eigen kring.* Kampen: Kok, 1930.

——. *Souvereiniteit in eigen kring: Rede ter inwijding van de Vrije Universiteit, den 20sten October 1880 gehouden, in het Koor der Nieuwe Kerk te Amsterdam.* Amsterdam: J. H. Kruyt, 1880.

——. "Sphere Sovereignty." In Bratt, *Abraham Kuyper: A Centennial Reader,* 461-90.

——. *Wisdom and Wonder: Common Grace in Science and Art.* Edited by Jordan J. Ballor and Stephen J. Grabill. Translated by Nelson D. Kloosterman. Grand Rapids, MI: Christian's Library Press, 2011.

——. "With All Thy Mind." In *Near unto God.* Translated by James C. Schaap. Grand Rapids, MI: Eerdmans, 1997.

Kuyper, Henriëtta Sophia Susanna, and Johanna Hendrika Kuyper, eds. *Herinneringen van de oude garde aan den persoon en levensarbeid van Dr. A. Kuyper*. Amsterdam: W. ten Have, 1922.

Legutko, Ryszard. *The Demon in Democracy: Totalitarian Temptations in Free Societies*. New York: Encounter Books, 2016.

Lever, Jan. *Creation and Evolution*. Translated by Peter G. Berkhout. Grand Rapids, MI: Grand Rapids International Press, 1958.

Levin, Yuval. *The Fractured Republic: Renewing America's Social Contract in the Age of Individualism*. New York: Basic Books, 2016.

Lodge, Henry Cabot. *Alexander Hamilton*. Boston, 1892.

Lugo, Luis E., ed. *Religion, Pluralism, and Public Life: Abraham Kuyper's Legacy for the Twenty-First Century*. Grand Rapids, MI: Eerdmans, 2000.

Mahoney, Daniel J. *The Idol of Our Age: How the Religion of Humanity Subverts Christianity*. New York: Encounter Books, 2018.

Manent, Pierre. "La tentation de l'humanitaire." *Géopolitique*, no. 68 (2000): 5-10.

Marshall, Paul. *God and the Constitution: Christianity and American Politics*. Lanham, MD: Rowman & Littlefield, 2002.

McGoldrick, James Edward. *God's Renaissance Man: Abraham Kuyper*. Darlington, UK: Evangelical Press, 2000.

Menninga, Clarence. "History of Geology at Calvin College." Lecture presented at Calvin College 125th anniversary celebration, April 10, 2001. Accessed July 19, 2021. https://studylib.net/doc/14496792.

Monsma, Stephen V. *Healing for a Broken World: Christian Perspectives on Public Policy*. Wheaton, IL: Crossway, 2008.

———. *Pluralism and Freedom: Faith-Based Organizations in a Democratic Society*. Lanham, MD: Rowman & Littlefield, 2012.

———. *Positive Neutrality: Letting Religious Freedom Ring*. Grand Rapids, MI: Baker Books, 1993.

Monsma, Stephen V., and Stanley W. Carlson-Thies. *Free to Serve: Protecting the Religious Freedom of Faith-Based Organizations*. Grand Rapids, MI: Brazos Press, 2015.

Monsma, Stephen V., and J. Christopher Soper, eds. *Equal Treatment of Religion in a Pluralistic Society*. Grand Rapids, MI: Eerdmans, 1998.

Mouw, Richard J. *Abraham Kuyper: A Short and Personal Introduction*. Grand Rapids, MI: Eerdmans, 2011.

———. *All That God Cares About: Common Grace and Divine Delight*. Grand Rapids, MI: Baker Academic, 2020.

———. *Calvinism in the Las Vegas Airport: Making Connections in Today's World*. Grand Rapids, MI: Zondervan, 2004.

———. *He Shines in All That's Fair: Culture and Common Grace*. Grand Rapids, MI: Eerdmans, 2001.

———. "Mine! Kuyper for a New Century." In *Comment Magazine*. June 1, 2007. www.cardus.ca/comment/article/mine-kuyper-for-a-new-century/.

———. *Uncommon Decency: Christian Civility in an Uncivil World*. Downers Grove, IL: InterVarsity Press, 1992.

Mouw, Richard J., and Sander Griffioen. *Pluralisms and Horizons: An Essay in Christian Public Philosophy*. Grand Rapids, MI: Eerdmans, 1993.

Mozur, Paul, and Ian Johnson. "China Sentences Wang Yi, Christian Pastor, to 9 Years in Prison." *New York Times*, January 2, 2020. www.nytimes.com/2019/12/30/world/asia/china-wang-yi-christian-sentence.html.

Murray, Charles. *Coming Apart: The State of White America, 1960–2010*. New York: Crown Forum, 2012.

Naber, S. A. *Levensbericht van Allard Pierson*. Amsterdam: Johannes Müller, 1898.

Nicholson, Robert. "Is the Struggle with Islam Reshaping the Modern World? An Interview with Shadi Hamid." *Providence*, September 25, 2018. https://providencemag.com/2018/09/struggle-islam-reshaping-modern-world-interview-shadi-hamid/.

Noll, Mark. *America's God: From Jonathan Edwards to Abraham Lincoln*. New York: Oxford University Press, 2002.

———. *Jesus Christ and the Life of the Mind*. Grand Rapids, MI: Eerdmans, 2011.

———. *The Scandal of the Evangelical Mind*. Grand Rapids, MI: Eerdmans, 1994.

Numbers, Ronald. *The Creationists: The Evolution of Scientific Creationism*. New York: Knopf, 1992.

Paris, Peter J. "The African and African-American Understanding of Our Common Humanity: A Critique of Abraham Kuyper's Anthropology." In Lugo, *Religion, Pluralism, and Public Life*, 271-72.

Parsons, William B., ed. *Being Spiritual but Not Religious: Past, Present, Future(s)*. Abingdon, UK: Routledge, 2018.

Pew Research Center. "Elaborating on the Views of AAAS Scientists, Issue by Issue." July 23, 2015. www.pewresearch.org/science/2015/07/23/elaborating-on-the-views-of-aaas-scientists-issue-by-issue/.

———. "Public's Views on Human Evolution." December 30, 2013. www.pewforum.org/2013/12/30/publics-views-on-human-evolution/.

———. "Strong Role of Religion in Views About Evolution and Perceptions of Scientific Consensus." October 22, 2015. www.pewresearch.org/science/2015/10/22/strong-role-of-religion-in-views-about-evolution-and-perceptions-of-scientific-consensus/.

Pinson, J. Matthew, Matthew Steven Bracey, Matthew McAffee, and Michael A. Oliver. *Sexuality, Gender, and the Church*. Nashville: Welch College Press, 2016.

Plantinga, Alvin. *Where the Conflict Really Lies: Science, Religion, and Naturalism.* Oxford: Oxford University Press, 2011.

Plantinga, Cornelius, Jr. *Engaging God's World: A Christian Vision of Faith, Learning, and Living.* Grand Rapids, MI: Eerdmans, 2002.

Pugh, Jeffrey C. *Religionless Christianity: Dietrich Bonhoeffer in Troubled Times.* London: T&T Clark, 2008.

Rainer, Thom S. "A Resurgence Not Yet Realized: Evangelistic Effectiveness in the Southern Baptist Convention Since 1979." *Southern Baptist Journal of Theology* 9, no. 1 (Spring 2005): 54-69.

Ramm, Bernard. *The Christian View of Science and Scripture.* Grand Rapids, MI: Eerdmans, 1954.

Rasmussen, Joel D. S., Judith Wolfe, and Johannes Zachhuber, eds. *The Oxford Handbook of Nineteenth-Century Christian Thought.* Oxford: Oxford University Press, 2019.

Rieff, Philip. *The Crisis of the Officer Class: The Decline of the Tragic Sensibility.* Edited by Alan Woolfolk. Vol. 2, *Sacred Order/Social Order*, edited by Kenneth S. Piver. Charlottesville: University of Virginia Press, 2007.

———. *My Life Among the Deathworks: Illustrations of the Aesthetics of Authority.* Vol. 1, *Sacred Order/Social Order.* Charlottesville: University of Virginia Press, 2006.

Rookmaaker, Hans. *Art Needs No Justification.* Leicester, UK: Inter-Varsity Press, 1978. Reprint, Vancouver: Regent College, 2010.

———. *The Complete Works of Hans Rookmaaker.* Edited by Marleen Hengelaar-Rookmaaker. 6 vols. Carlisle, UK: Piquant, 2001–2002.

———. *Modern Art and the Death of a Culture.* London: Inter-Varsity Press, 1970.

Schilder, Klaas. *Christ and Culture.* With a foreword by Richard Mouw. Translated by William Helder and Albert H. Oosterhoff. Hamilton, ON: Lucerna CRTS Publications, 2016.

Schleiermacher, Friedrich. *On Religion: Speeches to Its Cultured Despisers.* Edited by Richard Crouter. Cambridge: Cambridge University Press, 1996.

Schuurman, Derek. *Shaping a Digital World: Faith, Culture and Computer Technology.* Downers Grove, IL: IVP Academic, 2013.

Seerveld, Calvin. *A Christian Critique of Art and Literature.* Toronto: Tuppence Press, 1995.

———. *Rainbows for the Fallen World.* Toronto: Tuppence Press, 1980.

———. *Redemptive Art in Society.* Sioux Center, IA: Dordt College Press, 2014.

Seerveld, Calvin, and Nicholas Wolterstorff. "Two Writers Engage in Rainbow Action: Nick Looks at Cal; Cal Looks at Nick." *Vanguard* 10, no. 6 (November–December 1980): 4-5, 18.

Sire, James. Interview by Fred Zaspel. Books at a Glance, May 12, 2015. www
.booksataglance.com/author-interviews/interview-with-james-sire-author
-of-apologetics-beyond-reason-why-seeing-is-really-believing/.

Skillen, James W. "Civil Society and Human Development." In *In Pursuit of Justice: Christian-Democratic Explorations*, 19-40. Lanham, MD: Rowman & Littlefield, 2004.

———. *The Good of Politics: A Biblical, Historical, and Contemporary Introduction.* Grand Rapids, MI: Baker Academic, 2014.

———. *Recharging the American Experiment: Principled Pluralism for Genuine Civic Community.* Grand Rapids, MI: Baker Books, 1994.

———. *With or Against the World? America's Role Among the Nations.* Lanham, MD: Rowman & Littlefield, 2005.

———. "Why Kuyper Now?," in Lugo, *Religion, Pluralism, and Public Life*, 189-201.

Skillen, James W., and Rockne M. McCarthy, eds. *Political Order and the Plural Structure of Society.* Atlanta: Scholars Press, 1991.

Smith, Christian, with Melina Lundquist Denton. *Soul Searching: The Religious and Spiritual Lives of American Teenagers.* Oxford: Oxford University Press, 2005.

Smith, Gary Scott, ed. *God and Politics: Four Views of the Reformation of Civil Government.* Phillipsburg, NJ: P&R Publishing, 1989.

Smith, James K. A. *Awaiting the King: Reforming Public Theology.* Grand Rapids, MI: Baker Academic, 2017.

———. *Desiring the Kingdom: Worship, Worldview, and Cultural Formation.* Vol. 1, *Cultural Liturgies.* Grand Rapids, MI: Baker Academic, 2009.

———. *How (Not) to Be Secular: Reading Charles Taylor.* Grand Rapids, MI: Eerdmans, 2014.

Solzhenitsyn, Alexander. *The Gulag Archipelago.* New York: Harper & Row, 1974.

Stellingwerff, Johannes. *Dr. Abraham Kuyper en de Vrije Universiteit.* Kampen: Kok, 1987.

———, ed. *Geboekt in eigen huis: Bevattende een opsomming van de werken van Abraham Kuyper zoals vermeld in de catalogus van de bibliotheek van de Vrije Universiteit, een essay van J. Stellingwerff benevens twee herdrukte redes van Abraham Kuyper.* Amsterdam: VU Uitgeverij, 1987.

Strachan, Owen. *Awakening the Evangelical Mind: An Intellectual History of the Neo-Evangelical Movement.* Grand Rapids, MI: Zondervan, 2015.

Strauss, David Friedrich. *The Old Faith and the New: A Confession.* Translated by Mathilde Blind. New York: Henry Holt and Co., 1873.

Strauss, P. J. "Abraham Kuyper and Pro-apartheid Theologians in South Africa: Was the Former Misused by the Latter?" In Van der Kooi and De Bruijn, *Kuyper Reconsidered*, 218-27.

Stump, James, and Alan Padgett, eds. *The Blackwell Companion to Science and Christianity*. Chichester, UK: Wiley-Blackwell, 2012.

Summers, Stephanie, ed. "Fairness for All: Does Supporting Religious Freedom Require Opposition to LGBT Civil Rights?" *Public Justice Review* 9, no. 3. www.cpjustice.org/public/public_justice_review/volume/9-3.

Synod of Dort. *Decision of the Synod of Dort on the Five Main Points of Doctrine in Dispute in the Netherlands*. English translation available in "Synod of Dort." Christian Classics Ethereal Library. Accessed May 16, 2020. https://ccel.org/ccel/anonymous/canonsofdort/canonsofdort.iii.i.html.

Taylor, Charles. *A Secular Age*. Cambridge, MA: The Belknap Press of Harvard University Press, 2007.

Tiemstra, John, ed. *Reforming Economics: Calvinist Studies on Methods and Institutions*. Lewiston, NY: Edwin Mellen Press, 1990.

———. *Stories Economists Tell*. Eugene, OR: Pickwick Publications, 2012.

Troeltsch, Ernst. *The Social Teaching of the Christian Churches, Volume II*. London: Allen & Unwin; New York: Macmillan, 1931.

Turnbull, Herbert Westren, ed. *The Correspondence of Isaac Newton: 1661–1675*. Vol. 1. Cambridge: Cambridge University Press for the Royal Society, 1959.

———. *The Malaise of Modernity*. Toronto: House of Anansi Press, 1991.

Van den Brink, Gijsbert. *Reformed Theology and Evolutionary Theory*. Grand Rapids, MI: Eerdmans, 2020.

Van der Kooi, Cornelis, and Jan de Bruijn, eds. *Kuyper Reconsidered: Aspects of His Life and Work*. Vol. 3, VU Studies on Protestant History. Amsterdam: VU Uitgeverij, 1999.

Van Deursen, Arie. *The Distinctive Character of the Free University in Amsterdam, 1880–2005*. Grand Rapids, MI: Eerdmans, 2008.

Van Prinsterer, Groen. *Unbelief and Revolution*. Translated by Harry Van Dyke. Bellingham, WA: Lexham Press, 2018.

Vanderkloet, Edward, ed. *A Christian Union in Labour's Wasteland*. Toronto: Wedge Publishing, 1978.

Vandezande, Gerald. *Justice, Not Just Us: Faith Perspectives and National Priorities*. Edited by Mark R. Vander Vennen. Toronto: Public Justice Resource Centre, 1999.

Volf, Miroslav. *A Public Faith: How Followers of Christ Should Serve the Common Good*. Grand Rapids, MI: Brazos Press, 2011.

Walsh, Brian J., and J. Richard Middleton. *The Transforming Vision: Shaping a Christian World View*. Downers Grove, IL: InterVarsity Press, 1984.

William Elliot Griffis Collection. Special Collections. Alexander Library. Rutgers University. New Brunswick, NJ.

Witte, John, Jr. "The Biography and Biology of Liberty: Abraham Kuyper and the American Experiment." In Lugo, *Religion, Pluralism and Public Life*, 243-62.

Woldring, Henk E. S. "Kuyper's Formal and Comprehensive Conceptions of Democracy." In Van der Kooi and Jan de Bruijn, *Kuyper Reconsidered*, 206-17.

Wolters, Al. "What Is to Be Done . . . Towards a Neocalvinist Agenda?" In *Comment Magazine*, December 1, 2005. www.cardus.ca/comment/article/what-is-to-be -done-toward-a-neocalvinist-agenda/.

Wolterstorff, Nicholas. *Art in Action: Toward A Christian Aesthetic*. Grand Rapids, MI: Eerdmans, 1980.

———. *Art Rethought: The Social Practices of Art*. Oxford: Oxford University Press, 2015.

———. *Reason Within the Bounds of Religion*. 2nd ed. 1984. Reprint, Grand Rapids, MI: Eerdmans, 1999.

———. *Until Justice and Peace Embrace*. Grand Rapids, MI: Eerdmans, 1983.

Wood, John Halsey. *Going Dutch in the Modern Age: Abraham Kuyper's Struggle for a Free Church in the Nineteenth-Century Netherlands*. Oxford: Oxford University Press, 2013.

Young, Davis, and Ralph Stearley. *The Bible, Rocks, and Time: Geological Evidence for the Age of the Earth*. Downers Grove, IL: InterVarsity Press, 2008.

Zakaria, Fareed. *The Post-American World: Release 2.0*. New York: W. W. Norton, 2012.

Zuidervaart, Lambert. *Art, Education, and Cultural Renewal: Essays in Reformational Philosophy*. Montreal: McGill-Queen's University Press, 2017.

———. "Art in Public: An Alternative Case for Government Arts Funding." *The Other Journal*, January 3, 2009. http://theotherjournal.com/2009/01/03/art-in -public-an-alternative-case-for-government-arts-funding/.

———. *Artistic Truth: Aesthetics, Discourse, and Imaginative Disclosure*. Cambridge: Cambridge University Press, 2004.

———. "Macrostructures and Societal Principles." In *Religion, Truth, and Social Transformation: Essays in Reformational Philosophy*, 252-76. Montreal: McGill-Queens University Press, 2016.

GENERAL INDEX